Christians in the City of Hong Kong

Christians in the City: Studies in Contemporary Global Christianity

Series Editor: Dyron Daughrity

Christians in the City looks carefully at Christianity in many of the world's great cities. It draws on interdisciplinary methods including anthropology, ethnography, sociology, phenomenology, and history. The series marks a significant contribution to the growing body of scholarship on world Christianity, lived religion, material religion, urban studies, and globalization as it engages people on the ground, in their local setting. The cities covered are drawn from around the world: North America, Latin America, Africa, Asia, Europe, the Middle East, and Oceania.

Books highlight how Christianity is changing particular metro areas, as well as how those areas are impacting the Christian religion. Most major forms of Christianity are discussed: Pentecostalism, Roman Catholic, mainline Protestant, non-denominational megachurches, Eastern Orthodox, immigrant forms, and house churches. The net is cast wide in order to understand what is happening with Christianity as it engages the great urban centers of the world.

Forthcoming books:

Christians in the City of Kinshasa, Fohle Lygunda li-M
Christians in the City of Rio de Janeiro, Graham McGeoch
Christians in the City of Shanghai, Susangeline Y. Patrick

Christians in the City of Hong Kong

Chinese Christianity in Asia's World City

TOBIAS BRANDNER

BLOOMSBURY ACADEMIC
LONDON • NEW YORK • OXFORD • NEW DELHI • SYDNEY

BLOOMSBURY ACADEMIC
Bloomsbury Publishing Plc
50 Bedford Square, London, WC1B 3DP, UK
1385 Broadway, New York, NY 10018, USA
29 Earlsfort Terrace, Dublin 2, Ireland

BLOOMSBURY, BLOOMSBURY ACADEMIC and the Diana logo are trademarks
of Bloomsbury Publishing Plc

First published in Great Britain 2023

Copyright © Tobias Brandner, 2023

Tobias Brandner has asserted his right under the Copyright, Designs and Patents
Act, 1988, to be identified as Author of this work.

For legal purposes the Acknowledgements on pp. 13–15 constitute an extension
of this copyright page.

Series design by Rebecca Heselton

Cover images © Daniam Chou/Manson Yim/Tyler Lee/Unsplash

Bloomsbury Publishing Plc does not have any control over, or responsibility for,
any third-party websites referred to or in this book. All internet addresses given in
this book were correct at the time of going to press. The author and publisher
regret any inconvenience caused if addresses have changed or sites have ceased
to exist, but can accept no responsibility for any such changes.

A catalogue record for this book is available from the British Library.

A catalog record for this book is available from the Library of Congress.

ISBN: HB: 978-1-3502-6909-5
       PB: 978-1-3502-6908-8
       ePDF: 978-1-3502-6910-1
       eBook: 978-1-3502-6911-8

Series: Christians in the City: Studies in Contemporary Global Christianity

Typeset by RefineCatch Limited, Bungay, Suffolk

To find out more about our authors and books visit www.bloomsbury.com
and sign up for our newsletters

To my wife Gabi, in gratitude for our life together in Hong Kong.
And to the people of Hong Kong, in admiration of their resiliency
and strength.

Contents

Illustrations

Figures

Tables

Abbreviations

AG	Assemblies of God	神召會
AO	Asian Outreach	香港亞洲歸主協會
BTJ	Back-to-Jerusalem Movement	回到耶路撒冷
HKCCLA	Catholic Commission for Labour Affairs	香港天主教勞工事務委員會
CEM	China Evangelistic Mission	中華福音使命團
CIM	China Inland Mission	中國內地會
CCM	Chinese Christian Mission	中國信徒佈道會
CPC	Communist Party of China	中國共產黨
CCCOWE	Chinese Coordination Centre of World Evangelism	世界華福中心
CPPCC	Chinese People's Political Consultative Conference	中國人民政治協商會議
CUHK	Chinese University of Hong Kong	香港中文大學
CA	Christian Action	基督教勵行會
CMA	Christian and Missionary Alliance	基督教宣道會
CBN	Christian Broadcasting Network	視博恩
CCA	Christian Conference of Asia	亞洲基督教議會
CIC	Christian Industrial Committee	香港基督教工業委員會
CMO	Christian Mission Overseas	基督教華僑佈道會
CHSKH	Chung Hua Sheng Kung Hui (Anglican Church)	中華聖公會
CMS	Church Missionary Society	英國海外傳道會
CRM	Church Renewal Movement	香港教會更新運動
CHRF	Civil Human Rights Front	民間人權陣線
CCM	Contemporary Christian Music	當代基督教音樂
CWM	Council for World Mission	世界傳道會
CANs	Creative-Access Nations	創啟地區
DSCCC	Divinity School of Chung Chi College, Chinese University of Hong Kong	香港中文大學崇基學院神學院

ECC	Evangelical Community Church	
EFCC	Evangelical Free Church of China	中國基督教播道會
ELCHK	Evangelical Lutheran Church	基督教香港信義會
HKMLC	Hong Kong and Macau Lutheran Church	港澳信義會
ACF	Hong Kong Artistes Christian Fellowship	香港藝人之家
HKACM	Hong Kong Association of Christian Mission	香港差傳事工聯會
ACM	Hong Kong Association of Christian Musicians	香港基督徒音樂事工協會
HKCCCU	Hong Kong Chinese Christian Churches Union	香港華人基督教聯會
HKCC	Hong Kong Christian Council	香港基督教協進會
HKCI	Hong Kong Christian Institute	香港基督徒學會
HKCS	Hong Kong Christian Service	香港基督教服務處
HKCNP	Hong Kong Church Network for the Poor	教會關懷貧窮網絡
CTU	Hong Kong Confederation of Trade Unions	香港職工會聯盟
CCC	Hong Kong Council of the Church of Christ in China	中華基督教會香港區會
PHC	Hong Kong Pentecostal Holiness Church	五旬節聖潔會
HKSKH	Hong Kong Sheng Kung Hui (Anglican Church)	香港聖公會
HUP	Hymns of Universal Praise	普天頌讚
IM	Incubator Ministry	孵化箱事工
IEF	Industrial Evangelistic Fellowship	工業福音團契
ICA	International Christian Assembly	基督教國際神召會
IHOPKC	International House of Prayer in Kansas	國際禱告殿
JIL	Jesus Is Lord Church	
JHF	Jian Hua Foundation	建華基金會
JM	Jubilee Ministries	禧福協會
ME	Media Evangelism Group	影音使團

MCHK	Methodist Church Hong Kong	香港基督教循道衛理聯合教會
MIC	Methodist International Church	循道衛理會國際禮拜堂
NSL	National Security Law	國家安全法
OCLP	Occupy Central with Love and Peace	讓愛與和平佔領中環
OM	Operation Mobilization	世界福音動員會
OMF	Overseas Missionary Fellowship	海外基督使團
PHC	Pentecostal Holiness Church	五旬節聖潔會
P.I.M.E.	Pontifical Institute of Foreign Missions in Milan	宗座外方傳教會
RCCG	Redeemed Christian Church of God	
SDA	Seventh-day Adventists	基督復臨安息日會
SIC	Soccer in Christ	香港足球體育事工
SoCO	Society for Community Organization	香港社區組織協會
SMC	Sports Ministry Coalition	體育事工聯盟
SOP	Stream of Praise	讚美之泉
TBN	Trinity Broadcasting Network	三一電視台
TJC	True Jesus Church	真耶穌教會
TTM	Tsung Tsin Mission Church of Hong Kong	基督教香港崇真會
UFWD	United Front Work Department	中共中央統一戰線工作部
URM	Urban and Rural Mission	城鄉宣教運動
WKPHC	Wing Kwong Pentecostal Holiness Church	五旬節聖潔會永光堂
WCRC	World Communion of Reformed Churches	普世改革宗教會聯盟
WCC	World Council of Churches	普世教會協會
WMC	World Methodist Council	世界循道衛理宗協會
YMCA	Young Men's Christian Association	香港中華基督教青年會
YWCA	Young Women's Christian Association	香港基督教女青年會
YWAM	Youth with a Mission	青年使命團

Maps

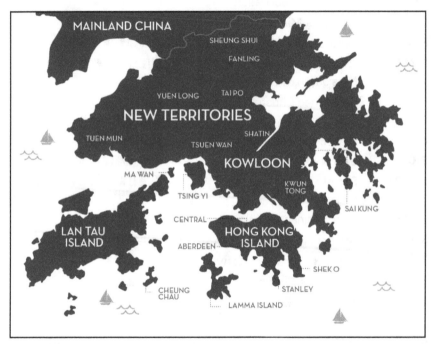

The Hong Kong territory with Hong Kong Island, Kowloon, and the New Territories including the outlying islands (design Erin Hung).

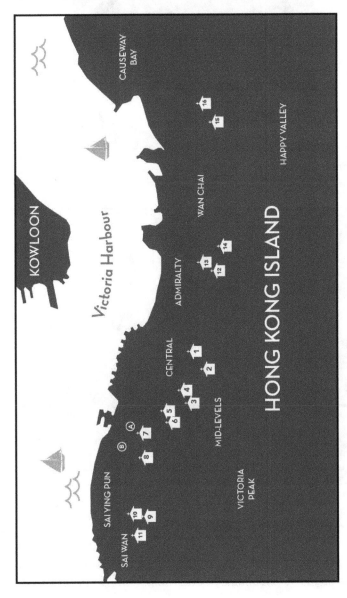

KEY

1. Anglican St. John's Cathedral
2. Catholic St. Joseph's Church
3. Catholic Cathedral of the Immaculate Conception
4. Anglican St. Paul's Church
5. Swatow Christian Church
6. Caine Road Baptist Church
7. China Congregational Church
8. Church of Christ in China Hop Yat Church
9. Hong Kong Rhenish Church
10. Tsung Tsin Mission Kau Yan Church
11. Saint Stephen's Anglican Church
12. Catholic Our Lady of Mount Carmel Church in Wanchai
13. Hong Kong Methodist Church
14. Hong Kong Union Church
15. Church of Christ in China Congregational Church
16. Anglican St. Mary's Church

A. Man Mo Temple
B. Shui Yuet Kung Temple

Northern part of Hong Kong Island, the historical center of the territory, between Causeway Bay and Sai Wan (design Erin Hung).

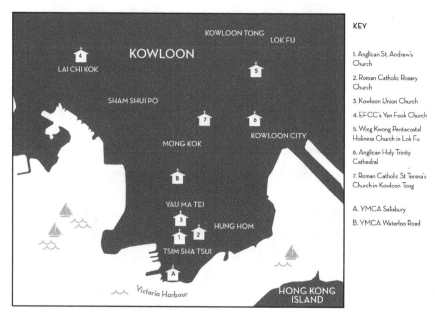

KEY

1. Anglican St. Andrew's Church

2. Roman Catholic Rosary Church

3. Kowloon Union Church

4. EFCC's Yan Fook Church

5. Wing Kwong Pentecostal Holiness Church in Lok Fu

6. Anglican Holy Trinity Cathedral

7. Roman Catholic St Teresa's Church in Kowloon Tong

A. YMCA Salisbury

B. YMCA Waterloo Road

Kowloon peninsula (design Erin Hung).

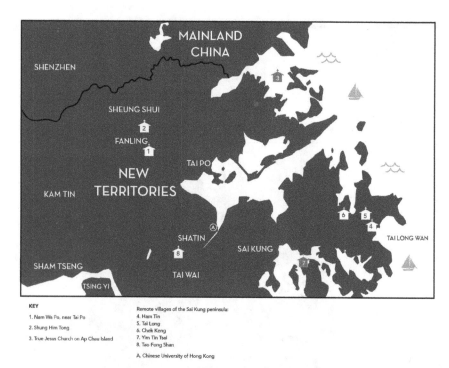

KEY

1. Nam Wa Po, near Tai Po

2. Shung Him Tong

3. True Jesus Church on Ap Chau Island

Remote villages of the Sai Kung peninsula:

4. Ham Tin

5. Tai Long

6. Chek Keng

7. Yim Tin Tsai

8. Tao Fong Shan

A. Chinese University of Hong Kong

Northeastern New Territories and the Sai Kung Peninsula, with some of the remote village churches (design Erin Hung).

Series Introduction

Dyron B. Daughrity, Series Editor

Christians in the City is a fascinating and cutting-edge series that looks carefully at Christians in many of the world's greatest urban centers. It draws on interdisciplinary methods including anthropology, ethnography, sociology, phenomenology, and history. The series marks a significant contribution to the growing body of scholarship on world Christianity, lived religion, material religion, urban studies, and globalization as it engages people on the ground, in their local setting. The cities are drawn from around the world: North America, Asia, Africa, Europe, Latin America, and Oceania.

The Series' books highlight how Christianity is changing particular metro areas, as well as how those areas are impacting the Christian religion. Many different although often overlapping forms of Christianity are discussed in the volumes: Pentecostal, Roman Catholic, mainline Protestant, non-denominational, Eastern Orthodox, immigrant churches, megachurches, charismatic, evangelical, independent, and house churches. The net is cast wide in order to understand better what is happening with Christianity as it engages the great urban centers of the world. Christian organizations in the city—universities, private schools, and faith-based charities—will be explored as well.

The Series features established as well as rising scholars. We have taken great care to choose authors who live in the cities under consideration, or at least have lived in those cities in the past. There is an intimacy that comes through in these volumes, and readers from those cities will recognize the streets, the sounds, the vibe, and the cultural accents that make cities unique. The volumes are written with crossover appeal—for audiences both inside and outside the academy.

Each volume contains interviews with leading figures from the city under consideration—as well as a broad array of laypeople—in order to gain a well-rounded perspective on these cities. There will be no shortage of material, as Christianity is not only the largest world religion in terms of adherents, but is also extremely widespread geographically, making it a diverse and complex religion that takes root in the soil of the cities it has been planted in.

The Series will consist of monographs on 25 of the world's great cities, with carefully chosen, exceptional authors who have an intimate understanding of the city they write about. As the list of books in the series expands, a global balance will be maintained. The current list of cities/volumes that have either been contracted or are under consideration are:

- *In North America*: New York, Los Angeles,* Boston, Houston,* Montreal*

- *In Asia*: Shanghai,* Hong Kong,* Seoul, Delhi, Manila

- *In Africa*: Cairo,* Addis Ababa, Kinshasa,* Lagos,* Johannesburg,* Nairobi*

- *In Europe*: Moscow, London, Athens

- *In Latin America*: Sao Paulo,* Rio de Janeiro,* Havana, Santiago, Mexico City

- *In Oceania*: Sydney*

- *Books already contracted.*

This Series has been several years in the making, and we are excited to see them now coming to light. Over half of the books are contracted, but the search continues for authors for the remaining volumes. We are open to proposals of other cities from potential authors.

Over half of the world's population lives in cities, and the expectation is that in coming years the number of people leaving the countryside for the city will only increase. Since its earliest days, Christianity was a religion of the city: Jerusalem, Alexandria, Antioch, Damascus, Corinth, Thessaloniki, and Rome. Established by the apostles themselves, that pattern continued. As Christianity expanded further, it gravitated towards cities: Aleppo, Edessa, Seleucia-Ctesiphon, Aksum, Etchmiadzin, and Constantinople.

The pattern continued, as the energy of the city attracted Christian missionaries, scholars, and laypeople in search of opportunity. As cities developed, Christians established bishoprics, cathedrals, and centers of learning in cities. Today, the great centers of Christian thought and influence are located chiefly in cities: Seoul, Addis Ababa, Rio de Janeiro, Dallas, Athens, Rome, and Moscow.

A series on Christians in the cities is timely, and promises to break new ground. There is an undeniable power in cities—a power to attract. And Christians continue to make their way, bringing with them manifold Christian practices, routines, rituals, and beliefs. In all of their diversity, they are united in one thing—they consider themselves Christians. And they live in the city.

For more information about this series, contact the Series Editor:
Dyron B. Daughrity
Professor of Religion
Pepperdine University
dyron.daughrity@pepperdine.edu

Introduction

Storms are the reason Hong Kong has become a global city. Its harbor, offering protection from fierce typhoons, attracted British colonialists to seize it from China in 1842 after the First Opium War. Storms are a fact of life in Hong Kong, the natural storms approaching from the south and the political storms approaching from the north—and a gigantic one, whose impact still cannot be fully assessed, has engulfed the city over the past decade. Storms have made Hong Kong what it is. The city navigated storms and channeled its energy into a resilient society and a prosperous economy, and whether the most recent storms will continue to make Hong Kong, or eventually break it, is yet to be seen.

Christians are a minority in this city geared towards trade, but they are remarkably visible in all parts of society. Though rather conservative and inward-looking, they have significantly contributed to social change throughout the city's history; fragmented in a multiplicity of denominations, independent churches and small fellowships, they share a common identity that stubbornly stands apart from the values of mainstream society. This book offers a comprehensive portrait of Christianity in the global city of Hong Kong and tells some of the stories, past and present, of this dazzling faith group—its journey through 180 years of local history, its unique character today, its continuous passion for individual and communal change, and the amazing vitality of people who, through heavy storms, have remained anchored in their faith.

What is Hong Kong? A short note for non-local readers: Hong Kong is both a city and a small territory on the southern coast of China, politically part of China, but governed as a "special administrative region." It consists of three parts: Hong Kong Island, the first location given the name "Hong Kong" and still the economic and political center of the territory; the Kowloon peninsula, the most densely populated part of the territory; and the New Territories, which include new towns, villages, large areas of mountainous uninhabited land and around 230 outlying islands. Nowadays, the name "Hong Kong" usually refers to the whole entity, both urban and rural, with the latter so strongly integrated into the urban infrastructure and lifestyle that they cannot be separated. Hong Kong is a city that, for 155 years, belonged to the British Empire and was returned to China only in 1997. While some see Hong Kong's handover to China as a long overdue redress of colonial injustice, many locals see it as simply a transfer of power from one master to the next. Originally, the independent administration of Hong Kong—summarized in Deng Xiaoping's famous slogans "Hong Kong people ruling Hong Kong" and "one country, two systems"—covered all areas of government except foreign and military affairs: currency, economy, taxes, judiciary, police, infrastructure, education, social welfare, and so forth. On this basis, post-1997 Hong Kong initially maintained a high level of civil and political rights. However, this administrative autonomy has been under increasing pressure, evidenced by the recent adoption of policies obviously designed by the central government.

In terms of economic and social development, Hong Kong is one of the world's most highly developed territories, ranking fourth worldwide in a combined measure of life expectancy, education, and per capita income.[1] Its stock exchange is the world's third largest in terms of capitalization, and it famously brands itself as the city with the most Rolls Royces. Yet, the city also ranks first among highly developed economies in terms of inequality. Indeed, elderly grannies pushing trolleys through the crowded streets to collect cardboard for a subsistence living are a common sight; government and NGO statistics show that more than 220,000 people (nearly 3 percent of the population) are living in sub-standard housing.[2]

Hong Kong is one of the most densely populated areas of the world, with around 7.5m people living on only 1,100 sq. km (410 sq. mi). In fact, the inhabited areas comprise only one-quarter of the whole land area. Large parts of the territory remain as untouched nature—pristine beaches, impenetrable forests, steep mountains, and outlying islands. Only a few minutes from the central business district are places of wilderness. Wild animals—monkeys, boars, and snakes—are frequently sighted, occasionally even in urban areas; migratory birds take rest in isolated areas of the territory; and attentive hikers may have a chance to come across rarer species of wildlife such as the porcupine, civet cat, or barking deer.

Culturally, Hong Kong is very Chinese (92 percent), yet also truly international. The most significant other ethnic groups are people from the Philippines and Indonesia (each 2 to 3 percent of the population), mostly employed as domestic workers; South Asians (around 1 percent), some of them descendants of colonial employees as well as more recent immigrants working in the construction industry; and Caucasians (less than 1 percent). The most commonly spoken language is Cantonese; other commonly spoken languages are English and Mandarin. While Cantonese and Mandarin both belong to the Chinese language family and have a nearly identical written language, the spoken languages are significantly different. Despite this predominantly Chinese population, the city has an international feel. This has not only to do with its long colonial history, but with the self-understanding of many Hongkongers, who proudly see themselves as a distinctive people, a hybrid of Chinese and Western.

In short, it is a city that enthralls its visitors with its pace and its contrasts: the urban jungle and the mountain peaks rising from the sea; the crowded streets, ubiquitous vendors, abundant eateries and street signs competing for attention; an amazing mix of tradition and modernity; and a hypermodern infrastructure permeated with remnants of traditional religion and culture. Woven into the complexity of this city is a Christian community that, although a minority, plays a disproportionally large role in social, political, and economic life.

The Many Faces of Christianity in Hong Kong

This book portrays the amazing diversity of Christianity in Hong Kong, introduces its people, and explains some of the factors that make this vibrant community move. Christians in Hong Kong stand at a crossroads of East and West, on the threshold of China, where they have witnessed unprecedented Christian growth in the last few decades. A looming shadow for some, a luring opportunity for others, China is part of what powers the people in Hong Kong and what drives Christian life. The book's eight chapters, then, approach Christianity in its diverse expressions of faith and in its manifold impact on society.

The first chapter provides a systematic overview of the material and spatial reality of local Christianity, discusses some of the underlying economics, and reflects on the different forms of Christianity as encountered in its material expressions. The second chapter introduces the large variety of denominational traditions, from spiritually progressive Christians to conservative evangelicals and Pentecostals, and discusses their places within society. It shows how these churches pragmatically live and work together while always maintaining a strong focus on their own congregations, and it identifies trends in local church life. The next chapter surveys international Christianity, from charismatic migrant churches to those catering to expatriates in the financial industry. It analyzes how these Christians contribute in unique ways to local society, and it examines why international churches attract many local Christians. The fourth chapter portrays the Christian presence in the cultural realm— entertainment, movies, music, and sports—and shows how the quest for identity has been a driving factor in Christians' cultural production.

Chapter 5 is especially important, as it introduces past and present Christian ministries in the social realm. It considers how Christian individuals, churches, and NGOs have contributed to all aspects of social care; it explains why Christians, despite their minority status, have played such a huge role in the city's social, medical, and educational services; and it shows how Christians have successfully maintained a double role, partnering with the government to improve the people's welfare while speaking out for social justice.

Chapter 6 discusses the missionary vision of local Christians. It reveals how the unique position of Hong Kong brought local Christians a calling to spread the gospel in an environment that is difficult to access. It tells the story of how Hong Kong has always been a safe place for missionaries to China; how Hong Kong has been a hub for channeling Bibles and Christian literature on their way north; and how local Christians have contributed to the growth of Christianity in mainland China.

Chapter 7—on Christians in the political realm—has been looming over the writing of this book ever since the beginning. This chapter summarizes the political developments of the past decades and highlights how Christians have played leading roles on both sides of the political spectrum, among the political establishment *and* within the movements for political change. It explains why Christians, although deeply divided over the 2014 umbrella movement, which called for universal suffrage, converged in opposition to the 2019 extradition bill. The chapter concludes that the Christian resistance to the erosion of civil and political rights is deeply linked to the question of Christian identity. Finally, the concluding chapter offers a few signposts of local theology in Hong Kong. It identifies the features of a "lived theology," traces the emergence of a local theology, and shows how two different strands of local theological production, postcolonial and Sino-Christian theology, both contextually express the Christian faith in Hong Kong. While the latter continues the tradition of dialogue between Christianity and Chinese culture (including philosophy and religion), the former reflects the deep ambivalence of local people as both Chinese and British. It considers how this hybridity, beyond the false dichotomy of East and West, is local Christians' unique contribution to global Christianity.

A Short History of Hong Kong Christianity

This is not a history book, even though historical information is intermittently offered.[3] As part of this introduction, it is enough to mention major historical developments in a few broad strokes so that the reader may find initial orientation. The history of Christianity in Hong Kong has, since the 1841 establishment of the first local Roman Catholic prefecture, been intimately intertwined with events in China. In the same way as British colonialists understood the island as a stepping-stone to China, the various mission societies saw Hong Kong as a logistical base and safe harbor. We may thus link the history of Christianity in Hong Kong to certain periods in China and distinguish a first period from 1841–1949, when the People's Republic of China was established; a second period from 1949–1978, when the churches in Hong Kong re-established themselves independently from China; a third period, 1978–1997, when China began to open up to the world and Hong Kong resumed its role as a hub for reaching out to China; and finally the last period from 1997 to the present.

During the first period, Christianity was spread through four major movements. The first movement was based on mainline churches and mission societies, which set up bases in Hong Kong starting in the 1840s. The first to start was the Catholic Church, followed by the American Baptist Mission (1842) as the first Protestant mission in Hong Kong; the next five years saw the arrival of the London Missionary Society, the (Anglican) Church Missionary Society, and German Pietists from the Basel Mission and the Barmen Mission. In the 1880s, the Wesleyan Methodist Mission and the American Congregationalists from the American Board of Commissioners of Foreign Mission arrived. The Catholic Church and these seven Protestant missions are the eight mainline denominational churches that still play a major role in Hong Kong Christian life.[4]

The second movement was the arrival of non-mainline churches, beginning in the late nineteenth century: among them was the Seventh Day Adventists (1888), the Pentecostal Church (1907), the Pentecostal Holiness Church (1909), and the Assemblies of God (1928).

A third movement, beginning in the early twentieth century, was the emergence of indigenous churches in mainland China independent of Western mission societies. These churches also spread to Hong Kong, as Chapter 2 will explain. Finally, the deteriorating situation in China and the beginning of the Second World War in Asia led several missions to move their activities fully or partly from China to Hong Kong, among them the Evangelical Free Church (1937) and the Christian and Missionary Alliance (1940).

The second period began in 1949 with the establishment of the People's Republic of China and the increasing political pressure on Christians, who were accused of complicity in China's past colonial humiliation. During the Korean War, the international church community supported the U.S., and pressure turned into persecution, leading to the forced departure of foreign missionaries from China. Many of them withdrew to Hong Kong, where they hoped to wait for a return to China while supporting Chinese Christians from outside. Important among the churches that moved to Hong Kong during this period were several Lutheran denominations. Hong Kong churches previously linked to denominations in China now became separated and had to set themselves up as independent churches. The period from 1950 to the 1970s was a time of unprecedented hardship in China, with several political campaigns aimed at purging Mao's enemies leading to the deaths of millions. This period brought a huge number of refugees to Hong Kong, which provided ample opportunity for Christians to serve locally, as Chapter 5 will show; from the Second World War until the 1960s, the city was largely a refugee society. Some mission agencies and Christian NGOs began to use Hong Kong as a base to reach out to the Chinese diaspora in other parts of the world, recalling the mission mode of the early nineteenth century, when missionaries were not yet allowed to serve in China and could only reach Chinese people through overseas Chinese communities.

The third period was made possible by the end of the Cultural Revolution and the death of Mao, both in 1976, and it truly began in 1978 with Deng Xiaoping's "reform and opening up" policy, which allowed a normalization of religious life in China. Churches in Hong Kong soon recovered their interrupted relations with their historical roots and reconnected with their fellow Christians on the mainland, and they contributed financially, logistically, spiritually, and theologically to the rebuilding of Christianity in China. In the 1980s many Christians in Hong Kong had high hopes for more significant changes in China, yet their excitement was increasingly overshadowed by the imminent handover to China and the uncertainty about future religious life in the territory. The fears of many Christians were realized with the violent crackdown on the 1989 democracy movement in China, and a wave of solidarity swept through Hong Kong, carrying many Christians along with it. However, the ensuing disillusionment with developments in China also led to the departure of many Hongkongers, including many Christians who found a warm reception in Chinese communities overseas. Many regard this third period as the transformation of a refugee society into a city of locally born residents—in other words, the time when Hong Kong acquired its unique local identity.

The years since 1997 have been an emotional rollercoaster for local Christians. First, there was hope, excitement and enthusiasm: about the tremendous growth of Christianity on the other side of the border, about the ministry opportunities enabled by this growth, and about China's entry into the global economy and its social opening up, which seemed to presage gradual changes in the social fabric. This positive wave crested with Beijing's hosting of the 2008 Summer Olympics, which filled many Hongkongers' hearts with a sense of national pride. Since then, however, the atmosphere has turned increasingly dark, with China's political intervention extinguishing most Hongkongers' hopes for democratization and the continuous development of civil and political rights. The growing repression of civil and religious movements in China, the intransigence shown towards the 2014 and 2019 social movements in Hong Kong, and the 2020 introduction of a National Security Law have made both Christians and non-Christians increasingly pessimistic, and caused many families and young people, including many active church members, to migrate.

A Note on Method and Style

Rather than offering a comprehensive methodological explanation of this book's approach, I would like to share some theories that have inspired my reflections and informed my writing in recent years. First, several scholars have emphasized the *importance of networks*, showing that important developments often happen through informally organized groups. Among these are the theologian David Hempton (in his lecture "Networks, Nodes and Nuclei: Towards a New Theory of Religious Change"), the historian Niall Ferguson (in his book *The Square and the Tower: Networks and Power, from the Freemasons to Facebook*), and the sociologist Saskia Sassen (in her book *The Global City*). While studies of Christianity traditionally focus on doctrines, theologians, denominations, the institution, or hierarchies, Hempton draws our attention to how Christianity has been growing as a movement from below that connects beyond borders. Hempton's approach helps us understand Hong Kong as a typical node within a network of interconnected people, a place where people meet and where the encounter of local and global creates new identities and new forms of expression. Local Christianity is a result of global mission networks, of local people groups appropriating and localizing this faith, and of both transmitting it along their networks. In other words, the flow of ideas and beliefs is not unidirectional, nor necessarily dependent on the exercise of superior power.

Second, inspired by several of my colleagues, I discovered postcolonial theology as an important form of contextual theological expression. A major issue of Hong Kong throughout its history has been how to locate itself between East and West; this also applies to Christianity, which has traditionally been perceived as a Western religion (which, of course, it is not). With the city's handover to China, the question of a local Christian identity gained additional relevance, leading to a search for a more contextual theology, in both theory and practice. Local theologians thus developed their postcolonial theological thoughts in response to this search, staying faithful to both Chinese and Western traditions, as both have played crucial roles in the making of local Christianity. Postcolonial theologians (whose local representatives will be discussed in Chapter 8) and cultural critics such as Kuan-Hsing Chen ("Asia as Method") have been critical about a common and confining binarian view of East and West because it is based on constructing an "other," as is typical in orientalism, and have instead developed approaches that take into consideration the ambiguity and hybridity of identities in cultural and religious life.

Third, the anthropologist James Scott analyzes the power of resistance in unequal power relations such as slave-and-master, feudal systems, or politically repressive environments and how people subject to repressive power express resistance in what he calls hidden transcripts. His insights are helpful as we think about how Christianity during Hong Kong's colonial period was a space for developing countercultural practices—even more so in the present context, as Hong Kong experiences unprecedented challenges to its way of life.

Finally, this book benefits from a recent trend in religious scholarship that pays more attention to practices than to doctrines and understands Christianity as a "lived religion." It considers all expressions of faith as less a divine matter than as one embedded in believers' daily lives and infused with secular and material concerns. The "lived religion" approach studies local Christianity in the messiness of its practices and conflicts.

This book is written for people both inside and outside Hong Kong—and of course for the many who pass through the city. While locals may find some of the information well-known, they will still discover unknown aspects of their community. This book uses the term "Christian" as referring to both Catholics and Protestants; I am passionately opposed to the misleading terminology that distinguishes "Christians" and "Catholics." Protestants and Catholics—not to mention Eastern Orthodox, and still a few other groups—are all Trinitarian Christians. Differences among various Protestant groups, or among different wings of the Catholic Church, are often larger than between ecumenical-minded Protestants and Catholics. That said, it is obvious that this book is focused more heavily on Protestant Christianity. This is due first to the fact that I am much more familiar with developments on the Protestant side; a second reason is that Protestant Christians form the majority of local Christians; thirdly, they are less homogenous than Catholics and thus display a broader spectrum of Christian expressions.

This study is based on many years of involvement in local church life, on participating observation, church visits, numerous interviews (both formal and informal) with major figures in the local Christian community, interactions with Christians from all walks of life, and on both English- and Chinese-language studies of local Christianity. I gained significant information from social media and the websites of churches and Christian groups. To improve readability, I have avoided hiding information of lesser importance in notes, using them mainly for citations. Instead, some detailed and factual information of interest only to the specialist is contained in smaller-font sections. Furthermore, the two longest chapters, Chapters 2 and 5, contain a significant amount of encyclopedia-like information on various churches and social ministries. Many readers may prefer to save time and skip to the conclusions of these two chapters. I acknowledge the impossibility of including everything I have learned in a single book. The limited space required the omission of many sections that would have deserved deeper analysis, among them on local evangelism, on Christianity in the corporate world, on Christians among the rich and super-rich, on class issues, and on what is called Hong Kong Christians' "captivity in the middle class."[5]

A note on language: Hong Kong's lingua franca is Cantonese, not Mandarin. While Mandarin uses a standardized form of romanization (pinyin), there is no standard romanization in use for Cantonese; a further challenge is that English and Chinese place names in Hong Kong are often completely different. For instance, the largest island is known in English as Lantau, but in Cantonese as *daai yu san* and in Mandarin pinyin *da yu shan*. For simplicity, I have retained the most common locally used expression in the text, rather than converting Cantonese names of places or persons into Mandarin romanization. Where I refer to names or places from mainland China, I use standard Mandarin pinyin. The same applies to the bibliography where I list authors following common use, i.e., names in Cantonese for local scholars and in Mandarin for scholars from the mainland.

Acknowledgements

A book like this necessarily reflects the unique experiences and interests of its author. A few words about my own background and place may help the reader better understand this book. Originally from Switzerland and ordained in the Swiss Reformed Church, I came to Hong Kong in 1996. Since then, I have had the privilege of being part of several very different communities: a conservative Christian NGO, the *Hong Kong Christian Kun Sun Association*, dedicated to the care for those in prison; a spiritually progressive theological institution, the *Divinity School of Chung Chi College, Chinese University of Hong Kong*; and the *Tsung Tsin Mission of Hong Kong* (TTM), a historic denomination that integrates conservative and progressive spiritual concerns. I have also served in various Christian and non-Christian NGOs, most important among them the *Society for Community Organization*. Engagement in such vastly different parts of society and the Christian community has provided encounters with all parts of Christianity.

The fact that I am originally not from Hong Kong is both a weakness and a strength. I will never fully grasp the amazing playfulness of the Cantonese language, I will never be as proficient as a local in dealing with spoken Cantonese and written Chinese, and I will always lack the deep familiarity with the myths and stories of Hong Kong's narrative fabric that comes only from having grown up locally. On the other hand, coming from outside may also help me see aspects of local faith, culture and society that are too obvious or not noteworthy enough to be perceived by people who have always lived here. I also have a certain distance that helps when trying to present a portrait of this variegated faith community. Most important for my understanding of local society are the two and a half decades of ministry as a chaplain in local prisons, where I have met people from all walks of life. Prisons are a magnifying glass, focusing our gaze on the innermost values and the deepest brokenness of a society. The people I have met in Hong Kong's prisons—from members of triad societies, the local mafia, and former street sleepers to international and local drug traffickers, affluent businesspeople and high government officials—have led me on a path of growing understanding of this unique context.

I am grateful for the diverse people who have taught me in my ministry and in academic life. I have benefitted from being surrounded by a group of culturally sensitive persons who have consistently explained to me the depth, intricacies, and idiosyncrasies of local culture and set me on a path of constant learning. I have been blessed by fellowship and friendship with a wide array of people, both Christian and non-Christian alike: young protesters and aged politicians; new immigrants from the mainland and refugees from Africa; tycoons and people at the margins of society; academics and school dropouts; locals, ex-pats and migrant workers; NGO workers, artists, lawyers, doctors and businesspeople; and domestic, construction, and transport workers. These people's stories and insights have been a constant source of inspiration, and they may rediscover themselves in the pages of this book.

I am particularly indebted to my colleagues and students at the Divinity School, who have helped me understand the more hidden aspects of Hong Kong church life. I am equally grateful for the enriching fellowship I have had with all my co-workers in church ministry—foremost those of the TTM, but also those of several other churches where I have served in preaching, speaking and joint prison ministry. I am beholden to the countless moving encounters with people behind bars, many of them Christian, who demonstrated something of the vitality and resiliency of local faith life. I have greatly benefitted from research papers written by my students throughout the years, most importantly those who participated in a local study tour in May 2021.

Among the many who directly or indirectly contributed to this book, I would like to name several colleagues and friends whose help I have particularly treasured. My colleagues Ying Fuk-Tsang, Yip Ching-Wah, and Kwan Shui-Man critically read parts of my book, gave me valuable advice and corrected a few mistakes. With his unique knowledge of the history of local Christianity, Ying Fuk-Tsang was a precious source of information. When I lacked crucial information on an issue, several people were flexible and fast in responding. My thanks go to Ray Wong Ka-Fai, my former colleague and now general secretary of the Church of Christ in China; Wong Fook-Yee, the former president of the Tsung Tsin Mission Church (TTM) and colleague in many church meetings; and Cheung Oi-Sze, my long-time colleague and now general secretary of the TTM. I am grateful for several people who helped me with important information for specific chapters: Donovan Ng Shan-Ho, for several decades the superintendent of the Hong Kong Pentecostal-Holiness Church, granted me an inspiring afternoon as he shared the story of the Wing Kwong Church; Chan Wai On patiently recounted the vision that led to the Flow Church; Lau Tsz Ho, from the Hong Kong Church Renewal Movement, helped me with his vast knowledge of statistical issues; Judy Chan and John Snelgrove advised me on international churches; my students Stanley Ho Wai-Hong, Chloe Luo Ning, Wins Law Siu Ling, Elim Mok and Donald Wong wrote papers on Christians in sport and in the entertainment industry, on Christian mission, and on the emergence of local theology that offered me crucial information; Steve Gaultney gave me inspiring advice at various points during the writing process; and Mimi Tang, a highly dedicated researcher with a passion for Hong Kong, was there whenever I needed some special information and generously compiled important information for Chapter 7. Several research assistants helped me with various parts of the book: Alison Hui Kar-Yan, who has worked many years at the Ray Bakke Centre for Urban Transformation at the Bethel Bible Seminary; Timothy Chan Ka, who helped me with research on international churches and with critical insights across several chapters; and Chamois Chui, who helped me collect information for several chapters. I am indebted to Lo Lung-Kwong, the former director of the Divinity School, who called me into the school's teaching fellowship. He generously offered me insights into various aspects of local Christianity and gave me critical advice on specific parts of the book. Donald Wong critically reviewed all the chapters and offered me detailed and encouraging feedback that inspired me to further improvements. Hans Lutz, a fatherly friend, fellow pilgrim and missionary from the Basel Mission has, since 1969, been deeply involved in Christians' social ministry in this city. His honest and critical thoughts on each chapter gave me a solid assessment and helped refine my portrait of Hong Kong Christianity. A special word of thanks goes to Luke DeKoster who, besides suggesting invaluable linguistic improvements, critically engaged with my thoughts and inspired me to be more precise. Finally, I am grateful for funding that has helped me in parts of this book. The Hong Kong's Research Grant Council supported me in a project on Chinese missions overseas, the findings of which informed Chapter 6. A Direct Grant from the Faculty of Arts, Chinese University of Hong Kong, supported a research project on international churches in Hong Kong, the findings of which contributed to Chapter 3.

1

Exploring Spaces

Historical Church Buildings, Modern Auditoriums, and Upper-Floor Churches

To start with the physical reality of Hong Kong Christianity may be surprising, but Christian faith as an incarnated faith interacts with its environment physically: shaping it even while its beliefs and practices are shaped by it. The Hong Kong city landscape is permeated by old and new church buildings, from the Anglican and Catholic cathedrals in the heart of Hong Kong Island to newly developed church buildings across the territory as well as village churches in the countryside. This chapter offers a panoramic view of the various material forms of Christianity's presence in the public space—worship sites, inscriptions, symbols, retreat centers, and cemeteries—and discusses underlying economic and other factors.

Church Buildings: Old and New, Urban and Rural

In the heart of historical Hong Kong stands the Anglican St. John's Cathedral, Hong Kong's oldest extant church, built in the neo-Gothic style and completed in 1849. It is surrounded by symbols of financial and governmental power: the skyscrapers of the Bank of China and the Hong Kong and Shanghai Bank, government offices, and a few steps further away, the old Government House. In the middle of the busy Central Business District, it stands as an island of tranquility and peace. Not far from it, along Garden Road—ironically now a busy highway—on the other side of the government's offices, stands the Catholic St.

Joseph's Church. Further west, on the steep slopes of the affluent Mid-Levels above Central, is another Anglican church, St. Paul's, built in the early twentieth century. Further up the hill, one reaches the Catholic Cathedral of the Immaculate Conception, built in the 1880s, also in the neo-Gothic style. Reflecting the history of colonial settlement, the same neighborhood houses major churches of other early denominations. Located on roads named Shelley, Caine, Bonham, and Bridges, after former colonial officials, they stand in a line from Central district moving westward: the Swatow Christian Church, the Caine Road Baptist Church, the Church of Christ in China Congregational Church, the Church of Christ in China Hop Yat Church, two Pietist-Lutheran churches—the Rhenish Church and, a bit further below, the Kau Yan Church of the Tsung Tsin Mission—and another Anglican church, Saint Stephen's, the first Chinese Anglican congregation. Not far in the other direction, in Wanchai, traditionally a poorer area, is the Chinese Methodist Church, and, further east, in the heart of Causeway Bay, the Church of Christ in China Congregational Church (on Leighton Road).

Crossing the harbor, a few minutes' walk from the shore, stands the Anglican St. Andrew's Church, again in neo-Gothic style, but with its red bricks, quite unlike St. John's. Completed in 1906, it reflects the extension of colonial power from Hong Kong Island to Kowloon. Even older is the first Roman Catholic Church on Kowloon side, the Rosary Church, a short walk east of St. Andrew's. First completed in 1901, the growing congregation erected a larger building only four years later. The Kowloon Union Church, just 500 meters north of St. Andrew's and built in 1931, completes the trio of historical church buildings in the southern part of Kowloon.

Moving north and away from the historical center, the physical appearance of churches gradually changes: fewer of the traditional, free-standing churches; more examples of less-recognizable churches seamlessly integrated into the urban jungle. Less than 15 percent of Hong Kong's 1,312 local Protestant church congregations worship in what looks like a church building. The vast majority of congregations are instead located in commercial or residential buildings, shopping malls, schools, social service institutions, NGO premises, rented conference rooms, or even industrial buildings.[1] This diversity of localities may lead to interesting associations. One church, a Pentecostal Tabernacle, houses a bank branch on its ground floor. The message of this connection appears clear: Hong Kong Christians, particularly Protestants, do not dread the financial world. Indeed, local Christians are pragmatic regarding their neighbors: banks, stores, restaurants, entertainment venues and offices are all part of life in a cosmopolitan city and may offer interesting synergies. In contrast, many of the ninety Catholic worship sites are in free-standing churches or chapels[2] and thus more separated from secular life.

Over the past decades, some congregations grew into urban megachurches with the means to acquire large spaces: among them are the North Point

Alliance Church; the Evangelical Free Church of China (EFCC) Tung Fook Church, which worships in a former cinema located in the busy Causeway Bay shopping district; the charismatic Bread of Life 611 Church in the old industrial center of Tsuen Wan; the Assembly of God's Kam Kwong Church in Yuen Long,

FIGURE 1.1 *The 2012 completed Congregational Church (Leighton Road) of the Church of Christ in China, in the heart of the busy Causeway Bay district (copyright Tobias Brandner).*

far out in the New Territories, which, in 2003, moved from its rural location to the city center of Yuen Long where it had purchased a grand theater; the EFCC's Yan Fook Church, Hong Kong's largest congregation, which owns a whole high-rise building in Lai Chi Kok; the Wing Kwong Pentecostal Holiness Church in Lok Fu, in the northern part of the Kowloon Peninsula, a rare example of a newly built free-standing church in a dense urban area (see Case study); and The Vine, a charismatic international church in Wanchai, which also worships in a former cinema.

More than half of all churches are located in commercial or residential buildings,[3] usually occupying one or more floors, sometimes right next to other churches or Christian NGOs: ecumenical togetherness all in one building. It is indeed a unique feature of local church life that many Christians worship in small upper-floor churches, in family-like congregations of a few dozen to one or two hundred. Forty-four percent of all local Chinese-speaking churches have fewer than 100 members.[4] One of the more remarkable (and rather atypical) upper-floor churches is the Sky City Church, located on the top floor of what was for many years Hong Kong's highest skyscraper, Central Plaza in Wanchai. The building's co-owner, the city's largest property developer Sun Hung Kai, offers the hall to the congregation for their Sunday worship. The majestic view over city and harbor renders any Christian decoration redundant.

Moving out into the remote rural villages, we see free-standing churches dominate again, some abandoned and reclaimed by nature, others still used for regular worship. This reflects local mission history: some early missions, worried about the moral pitfalls of city life, aimed more at the rural population. Several such villages are firmly steeped in the Christian faith. One example is Nam Wa Po, near Tai Po: a traditional Hakka-speaking farming community, where more than one hundred years ago the village chief brought the whole village to the Christian faith. The Nam Wa Po church is still part of the Tsung Tsin Mission (TTM), which grew out of the Basel Mission's ministry. A few kilometers north is Shung Him Tong, another firmly Christian Hakka village that grew out of the ministry of the Basel Mission and that has been beautifully portrayed by the anthropologist Nicole Constable.[5] Another example is the True Jesus Church in Ap Chau, literally "duck island," also called Robinson Island due to its remoteness, established in 1952 by a fishing community in the far away seas of the northeastern New Territories. The church stands at the beginning of the development of the island community. Villagers introduce the island to visitors by saying, "There is a church, a school, a water cistern,"[6] a description of the simplicity of their church-centered life. Unlike Nam Wa Po and Shung Him Tong, Ap Chau today has very few residents; all the villagers have moved to urban areas or migrated to the UK, although they did bring their faith along, establishing several True Jesus Churches where they went. Several Catholic chapels in remote villages of the Sai Kung peninsula in the Eastern New Territories such as the ones in Ham Tin, Tai Long and Chek Keng are abandoned, but others are still maintained by devout villagers.[7] They were built by Catholic missionaries from Italy, who started their ministry in this rural area in the 1860s. Some of the communities, such as the one on the small island of Yim Tin Tsai, became entirely Catholic. Near these chapels one can discover old graves built in traditional *feng shui* style, yet with Christian symbols replacing some of the indigenous religious elements and reflecting an early form of architectonic inculturation.

Inscriptions, Sacred Mountains, and a Theme Park

Christianity in Hong Kong is visible not only through actual church buildings, but also through church-run schools and social service centers, which are simultaneously used for Christian community life. Local churches have devised creative strategies to gain further visibility, such as attaching a large sign to the outside of a building, similar to the signs for other services such as restaurants, entertainment venues, and shops. Some churches (or even individual Christians) have sponsored biblical messages on the top of buildings or on strategically placed billboards, the most visible one proclaiming "Jesus is Lord" across the entire façade of a Jordan Road building. In some places, Christian crosses adorn prominent locations as a sign of the Christian presence in the city.

The most famous such cross stands on Tao Fong Shan, the "mountain from which the wind of the Tao blows,"[8] in the New Territories. It keeps watch over Shatin, one of the oldest of the "new towns" built in the 1970s to accommodate Hong Kong's ever-growing population. Tao Fong Shan has a long history as a sacred mountain, with early missionaries settling at its base and with a famous Norwegian missionary, Karl Ludwig Reichelt (1877–1952), setting up the *Christian Mission to Buddhists* there in 1930. Reichelt's center welcomed pilgrims and monks from China to learn about the Christian faith and to engage in spiritual exchange. The centerpiece is a beautiful chapel built in the traditional style of a Chinese pagoda, with the altar featuring drums, bells, and gilded characters, as in Chinese temples. The whole area, including the chapel, conference halls, and guest rooms is a respite from hectic urban life.[9] Today, the *Tao Fong Shan Christian Center* extends the spiritual hospitality of this place, while the *Institute of Sino-Christian Studies*, which shares the premises, inherited the tradition of theological exchange with Chinese scholars. On the same hill, the Lutheran Theological Seminary has a magnificent campus (completed in 1992) built in traditional Chinese style, thus extending the tranquility of the neighboring Christian Center.

Another—although very different—"sacred mountain" lies on Lantau Island. Sunset Peak, or Tai Tung Shan (Great Eastern Hill), has two dozen mountain cabins spread across its peak area, 800m above sea level. These cabins were built in the 1920s by early mission agencies to provide a mountain retreat for their workers, similar to other places in the British Empire where colonial officials established resorts to escape the sweltering heat of the lowlands for cooler mountain air.[10] For many generations of missionaries, these houses offered a precious retreat and an opportunity for communal devotional life combined with a mountain holiday. Descendants of missionary families have fond memories of their childhood summer vacations on the hill, playing across the hillside and visiting their fellow mountain dwellers.[11] Today, only a few of the cabins are still owned by mission agencies or churches, while most have passed into secular ownership.

The Saddle, as Sunset Peak is called by its inhabitants, has one drawback: an inclination to dense fog. In this regard, another traditional missionary retreat, picturesque and mild Cheung Chau to the southwest of Hong Kong Island, one of the larger islands, is more fortunate. In 1919, a government ordinance reserved parts of this island as a vacation reserve for British and

FIGURE 1.2 *Western entrance to Jordan Road, in the southern part of the Kowloon Peninsula (copyright Gabi Baumgartner).*

American missionaries—similar to the infamous ordinances barring Chinese and Eurasians from living on the Peak. These segregationist ordinances were repealed only in 1946.[12] Today, Cheung Chau is densely populated by a mix of local villagers and expats who seek some distance from the hustle and bustle of the city, but the dense presence of churches and Christian institutions still bears witness to the island's historical background.

A more tranquil environment can be found in some of the Roman Catholic retreat centers. The Catholic Trappist monastery, on the eastern flank of Lantau, is an important monastic center offering a quiet place and spiritual guidance. It is famous beyond the faith community for its milk, consumed in many local households. Nowadays, the monks are too old to milk the cows, but they still have a significant stake in the dairy company that carries on their brand. Other Catholic retreat centers are the Jesuits' Xavier House on Cheung Chau; the Holistic Retreat Centre in Shek O, a remote seaside village on Hong Kong Island, beautifully overlooking the ocean and led by Carmelite priests from Indonesia; the St. Paul's House of Prayer near Sheung Shui, close to the border with mainland China; and, until recently, the Maryknoll Convent, located on a small hill in the middle of Stanley Village, on the expensive south side of Hong Kong Island. This significant building has, however, been sold to a developer and is going the way of so many other historic buildings in Hong Kong: demolition and redevelopment.

Similarly serving recreational, but also evangelistic purposes, is a non-commercial theme park centered on Noah's Ark, built adjacent to a large residential development on Ma Wan Island. The island lies between Tsing Yi and Lantau, at one end of the famous Tsing Ma Bridge that connects the downtown city with Lantau and the airport. The theme park, financed by three wealthy Christians and several Christian organizations, opened in May 2009 and offers a full-scale replica of the biblical Ark. It promotes Christian values such as love, social harmony, and care for the environment, and offers an easily accessible biblical message—not least for visitors from mainland China.

Christian Cemeteries

From places of rest and recreation to places of eternal rest:[13] Cemeteries are important places in local faith life. With the fast-changing city offering little in terms of holy sites, the graves of important missionaries have become important pilgrim sites for local churches and, sometimes, even for international visitors, as in the case of the Happy Valley grave of Robert Semple, the husband of the founder of the Foursquare Gospel Church.[14] To properly understand the important role played by Christian cemeteries, three factors need to be considered. First, matters related to death have always been strongly regulated by the government. The early colonial government's policies regarding the burial of the dead revealed the same tendency towards hierarchical and segregationist regulations based on ethnicity, religion, and class, as did policies regarding the living.[15] In Hong Kong's early decades, colonial officers and Christians enjoyed the privilege of being buried in urban colonial cemeteries, such as the one in Happy Valley. Minority groups of other religious faiths were allocated space in minority cemeteries. In contrast, the government neglected the proper burial needs of the local population, and it was not until 1871 that the first officially designated burial ground for local Chinese was opened, though only the social elite could afford it.[16] Before that, Chinese burials happened outside of colonial regulation. The poor were the last to have access to urban burial sites.[17] Ethnic and faith-based segregation in arrangements for the dead remains common today.

Second, the major factor in all parts of life—and death—in Hong Kong is the scarcity of land (see next section). Since the late 1950s, the government has been promoting cremation as a way to save space,[18] and although it met initial resistance as it stood in contrast to traditional Chinese burial practices,[19] it has become the norm, with over 90 percent of the dead now being cremated. Since the 1960s, cemeteries with urn graves and, increasingly, columbaria have become the norm. Yet, despite such shifts in the management of the dead, the scarcity of space remains a major problem, with an urn niche in a privately run columbarium costing up to HK$1.8 million (US$230,000)/ft^2, more than prices in the most expensive residential areas.[20] The government does offer affordable burial space in public columbaria, but only after an embarrassingly long wait of several years, which means that the ashes need to be kept at home or in another unsuitable location such as a store room. As a mortuary worker explained: "No one sets up a coffin at home, so why would you put an urn there?"[21] In response to the acute shortage of burial space, the government has promoted the scattering of ashes in a publicly managed Garden of Remembrance or even in designated waters. The situation is different in the rural parts of Hong Kong, where original villagers are allowed their own burial grounds under special rights granted by the colonial government to gain their loyalty and support, a policy which has not changed even after Hong Kong's handover to China.

Third, all matters relating to death are of tremendous importance in traditional Chinese contexts, where the veneration of ancestors and the belief in the continuous existence of the dead in the form of the soul are core elements of popular faith. According to this belief, death is not an end to life, and interaction between the living and the dead continues beyond death.[22] Responsibility for the proper veneration and commemoration of the dead lies primarily with male descendants. A proper funeral, burial, and sacrificial offerings to the dead are important both for the deceased and for the living. It facilitates the deceased's safe passage to the realm of the departed, it ensures good fortune in the afterlife, it wards off potential harm by unsatisfied ghosts of the dead, and it may result in blessings for the living.[23]

This enormous concern for life after death is, spiritually and theologically, reflected in the great importance local Christians attach to the question of salvation: The belief that conversion gains a place in heaven, a common theological motif among evangelical Christians, finds fertile ground in this context and is commonly mentioned in conversion narratives. On the material level, it is expressed in the priority placed on proper burial rites and locations. Obviously, Christian churches that can provide access to attractive places for burial, have a significant spiritual and material advantage.

Two large cemeteries under the management of the Hong Kong Chinese Christian Churches Union (HKCCCU), one of two local ecumenical bodies, offer burial space exclusively to members of Christian churches. They are located on the south side of Hong Kong Island, in Pokfulam, and in the northern part of Kowloon, in Lok Fu. Similarly, the Roman Catholic Church manages five cemeteries across Hong Kong. The cost of an urn niche in a Christian cemetery, if one qualifies, is significantly lower than it would be in a private columbarium. In rural Hong Kong, a small number of older churches such as the Church of Christ in China's Chuen Yuen Church, which is now in the heart of the old industrial area of Tsuen Wan, the CCC's Tuen Mun Church, the CCC's Cheung Chau Church, and the TTM's church in the old Hakka village of Shung Him Tong near Fanling benefitted from the special rights granted to villagers and were given permission to establish their own cemeteries. The church cemetery in Shung Him Tong opened in 1931, and it has been a source of pride and security for its members ever since.[24] At the same time, such churches need to keep a close watch on who is a proper member and thus qualifies for a precious free burial space. Whether in urban or rural Hong Kong, the opportunity to acquire a burial space has been a factor attracting people to Christianity. Indeed, some elderly people have been suspected of converting to Christianity on their deathbeds for just this reason. As a consequence, Christian ministers' and family members' desire to evangelize and baptize the dying stands in tension with suspicious church council members' protection of prized Christian burial spaces.

Christians and Money: Church Economics

Land—or rather its scarcity—is the crucial economic factor in church budgets and in most local citizens' lives. The limited land in a territory of only around 1,100 sq. km, and policies that release land only in small parcels, have made Hong Kong the world's most expensive property market. All land, with very little exception, belongs to the government, which derives a significant part of its income from the sale of land. Around one-third of the government's annual budget comes from land revenue, including land premiums, annual rent, rates, and property taxes.[25] Every year, the government auctions plots of land to developers who then sell the properties—at a significant profit—to the public. The reputation of Hong Kong as a low-tax haven is thus only superficially true because the people simply pay the government in a different form, through sky-high property prices. The same superficial truth applies to the common view of Hong Kong as economically non-interventionist: Owning the land gives the government huge power to intervene in economic and social affairs through zoning rules, by imposing lease terms, and by categorizing land for residential, commercial, industrial, or communal use.

To be exact, the government does not sell land, but only leases it. In the past, leases have mostly been for 99 years (or 999 years, in a few nineteenth-century cases),[26] but they are commonly extended after expiring. During the current period of Chinese sovereignty, leases have been granted until 2047, which is, for now, the duration of the "special administrative region." The leasing of the land allows the government to retain significant authority by attaching terms to its use. Change of use requires governmental permission and the payment of a premium. To construct a church building, a congregation thus needs to ask the government for land. If the government accepts the application, it will lease land to the church for free (or for a low fee) under the condition that the land be used only for religious or charitable purposes such as social services. An exemption to this rule is the historic St John's Cathedral, which stands on land given as freehold to the church, although still under the same land-use conditions.[27] Land leases from the early colonial years have fewer terms attached, which gives older churches more flexibility to redevelop their premises and benefit from the astronomically high property prices. Indeed, in past decades, several significant redevelopment projects have given some churches a huge windfall. Among them are the Baptist Convention of Hong Kong, which funded the development of a new theological seminary on the outskirts of the city by the redevelopment of their downtown premises in Homantin in the 1990s. The Catholic Our Lady of Mount Carmel Church in Wanchai turned its church building into a 42-storey residential building in the late 1990s.[28] The historic Hong Kong Union Church, which traces its history to an English-language gathering that began in 1843 and was initiated by the early missionary and famous sinologist Dr. James Legge, had its free-standing church on Kennedy Road torn down in 2017 and replaced by a 22-storey residential block, with the church occupying the first five floors. This is a common practice.[29] With prices of more than US$10 million for a 1,500 sq. ft. flat, one may imagine the revenue for a church that was already (based on its members' wealth) among the world's most affluent churches. Property development is a practice also used by NGOs, as shown by the YMCA's two highly profitable hotels, one of them right next to the famous Peninsula Hotel.

Churches also benefit from having invested in the market when property was more affordable. The constant rise in prices over the decades has allowed some churches to accumulate significant wealth, and steady rental income has been an important source of support for many social, educational, and missionary projects. In recent years, due to the scarcity of land, the government has rarely granted land for free-standing churches, forcing many churches to meet in schools or social-service centers. Churches in such venues benefit in two ways: free worship space and the chance to evangelize students (and their families) or social-service recipients.

Of course, not all churches have the privilege of owning property; most depend on tithing to fund regular ministry. A common rule is that one-tenth of a person's income is donated to the church, and randomly interviewed church leaders report that anywhere from 10 percent to nearly 100 percent of the people in their congregation's tithe at that level. Many estimate that the average giving stands at 5 percent of family income. Factors influencing the practice of giving are household wealth, with poorer congregants finding it more difficult to contribute the full tenth; the public listing of donation information, which creates social pressure to give "appropriately"; and the emphasis on a church's teaching on proper tithing. Yet, even if members give only 5 percent, churches can be financially sustained with a small number of members.

A Case Study: The Wing Kwong Pentecostal Holiness Church

The Wing Kwong Church (WKPHC) is in many ways unique, yet, its story of church construction and tithing, of negotiating faith, economic, and material realities, is not completely untypical. The church was established in 1976 within the school premises of the Wing Kwong College in Lok Fu. The early members of the church were mainly secondary-school students, gathering around their charismatic pastor, Donovan Ng Shan-Ho, a young seminary graduate. Since then, the church has grown to more than 6,000 members.

In the 1990s, the church took a huge step of faith, acquiring land near the school for their own building. This was both an expression of trust in the continuous growth of the church, and a statement to society that the Christians gathered in this church were dedicated and generous—not to mention a testimony of faith at a time when many Hongkongers, worried about the impending political change, left the city. The land was bought under the category of "government, institution, or community purposes" (GIC). The church began fundraising in 1993, when it had a membership of around 2,300, and purchased the land in 1995 for HK$87 million (US$11.2 million), gaining a lease with few conditions attached. Construction was completed in 2001, with the total cost (including the land) amounting to HK$240 million (US$30.9 million). The church takes special pride in the clock tower, the large auditorium that accommodates 1,800 worshippers, and the beautifully designed egg-shaped smaller chapel for baptisms and marriages.

"I rejected all money offers from outside," says Rev. Ng, "I wanted to buy the land and build the church entirely with funds from our own congregation, for the glory of Jesus Christ and for our own good name." As a basic requirement, every member of the church paid HK$30,000 (US$3,860), and the remainder was covered by tithing and special donations. Today, the church receives up to HK$100 million (US$12.9 million) annually from tithing. "My policy of pastoring is that you don't need to open the private account of each member and try to grab money for the church," Rev. Ng says. "Let them keep their money. You only have to get their heart. If you ask too early for their money, they will just get suspicious that you are after it."

The church has therefore established an elaborate system that allows donations to the church only after a slow process of several steps: A "newcomer" enjoys certain privileges but is not allowed to donate. A "believer" becomes more actively involved and is allowed to join cell groups but is still not allowed to tithe (though special offerings for the charitable ministry of the church are permitted). During this stage, a person goes through a catechetic process of thirteen lessons to learn the basics of the Christian faith. If he or she wants to become a full member of the church, she may, as a third step, apply for permission to offer the tithe. After being thoroughly interviewed by a cell-group leader and a church elder and approved by a pastor, an applicant may eventually be allowed to tithe. After a further period of one year of regular tithing, this person may apply for baptism, at which time she becomes a full member of the church.

Our observations regarding church economics may be summarized in a few points: First, the long-lasting presence of Christian churches in the territory, the purchase of property by early mission societies who passed it on to local churches, the continuous growth of property values, and highly disciplined tithing give churches in Hong Kong considerable economic power. Although churches are, like everyone else, affected by economic crises, the wealth of Hong Kong churches gives them powerful visibility and significant clout to influence the city through social, educational, and missionary projects. The churches' financial position also offers some security against unpredictable church–state relations.[30] Secondly, while not everyone may observe the full

FIGURE 1.3 *The Pentecostal Holiness Wing Kwong Church, in Lok Fu, in the northern part of the Kowloon Peninsula (copyright Gabi Baumgartner).*

ten-percent tithe, many Christians in Hong Kong donate generously. This generosity grows out of several motives: obedience to the rules of the church; a transparent system where fellow church members often know the amounts donated by others; a culture of seeing the church as a family, where responsibility and mutual support is highly valued (more on this in Chapters 2 and 8); the public prestige or "face" that comes with generous donations; a religious consciousness that connects generous giving with an abundance of blessing; and, significantly, the will to offer a powerful testimony through faithful giving as individuals and as church communities. Third, the overall wealth of local churches is a relatively recent phenomenon. It developed parallel to Hong Kong's enormous economic growth—an average of around 9 percent per year—from the 1960s through the 1980s.[31] This wealth stands in contrast both to earlier decades and to the abysmal hardship under which many grassroots Hongkongers still live. Fourth, church growth, wealth accumulation, and, with this, the ability to build large church premises carries positive connotations. It symbolizes success; it may be seen as divine grace bestowed upon a church, and it witnesses to a congregation's faith, courage, love, and unity.[32] Fifth, this significant and solid wealth risks entangling churches in potential conflicts arising from financial interests. Some churches have been criticized for showing off too much wealth and for putting too much emphasis on questions of material status. A typical criticism is that church development projects, such as the one by the Hong Kong Union Church, sacrifice historically remarkable buildings for more income. Finally, there is a huge wealth disparity among the churches, reflecting the wealth gap in the wider society. Several ultra-rich churches, mostly on Hong Kong Island, stand alongside a poorer majority, i.e., churches operating on a rather simple basis without much reserves. Little inter-ecclesial sharing happens, and most congregations dispose of their wealth autonomously.

Religious Geography

Our survey of the material realities of local Christianity contributes some building blocks to the question of religious geography: How has local Christianity spread geographically, and what does this spread signify? Christianity has benefitted from a government that related more naturally to the Christian faith and that held an overall sympathetic view of it. Not all aspects of Christian life and ministry have received favorable treatment though, as the following chapters will show. Yet Christianity in Hong Kong has clearly had important advantages in its physical development, most obviously in the case of cemeteries, but also in other areas such as the leasing of land and the past use of Cheung Chau as an exclusive retreat.

The location of churches reflects the history of colonial settlement and the colonial organization of the community, which allocated different spaces to different faith groups. An example is the simultaneous construction in the 1840s of St. John's Cathedral and Man Mo Temple, the oldest Daoist temple, dedicated to the god of literature and the god of martial arts. While St. John's is situated in the very heart of the central business district, Man Mo Temple is further west in Sheung Wan, which, in early times, was designated for Chinese residents and where also other Daoist religious sites such as the Pak Sing Ancestral Hall and the Shui Yuet Kung Temple stand. Such spatial separation of the focal points of different faith groups, whether spontaneously or through governmental allocation, can also be observed elsewhere: On Lantau Island, many Buddhist temples stand on the island's western slopes, from Shek Mun Kap towards the Big Buddha in Ngong Ping and from there further westwards towards the old fishing community of Tai O. Christians, in contrast, settled more on the east side, on Sunset Peak and further east.

A further building block of Hong Kong's religious geography, which has economic and political implications, refers to the territorial distribution of the churches. It is a characteristic of the Roman Catholic Church to spread more evenly over all of the city's eighteen districts, including remote rural territories and islands, reflecting an approach that emphasizes sacramental presence. This more even spread partly also applies to mainline Protestant churches with a long historical presence in the city. Many of their churches use church-based schools and social services in relatively poorer areas as their worship sites, where they attract a less affluent population. With this, they remain trapped in a vicious cycle of insufficient donations and the inability to purchase their own premises. In contrast to them, though, many other Protestant churches tend to concentrate on the urban areas, with 45 percent of their churches located in five densely populated districts (Yau Tsim Mong, Sham Shui Po, Kwun Tong, Shatin, and Hong Kong Island East),[33] which may express the Protestant concern for convenience and practicality in the spread of faith, but also reflects an evangelical concern with claiming the city space for Christ. The disproportional presence of Protestant churches in inner-city areas is also caused by many of the evangelical and charismatic churches, many of which are independent of denominational affiliation, choosing such locations for their churches. Many purchased premises in central locations where they attract the upper-middle class and the ultra-rich, a situation which puts them on a path of steady income through donations.

Contextualization of Sacred Space

A final aspect that deserves consideration is the question of contextualization. What does it signify when Christians celebrate their worship in Gothic-style churches, or on the top floor of an office tower, on the second floor of a residential building, in a former cinema, in a commercial center, in a social welfare center, or in a school? How do local Christians establish sacred space within the profanity of a shopping mall, and with a bank, a McDonald's, an employment agency for domestic workers and a tutorial center as neighbors? How does local culture find reflection in the physical realities of local Christianity?

The earliest churches—St John's, the Catholic Cathedral, and some of the early historical churches—speak a decisively Western architectural language,[34] which makes Christianity appear as a foreign religion without local connections. Other churches, trying to relate positively to the Chinese context, express themselves by borrowing from indigenous religious traditions. Their architectural message is that Christianity is compatible with Chinese culture. An early proponent for a shift towards a contextual Chinese architecture was the visionary Anglican Bishop Ronald Owen Hall, the local Anglicans' longest-serving bishop (1932–66).[35] Famous examples of churches in a decisively Chinese style are the Tao Fong Shan chapel, the Catholic Holy Spirit seminary (1931), the Anglican Holy Trinity Cathedral and St. Mary's Church (both completed in 1937), and the Life Lutheran Church Yuen Long (1959). Their architecture contains clear Chinese religious and cultural references. St. Mary's, with its green-tiled multilayered roof and massive rosewood altar, features particularly striking similarities to Chinese imperial and religious architecture.[36] Architectural style was very much a matter of dispute, as the parallel construction of the Roman-Catholic Holy Spirit Seminary in Aberdeen and St Teresa's Church in Kowloon Tong shows: The former was led by Jesuits who opted for a Chinese style building; in the case of the latter, an Italian bishop and a parish mostly consisting of Portuguese rejected a Chinese-style design and replaced it with a project in Italian Romanesque style.[37]

Proper contextualization is still controversial. While these early attempts at adaptation to the Chinese context are aesthetically attractive, a younger

FIGURE 1.4 *The Anglican St. Mary's Church, in Causeway Bay (copyright Tobias Brandner).*

FIGURE 1.5 *Christ Temple on Tao Fong Shan (copyright Tao Fong Shan Christian Centre).*

generation, critical of being identified with classical Chinese culture, challenge them. They prefer to emphasize local culture in contrast to what they perceive as an essentialized Chinese-ness that defines Chinese culture in classical form. A young local Christian explained it in the following words: "After 1997, and after the recent political crisis, Hong Kong people are rebuilding their own identity, and this identity strongly distinguishes Hongkongers from China. Traditional architecture may therefore not represent this new identity." Many Hongkongers indeed joyfully embrace a hybridity, a mix of East and West that is forfeited in these elaborate forms of contextualization.

The more profane upper-floor churches in residential or commercial high-rise buildings reflect a different kind of contextualization, one that relates not so much to an elitist culture and to Chinese religious tradition as to locals' lived reality. Their integration into the ordinary lives of people makes them appear closer to secular life or, theologically speaking, more incarnational and less reflecting the profane-sacred dichotomy. The embeddedness of the religious life in the secular context of schools, malls, and social centers, may underline the pragmatic character of religious acts. The absence of a free-standing, solemn building may, unconsciously, cause these churches to understand spirituality more as an inward psychological experience. At the same time, the church's location in a shopping mall or in a commercial building may contribute to the commodification of the Christian faith, as it appears as simply another service sold and purchased like those offered in the neighboring shops, the bank, the food center, or the employment agency.

An important factor in the physical reality of these upper-floor churches is economic efficiency and multi-functionality, allowing church space to be used for various forms of activity and interaction. While the interiors of these churches do contain religious symbols such as crosses, banners with biblical messages, posters, and false windows with Christian images, the dominant feature is convenience. They are simple rooms for Christian instruction, mirroring the Confucian concern for learning that is also alluded to in the Chinese word for "church," which translates literally as "teaching community." Their simplicity, their functionality, and their conveniently constructed sacrality do not foster the same kind of attachment to a sacred place as churches with a longer history would. Indeed, due to rapid development, many churches are forced to move frequently; consequently, they maintain flexibility and keep a strong sense of the impermanence of sacred space.[38]

While these churches' proximity to the lived reality of ordinary people may make them more accessible to newcomers and religious seekers, the smaller congregations exude a coziness and familiarity that may deter newcomers from joining because it feels like stepping into an already established family. At the other extreme, some modern churches use large auditoriums for worship, similar to a concert hall or a cinema with comfortable chairs. This makes worship appear not arduous but pleasurable, comparable to the consumption of any other cultural product such as a music concert or a movie, appealing to new customers who might like to try out a religious offer in a non-committal way. Regardless of the physical environment, both kinds of church express a cordial informality that contrasts with the solemn and formalized interaction of more liturgical churches. Ironically, in this informality, they resemble the hustle and bustle of a traditional temple more than the atmosphere of a traditional church building, where quiet and spiritual earnestness dominate.

To conclude, our exploration of the material realities of Hong Kong Christianity has shown a strong physical presence across the territory with churches benefitting from favorable government policies, a historically long presence, and believers' practice of generous giving. Local Christians have developed creative vitality in navigating spatial restrictions in a city with the world's most expensive property prices. In a dynamic religious marketplace, Christianity appears as one option among many, visible and vibrant yet well integrated, not dominating the city space. The downside of (particularly Protestant) churches' smooth integration into the urban context is the danger of commodification, that is, religious experience simply becoming another service to be consumed.[39] Negotiating the economic realities of Hong Kong, local Christians largely show a pragmatic—and surely in no way hostile—attitude to money, wealth, and economic strength. This flexible attitude toward finances has been visible in local Christians' faith since earliest times, as the following story shows. Ho Fuk Tong, also known as Ho Tsun Shin, was an important co-worker of James Legge and accompanied him when he moved from Malacca to Hong Kong. In 1846, he was ordained by the London Missionary Society, making him the first locally ordained Chinese pastor. Soon after his arrival, he began to invest small sums in local properties and continued to do so until his death in 1871, leaving behind one of the largest estates in the city at the time. He held these properties under various aliases, which led to a contestation of his will after his death. Whether the reason for doing so was to conceal his property from the Western head of the mission, who would not have appreciated his interest in money and might have targeted him for the mission's fundraising, as a barrister in the court suit over the interpretation of his will suspected, remains a matter of speculation.[40]

2

Mainline, Evangelical, and Pentecostal

A Labyrinth of Denominations

In the large Methodist church in downtown Wanchai, worship starts with the nineteenth-century hymn "The Church's One Foundation" in Chinese. The choir, in white robes with green hems, enters in solemn procession. Led by a female lay leader, the worship is both earnest and grave, following the lectionary of traditional churches. Across town, in the Tsuen Wan district, on the twentieth floor of a modern office building, the Praise Assembly is already in full swing half an hour before the actual start. The band on stage rehearses and the hymns of praise and adoration emotionally prepare the worshippers for two hours of immersion in a festive celebration. Local Christians worship in all atmospheric shades, from solemn to ecstatic. What nearly all have in common, across the dozens of denominations and church networks, are long sermons and the strong presence of lay leaders.

Hong Kong has traditionally been a place of transit, where refugees from China found temporary shelter to rest and recharge before moving on to greener pastures. Even though most of these immigrants stayed longer, put down roots and established networks of belonging, an atmosphere of restlessness and impermanence continues to permeate many aspects of society. What endures are family ties and seasonal festivals—surrounded by volatility, with businesses coming and going, and people experiencing quick economic growth and equally sudden loss. This fluidity creates a unique pace and a pragmatic and flexible mindset that has fascinated many visitors to this city. The impermanence of local life has also been a crucial factor in shaping the ecclesial landscape, with churches springing up, growing, dividing, and always reaching out to new shores.

In this context, a host of churches and denominations emerged and have lived side by side: Catholics, Anglicans, Baptists, Lutherans, Presbyterians, and Methodists, who all came in the first decades of the territory's colonization; Pentecostals, who set up their local base in the early twentieth century; Chinese indigenous churches such as the True Jesus Church and the Little Flock, in the first decades of the twentieth century; a great number of churches and missionaries who withdrew from China during the 1940s and 50s and established local churches; more recent Pentecostal-charismatic groups such as the Bread of Life Church or the Praise Assembly; numerous locally founded independent churches; and several groups of Christians disenchanted with other churches. This chapter leads through the multi-colored landscape of local churches and denominations and discusses their place within local history and society. After an overview of Christian demographics, it summarizes significant historical developments and offers factual information about the various denominations, surveys and assesses major churches in Hong Kong, and identifies recent trends, with the focus on churches that worship in a Chinese language. The next chapter will consider the city's international churches.

Demographics of Christianity

Hong Kong is a highly fluid city with people moving in and out, and with religious change frequently taking place. Any numerical claims should thus be read with caution. Estimates regarding the number of Christians range from 6 percent to more than 20 percent. The large difference is due to different methodologies. The lower numbers are the result of churches reporting membership and worship attendance while the higher numbers are based on surveys of people's belief. Among the inherent difficulties of demographics is the problem of definition and of mobile membership.

The government estimates the Christian community to number around 1.2 million, or around 16 percent of the population, with around two-thirds Protestant Christians, including Pentecostals and Evangelicals, and around one-third Catholic. The small Greek, Russian, and Coptic Orthodox communities have a demographically negligible presence in the territory.[1] However, this information is not gathered by the government—it is supplied by the Hong Kong Christian Council (the HKCC, an association of the Protestant mainline denominations) and from the Catholic Diocese. A census by the Hong Kong Church Renewal Movement, based on questionnaires sent to churches and referring only to local Protestant churches, finds that 4 percent of the city's residents are members of a church, and 3.6 percent join in worship on an average Sunday.[2] Applying the government's two-to-one Protestant–Catholic ratio, Hong Kong Christians end up with an underwhelming 6 percent of the population.

On the other side, studies based on self-reporting instead of on church membership or worship participation report significantly higher numbers. A study conducted in 2009 and 2012 by the Chinese University based on telephone surveys and territory-wide random sampling concluded that around 24.4 percent of Hongkongers are Christians (2009), with 18.6 percent Protestants and 5.8 percent Catholics.[3] In 2018, the Ray Bakke Centre for Urban Transformation at the Bethel Bible Seminary conducted a meta-analysis of over a thousand journal articles on studies in Hong Kong covering various fields, some of them also offering data on religion. Their research estimates that between 24.1 and 31 percent are Christians, again with a large majority Protestants.[4] The most recent study, conducted in 2021 by the HKCC and the Divinity School of Chung Chi College, CUHK, like the earlier study based on self-declaration, concludes that 22.4 percent are Christians (17.2 percent Protestant; 5.2 percent Catholic).[5] This 2021 study takes, at least partly, recent developments such as the Covid pandemic and the migration after the introduction of the National Security Law into account.

The key point to note is the large gap between the 20 percent (or more) self-professed Christians and the as few as 6 percent of the people (or 4 percent, for Protestants) who attend church and maintain a membership. This points to a significant number of de-churched or unchurched Christians,[6] that is, Christians who have left the church for various reasons or whose lifestyle makes attendance or membership difficult, but who still identify with the Christian faith.

How can Christians demographically be further described? In shortest form: Christians are older and female, and they are better educated and earn more than the average Hongkonger.

According to the 2021 research,[7] the *gender ratio* of Christians is 62 percent female vs 38 percent male. Christians are on average older than the overall population, with 52 percent over 50 years, compared to Hong Kong's median age of 44.8 years. This is a notable change from the 2009 study where Christians were on average in the range of 40–44 years, while the average age of non-Christians was between 45 and 49 years.[8] The education level of Christians is significantly higher than that of the average populations: 55 percent have a tertiary education (vs. 32.7 percent overall).[9] Christians are earning significantly more than the average population: While the median income in Hong Kong is HKD 18,400 or around 2,350 USD (June 2020),[10] only 36 percent of Christians earn less than HKD 20,000. The median household in Hong Kong is HKD35,000. However, 61 percent of Christians have a household income above this amount.[11]

Denominations and Spiritual Orientations

With 1,312 congregations and 69 denominations,[12] nearly every tradition is present in Hong Kong. This has, first, to do with the character of the city: An open-minded population that welcomes innovation and that provides a vibrant marketplace for everything, including spiritual paths. It has, second, to do with the city's relationship to China, until 1949 a main target of world mission, for which the city was a steppingstone. It has, third, to do with post-1949 China, which expelled all missionaries and mission agencies, prompting an exodus of many of them to Hong Kong.

To introduce the city's large number of churches and denominations in a meaningful way is a difficult task. There are high churches and low churches; traditional liturgical and modern charismatic churches; churches with and without ordained ministry; institutionalized churches and those that understand themselves more as fellowships; churches with different polities—episcopal, presbyterian, and congregational churches; inclusive and exclusive churches; politically conservative and progressive churches; grassroots and affluent churches. While classifications never do justice to the complex reality, they help identify common characteristics. This chapter introduces the city's major denominations divided into the categories of Roman Catholics, ecumenical, evangelical, and Pentecostal-charismatics, followed by independent churches and, finally, increasingly fluid ecclesial forms.

Ecumenical churches are those who, as churches, not just as individual Christians, make efforts to connect to other churches and to the international Christian community, and whose theology has a measure of inclusiveness towards different truth claims. They stress the need for churches to strive for communal relatedness beyond individual churches and denominations, beyond particular cultures and social groups, and beyond individual subjectivity. Modern ecumenism has always included these three dimensions—interconfessional, intercultural, and intersubjective.[13] Locally, they gather in fellowship in the ecumenical Hong Kong Christian Council (HKCC), an affiliated member of the World Council of Churches, and carry on the multi-faceted worldwide ecumenical tradition.

Evangelicals are people who, to loosely follow the four marks that Bebbington identified as defining,[14] emphasize conversion experience, missionary activism, some form of biblical inerrancy, and the atonement through Christ's sacrifice on the cross. It is not accidental to speak of ecumenical *churches* on one hand and of evangelicals, that is, *individuals* on the other hand because evangelicals emphasize individual faith more than the corporate dimension of the church. Following a famous tongue-in-cheek definition of fundamentalists as "evangelicals who are angry about something"[15] and aware of the complicated history of evangelicalism and fundamentalism—modern evangelicalism as a movement emerging from the socially progressive evangelical awakening of the early nineteenth century, developing into socially conservative fundamentalism in the late nineteenth century, and reemerging as corrective to the fundamentalist rejection of all that is modern—we will treat *fundamentalists* as a sub-group of evangelicals.

The evangelical churches are not members of the HKCC, but most of them joined the 1915 founded Hong Kong Chinese Christian Churches Union (HKCCCU). This body should, however, not be seen in opposition to the ecumenical HKCC because first, the HKCCCU's founding members were mostly the same as the HKCC's, and the two bodies still have overlapping members, and second, the HKCCCU never did position itself as HKCC's counterpart. The differences between the two bodies are, first, that the HKCC brings different *denominations* into one council while the HKCCCU gathers individual *congregations*; second, that the HKCCCU has many evangelical members, which do not join the ecumenical body; and third, the HKCCCU refrains from developing a joint vision or expressing statements on matters of public concern, leaving this instead to individual churches.

The term "*Pentecostal-charismatic*" covers a wide field of believers, from historical Pentecostal denominations to younger charismatic or "Third Wave" groups. They have, similar to evangelicals, a passion for mission and evangelism, but they are, as they call it, "open to the work of the Holy Spirit" and demonstrate a more expressive and fluid form of faith that welcomes physical dimensions of faith expressions. They are Christians who are "concerned primarily with the *experience* of the working of the Holy Spirit and the *practice* of spiritual gifts."[16]

While various denominations loosely follow these spiritual orientations, they do not strictly identify with one or the other. A specific denomination may have an affinity for a specific spiritual orientation; however, an individual congregation may follow a different direction while still maintaining core characteristics of the original denomination. As a result, to understand churches, one needs to consider not only their denominational identity, but also what we may call their "post-denominational identity," that is, whether a church is ecumenical, evangelical, or Pentecostal-charismatic *in its faith practice*. For example, St. John's Cathedral, founded by the Anglican low-church Church Missionary Society (CMS), has gradually moved towards high-church Anglicanism, yet it is, theologically and practically, ecumenical and inclusive. On the other side of the harbor, the equally Anglican St Andrew's Church is low-church in its liturgical practice and evangelical in its beliefs, while incorporating elements of megachurch Christianity in its worship practice.

Catholics

The oldest and by far the single largest local tradition is the Catholic Church. It is, in its own way, an ecumenical church that relates to a worldwide faith community, cares for ecumenical church relations, emphasizes the corporate dimension of faith, and successfully integrates various spiritual currents.

Its 52 parishes with 90 worship places count around 580,000 believers, around 70 percent of them local Chinese—a local Catholic population of 401,000 plus an estimated 200,000 Filipino Catholics from among the overseas domestic workers.[17] However, some of these Filipino migrant workers might in fact worship in Protestant communities.

Although the Catholic Church was the first to enter the territory, just three months after Captain Charles Elliot declared Hong Kong part of the British dominion, it did, initially, not aim at local missionary work. It saw Hong Kong simply as a base outside Portuguese-controlled Macau intended to provide financial and logistical support to missionaries in China. It also wanted to provide spiritual support to local British soldiers from Ireland and Portuguese Catholics from Macau. In an amazingly short time, the first apostolic prefect, Theodor Joset, a Swiss national, began the construction of a mission house on Wellington Street, built in 1842, and a church that was completed after his death in 1843.[18] Within another two years, Joset's successor Feliciani built a cemetery, several houses, and a church in Wanchai. The Our Lady of Mount Carmel Church in Wanchai traces its history to these first years of local activity. Only after 1860, when the missionaries of the Pontifical Institute of Foreign Missions in Milan (P.I.M.E.) started their ministry, did the church direct its mission toward the local population, first among the Hakka people in the remote Tai Po and Sai Kung areas.[19] In 1874, the church was upgraded from an apostolic prefecture to a vicariate and, after the Second World War, to a diocese.

The history of local Catholicism is indissolubly linked to religious orders, which still make up 60 percent of the local priesthood. From the early Franciscans (1842), Paris Foreign Missionaries (1848), Sisters of St. Paul de Chartres (1848), P.I.M.E. missionaries (1858), Canossian Daughters of Charity (1860), Dominicans (1861), and Lasallians (1875), to the later Maryknoll Fathers and Brothers (1918), Maryknoll Sisters (1921), Jesuits (1926), and Salesians (1927), to name only a few,[20] with over forty religious institutes Catholic Christianity has as many religious agents as Protestants have mission agencies, but while the number of Protestant missionaries in Hong Kong has declined, non-local priests from religious orders continue to be a characteristic

FIGURE 2.1 *The Catholic Cathedral of the Immaculate Conception in Central (copyright Ricardo Balsani Ferraz).*

of local Catholicism. Today, just 45 percent of the priests in the diocese are ethnically Chinese, and it is only since 1969 that the diocese has had a local as bishop. This slow process of indigenization is not unique to Hong Kong but is a feature of Catholicism globally, which took decisive steps towards local leadership only after the Second Vatican Council. Yet, for local Catholics, diversity among their priests is an asset rather than a weakness: the fellowship and close cooperation of local and international priests reflects parishioners' self-understanding as citizens of a global city and as part of a transnational faith community, a connection which inoculates them against the promotion of a national identity (see more in Chapter 7).[21] On this basis—as a church both local and global, in a unique geographical and political position—the Catholic Church in Hong Kong has served as both a bridge between the universal church (headed by the Pope in Rome) and the government-approved church in China, and as a bastion of resistance against the patriotic claims of the central government.

The longest serving local church leader was John Baptist Wu Cheng Chung (1925–2002), a Hakka native from Eastern Guangdong who came to Hong Kong in 1946. He became the fifth bishop of the Hong Kong diocese in 1975, and in 1988, the first bishop of Hong Kong to be elevated to the position of cardinal. Among his achievements were the resumption of relations with the church in China and a strong emphasis on lay leaders. His successor, Bishop Joseph Zen Ze-Kiun (born 1932), is a native of Shanghai who fled to Hong Kong during the Chinese civil war in the late 1940s. A member of the Salesian order, he has been an outspoken critic of religious policies in mainland China, a prominent voice in the local movement for democracy, and something like the conscience of Hong Kong.[22] While his unabated criticism of the local and Beijing governments alienated some, many Christians (and non-Christians) were grateful for his persistent defense of social justice and the church's independence. Despite his high ecclesial position, he follows a simple and apostolic lifestyle, evidenced by his regular travels by public transport to remote prisons to visit inmates. His simplicity, and his care for the poor and the suffering, gives credibility to his prophetic voice.

Ecumenical Denominations

Most of the oldest churches in Hong Kong, sometimes called "historic" or "mainline" churches, among them Anglicans, Calvinists (Reformed or Presbyterians), Lutherans, and Methodists, belong to ecumenical Christianity. The *Anglican Church* is not the oldest Protestant church in Hong Kong—this honor goes to the Baptist Church—and it is by far not the largest local church. Yet, for many years, it has played an important and quasi-official role as the church of the colonial establishment. Its history goes back to 1843, with Vincent Stanton as the first Colonial Chaplain sent to the city from Macau. Initially, the Hong Kong diocese, established in 1849 as the Diocese of Victoria, included all of China and Japan—until today the Anglican Communion's largest diocese ever.[23] Later, it was divided into several dioceses, which eventually formed a nationwide church organization, the Chung Hua Sheng Kung Hui (CHSKH, 1912). In 1951, the Hong Kong and Macau diocese, the Hong Kong Sheng Kung Hui (HKSKH), was established, becoming the smallest Anglican diocese. Since 1998, local Anglicans have been an independent province of the Anglican Communion, its thirty-eighth Province. It is headed by an archbishop who oversees three local dioceses plus the missionary area of Macau.

Major congregations on Hong Kong Island are: St. John's Cathedral; St. Stephen's in Sheung Wan, the first Chinese Anglican church, founded in 1865; affluent St. Paul's in Central, adjacent to the prestigious St Paul's College; and St. Mary's in the busy Causeway Bay district, built in traditional Chinese style; on the Kowloon side St. Andrew's; All Saints' Cathedral, in the heart of the sprawling Mongkok district, consecrated in 1927 and the cathedral of the diocese of West Kowloon; and Holy Trinity in Kowloon City, like St. Mary's built in traditional Chinese style and the cathedral of the diocese of East Kowloon.

The Anglican Church has always been an important pillar of local ecumenical Christianity and embraces, as elsewhere, a broad diversity of theological beliefs and spiritual practices. This ecumenical breadth is not without tension, as witnessed when a former member of the clergy of St. John's sneered that people at St. Andrew's, not being liturgical enough, are hardly proper Anglicans anymore. On the other side, the evangelical Christians of St. Andrew's would be uncomfortable with St. John's barely concealed inclusiveness towards sexual minorities. Although deeply linked with the colonial establishment, the Anglican Church has contributed significantly to the contextualization of the Christian faith. Bishop Ronald Owen Hall played a particularly crucial role in integrating Christianity with Chinese culture during his long tenure (1932–66).[24] His deep respect for the Chinese culture finds expression in his statement that "all China's past is her Old Testament,"[25] suggesting that China's past may, like the history of Israel, lead to Christ. Hall developed a close relationship with Karl Reichelt, the founder of the Christian Mission to Buddhists on Tao Fong Shan and lived for most of his bishopric in a house built on the hill.

Bishop Hall was an exceptional figure in twentieth-century global Anglicanism, as shown in his extraordinarily courageous ordination of Florence Li Tim Oi as the first woman priest of the worldwide Anglican Communion in 1944,[26] an idea first conceived by Bishop Mok Shau Tsang, the first Chinese bishop consecrated in the diocese. This visionary ordination showed the willingness of Chinese Anglicans to respond creatively to a difficult situation, in this case a serious staffing shortage. Although Florence Li had to resign her priestly license after the war due to objections from Canterbury, her priestly orders were restored in 1984. Chinese Anglicans' acceptance of women in ministry was also evident in the ordinations of local women in the 1970s.[27] At a time when Anglicans elsewhere were still stuck in tense debates on this topic, the Hong Kong diocese assumed a pioneering and progressive role.

Since the handover, the senior clergy of the local Anglican Church has related to the new political authorities with the same loyalty as it showed to the colonial government. The archbishop even became a local delegate to the Chinese People's Political Consultative Conference, a kind of second chamber of the national parliament. A senior Anglican clergyman explained privately that "[i]t is part of the DNA of Anglicanism to be pro-government." In recent years, with church–state relations gradually changing, this strongly pro-government position has triggered considerable discontent among many Anglicans, both lay people and priests.

The *Hong Kong Council of the Church of Christ in China* (HKCCCC or shorter CCC) has always been a core pillar in ecumenical Christianity. The church is rooted in the ministry of the London Mission: In 1843, James Legge moved the mission station from Malacca to Hong Kong, the beginning of a

FIGURE 2.2 *The 1926-built Church of Christ in China's Hop Yat Church in Bonham Road, in the affluent Mid-Levels above Central; behind it the 2019 completed futuristic building of the Ying Wa Girls' School that has been offering local girls' education since 1900 (copyright Raffaella Endrizzi).*

movement towards the formation of an indigenous and united church in China, the Church of Christ in China, that was formally established in 1927.[28] Driving forces were Presbyterians, Congregationalists, and the London Mission; they were joined by representatives of other mission boards, among them British Baptists and Canadian Methodists. At the time of the church's founding, they accounted for about 30 percent of China's Protestant community.[29] The Hong Kong Council formed in 1953, after it had to separate from its sister churches north of the border when the latter joined the government-sanctioned organization of mainland churches, the "Three-Self Patriotic Movement." This Hong Kong Council carried on the tradition of an ecumenical and indigenous Chinese church. It included the local churches that had been part of the CCC's national network and a few new churches from the same background.

The CCC's first general secretary was Rev. Peter Wong, who had migrated to Hong Kong from Guangzhou in 1956. During his long years of service (1957–84), he shaped the church's development and was deeply involved in local, regional, and global ecumenical relations. Theologically, the church shares beliefs with the Reformed tradition and the major ecumenical bodies of which it is a member, the World Council of Churches (WCC), the Christian Conference of Asia (CCA), the Council for World Mission (CWM), the World Methodist Council (WMC), and the World Communion of Reformed Churches (WCRC).

Another core pillar of ecumenical Christianity is the *Methodist Church*. Its history[30] begins with the British Methodist missionary George Piercy, who came to Hong Kong in 1851. However, he soon moved on to serve on the mainland; it was not until 1882 that a group of Methodist Christians from Guangzhou began to establish the local Methodist church. The earliest congregation was an English-language church built in 1893 on Magazine Gap Road. The earliest Chinese chapel moved among various locations until finally setting up a major church in Wanchai (1936). This is Hong Kong's oldest Methodist congregation and a central church of the denomination. Like other denominations, local Methodists separated from the mainland church after 1949 and continued to develop independently. In the 1950s, the American Methodists—who had worked mainly in Shanghai and Fuzhou—withdrew to Hong Kong and began a ministry among the Mandarin-speaking immigrants from mainland China. The British and Americans merged in 1975 to form the Methodist Church Hong Kong. Clearly rooted in a distinctive denominational tradition, it is a spiritually progressive church with a strong ecumenical vision of inclusiveness and service in the world. Proud of its origins in the ministry of Chinese (i.e., not Western) missionaries and inheriting Wesley's tradition of dissent, the church emphasizes its independence from the government and its reliance on local support rather than on government subventions. An example of this tradition of dissent, independence, and passion for the community is Lo Lung Kwong, a charismatic church leader who played an important role in the church's social-justice ministry and who led the fundraising for three local church redevelopments. Historically related to the Methodist church through the Holiness tradition and also part of the ecumenical community is the small *Salvation Army*, which began its local ministry in 1930.[31]

The *Lutheran community* consists of six separate denominations, five of which compose the Hong Kong Lutheran Federation: the Tsung Tsin Mission Church (TTM), the Rhenish Church, the Evangelical Lutheran Church (ELCHK), the Hong Kong and Macao Lutheran Church, and the Lutheran Church Hong Kong. This separation reflects the strong denominational and less ecumenical character of local Lutherans. These churches, established by different mission societies, never entered into a church union as the Methodists did, and only two, the TTM and the ELCHK, joined the ecumenical HKCC. The two oldest Lutheran denominations are the TTM and the Rhenish Church, whose first missionaries (from the Basel and the Barmen Missions, respectively) arrived on the same boat in 1847. Both churches stand in the Pietist tradition, a more ecumenical form of Lutheranism that incorporates Reformed elements. The two groups aimed at two linguistically different Chinese populations—the

FIGURE 2.3 *The 1998-completed Chinese Methodist Church, in the heart of Wanchai, with its 23-storey tower for church and commercial use (copyright Tobias Brandner).*

Basel missionaries went to the Hakka (and, for a short initial period to the Hoklo in the Chaozhou area), while the Barmen missionaries worked among the Cantonese. A major church of the TTM, the Kau Yan Church has the honor of being the oldest Chinese church in Hong Kong with a continuous history going back to 1852. In 1924, in the process of an increasing movement towards independence from Western missions, the members of the Basel Mission Church established the Tsung Tsin Mission Church, meaning "the church worshipping the true God."[32] Due to political changes, the local conference in 1951 became independent of its counterparts in China. Since then, it has continued to understand itself as the church of the Hakka people worldwide, even though hardly any local TTM members still speak the Hakka language. The Rhenish Church initially served mainly in the Pearl River Delta; it began its local ministry only in 1898 and established its local district council in 1929; like the TTM, it separated from its churches in Guangdong and became a locally registered church in 1951.[33]

The largest among the Lutheran churches is the *Evangelical Lutheran Church*, which has its roots in European and American missions in China. The church was formally established in 1954 and, like the other Lutheran churches, has developed mainly through social services and educational ministries. The ELCHK still has strong connections with the German, U.S., Finnish, and Norwegian Lutheran churches. Most of its congregations are rather small and located in less affluent areas of Hong Kong such as Yuen Long, Tuen Mun, and Tin Shui Wai. The *Hong Kong and Macau Lutheran Church* (HKMLC) traces its history to the Norwegian mission in central China, which relocated to Hong Kong in 1949 and worked among the large number of Chinese refugees. Only in 1978 did it become a fully independent church. Its congregations also lie in less affluent areas—Tseung Kwan O, Kwun Tong, or Sham Shui Po. The most conservative of these Lutheran churches is the *Lutheran Church Hong Kong Synod*, established by the Lutheran Church Missouri Synod, an American denomination which still excludes women from pastoral ordination. Its history mirrors that of the ELCHK and the HKMLC: it began in 1913 in Szechuan and Hubei, relocated to Hong Kong in 1949, and subsequently ministered among poor refugees. Finally, outside of the intra-Lutheran communion, and like other conservative Lutherans rather belonging to evangelical Christianity, is the *South Asian Lutheran Evangelical Mission* that was founded in 1977 by another American denomination, the Wisconsin Evangelical Lutheran Synod.

Evangelical Denominations

Most Christians in Hong Kong would describe themselves as evangelical, and most churches are, in fact, evangelical in their theology and conservative in their moral teaching. This refers not only to the three largest local Protestant denominations—Baptists, Christian and Missionary Alliance, and Evangelical Free Church of China—but also to many of the Lutheran denominations introduced above.

The history of local *Baptists* began in 1842 with the first Protestant missionaries to take up residency in Hong Kong: Issachar J. Roberts, in February 1842; J. Lewis and Henrietta Shuck in March; and William Dean and his wife, arriving from Bangkok, later in 1842. They opened the first chapel in July 1842 on Queen's Road West, Wellington Street.[34] However, the ministry was soon discontinued and resumed only in 1880, when the Dutch missionary John W. Johnson and his wife moved from the mainland to engage in local mission work. Growth was slow, and in 1938, when the Baptist Convention of Hong Kong was founded, the church still had only six congregations with around 1,700 members.

Significant growth has happened since the 1940s, and today, the *Baptist Convention of Hong Kong* is the largest Protestant denomination. Around two-thirds of the local Baptist churches are members of the convention. Its largest congregations are the Kowloon City Baptist Church and the Shatin Baptist Church, each with around 4,500 people regularly attending Sunday services, and the Hong Kong Baptist Church (Caine Road) with around 2,000 regular attendees.[35] Like other denominations, Baptist Christians have established schools and social services, and their tertiary college even gained university status (1994). One factor for the strong growth of Baptist churches is the several large-scale evangelistic gatherings that the church conducted in the 1960s and 70s; another factor is their congregational independence that appeals to local Christians. Together with other evangelical churches, Baptists in Hong Kong have been vocal in promoting their understanding of traditional family values and opposing sexual minorities. Due to their congregational nature, different Baptist churches may differ widely in spiritual, theological, and political orientation.

The second-largest evangelical denomination is the *Christian and Missionary Alliance* (CMA or simply Alliance Church), which is rooted in the late nineteenth-century pre-Pentecostal Holiness movement but has moved into broader evangelical Christianity. Initially, Hong Kong was simply the church's base for ministry in China. During the Second World War and the civil war in China, many church leaders and members sought refuge in the city and, in 1940, started their first congregation in Kowloon Tong. Today, the largest CMA church is the North Point Alliance Church, which began in 1952 and, through steady growth, has become one of the largest churches in the city, with 6,000 members and even more regular attendees. An important figure not only in the North Point congregation but in the denomination as a whole was *Philip Teng* (1921–2013), one of the most prominent leaders of evangelical Christianity in twentieth-century Hong Kong and beyond. He was one of the founding chairs of the 1974 Lausanne Congress on World Evangelization and played a major role in both bringing the city's evangelical Christians together and mobilizing Chinese churches to engage in global mission. A result of this evangelical and missionary concern was the Chinese Coordination Centre of World Evangelism (CCCOWE), which he co-founded.[36] He was the interpreter for Billy Graham during his China tour in 1988. Characteristics of the Alliance Church are a strong emphasis on evangelism, spiritual leadership by a church board led by the senior pastor (i.e., in contrast to many churches' lay leadership, which can easily lead to tension between lay leaders and ordained clergy), and a conservative moral teaching advocating traditional family values.

The third major evangelical church is the *Evangelical Free Church of China* (EFCC), which has its roots in Scandinavian evangelicals who had migrated to the U.S., where they founded a free church in the 1880s and, soon after, began mission work in China. Local ministry began in 1937 and, since 1949, the EFCC's ministry has remained limited to the city. Continuous church planting and a strong growth orientation have turned the EFCC into one of the largest local denominations. At one point in the 1980s, the Waterloo Hill congregation single-handedly planted seven new churches in only six years. The EFCC's close link to the other major evangelical churches, the Baptist and Alliance, is visible in a joint "holiness campaign," launched in the late 1990s, promoting sexual purity and traditional family values. Similar to the Baptists, the EFCC congregations also span a wide spectrum, from many small and medium ones to several large ones, among them the strongly charismatic Tung Fook Church in busy Causeway Bay, the conservative Kong Fok [sic] in the Central Business District, which counts many government officials and other establishment figures among its members, and Yan Fook Church, which, since its beginnings in 1987, has grown into possibly the city's largest church, having more than 5,000 members and double that number joining Sunday worship in a skyscraper in Lai Chi Kok. For many years led by meanwhile retired senior pastor Patrick So Wing-Chi, the church employs around ninety full-time pastors. To enhance coherence, the church has even established its own theological seminary.

Among the many other evangelical denominations, a relatively large and moderate one is the *Union of the Swatow Christian Churches*, founded by Baptist and Presbyterian Christians from the Chaozhou (Swatow) area in eastern Guangdong, an area with its own Chinese language and a distinct culture. Traditionally, Chaozhou people worked in fishing and trade, and many settled in Southeast Asia, from Indonesia to Thailand, where many ethnically Chinese speak the Chaozhou language. The earliest evangelistic activities in the area go back to Rudolf Lechler (1824–1908) from the Basel Mission and, since 1858, English Presbyterians and American Baptists. The first gathering place for Swatow Christians in Hong Kong was established in 1909. In 1948, the different traditions of Swatow Christians resolved their theological differences to form a union and have grown gradually since then. Closely related is the *Lock Tao Christian Association*, named after Lock Road (*tao* = road), where their first meeting point was established in 1945.

Another relatively large evangelical denomination is the CNEC, whose name originally stood for China Native Evangelistic Crusade, but later for Chinese Native Evangelism Commission, and eventually for Christian Nationals' Evangelism Commission. Its history begins in the mainland's Guizhou Province in 1943.[37] With its strong passion for mission in the western parts of China where it established several churches and a small Bible school in Xinjiang, the CNEC played an important role in the early stages of Chinese overseas mission.[38] In 1949, it relocated to Hong Kong where, during the early period, it spread through regular evangelistic crusades conducted in local theaters. In 1952, it established the Bible Seminary of Hong Kong. In only one decade the CNEC grew to twelve churches spread across all parts of the city. In later decades, the CNEC grew like other churches through educational ministries.

On the conservative evangelical—or, rather, fundamentalist—side of local evangelical Christianity stands the *Peace Evangelical Church*, which has a significant following. Its theology is strictly separatist, and it rejects cooperation with churches with "impure" beliefs.[39] It cultivates traditional gender roles, with women subject to men and excluded from conducting the sacraments. With ordained ministry only recently adopted, congregations have long been led by elders and deacons. The church believes in the inerrancy and literal inspiration of the Bible, rejects speaking in tongues and other charismatic practices, and exhibits a premillennialist eschatology.

Even more radically separatist is *The Church of God in HK*, which had been involved in some controversy due to its enthusiastic evangelism among students and its rejection of other Christians. In an assessment of the church, Luk Fai, a senior pastor of the CCC, points out several theological differences from mainstream Christianity, such as an emphasis on human action that possibly ignores the sinful nature and limitations of human beings, a strict separatism that ignores the concerns of the world, and an emphasis on the own church's purity that implies that other churches are sects. Yet, while maintaining that the church is narrow and may hinder the spiritual growth of its members, he attests the church has an overall orthodox character.[40] Its separatist nature was also reflected in its continuous ignoring of requests for interviews, for church information, or for a church visit.

Several evangelical churches relate to the conservative wing of the Reformed (or Calvinist) tradition. Among them is the *Cumberland Presbyterian Church*, brought to China by a Chinese-American Christian in the early twentieth century, from where it came to Hong Kong in the early 1950s. A more conservative church in the same tradition is the *Reformed Evangelical*

Church Hong Kong, founded by the famous Indonesian Chinese evangelist Stephen Tong Tjong Eng. On the Baptist side, the *Hong Kong Universal Missionary Baptist Association* (previously known as the Association of Baptists for World Evangelism) began its local ministry when its China missionaries withdrew to the city after the war. The *Hong Kong Conservative Baptist Church Association* even carries its conservative orientation in its name. It was founded by American Baptists in 1963 who were dissatisfied with other U.S. Northern Baptists' lack of emphasis on the inerrancy of the Bible. The *Mission Covenant Church of Hong Kong* was founded by pietist missionaries from Norway who began their local ministry after being forced to leave China in 1949. Several other local evangelical denominations are independent of global networks and might be better categorized as independent churches.

Pentecostal-Charismatic Denominations

Pentecostal-charismatic Christianity includes historical Pentecostal churches, more recently emerging charismatic churches that emphasize the work of the Holy Spirit in various ways, and even Catholic charismatic groups. The history of local Pentecostalism begins in 1907 with the visit of the Americans A.G. and Lillian Garr, who had been inspired by the Azusa revival.[41] Their preaching inspired a local Congregationalist, Mok Lai Chi to establish the Apostolic Faith Mission, which in 1910 was renamed the Hong Kong Pentecostal Mission, probably the first indigenous Chinese Pentecostal church in Asia.[42]

Hong Kong's largest Pentecostal denomination, the *Assemblies of God* (AG), traces its beginnings to an American missionary, *Mattie Swan Ledbetter* (in Chinese Lai Ai Hua), who had first come to the city in 1912 but soon moved on to the mainland. A difficult life in Foshan, near Guangzhou, eventually took its toll and in 1928 she returned to the city to preach the gospel in Hong Kong.[43] The oldest local AG church is the First Assembly of God Church, established in 1951 on Argyle Street, Mongkok. The largest, the Yuen Long Kam Kwong Church, has over 5,000 members. While some of the congregations have maintained traditional Pentecostal practices such as speaking in tongues, some have become more evangelical and thus more cessationist (believing that the supernatural gifts of the Holy Spirit ended with the apostolic time and the emergence of the Bible). Still others practice the gifts of the Holy Spirit occasionally, for instance during special revivalist sessions, or recover them after a period of neglect. How much a congregation emphasizes Pentecostal practices largely depends on the senior pastor. The AG follows a congregational polity with only a very loose trans-congregational structure. Differences in teachings, personal tensions among church leaders, and a complicated mission history, with missionaries of Canadian and American affiliation flocking to the city from China after 1949, have resulted in repeated church divisions. As a result, today there are four different AG associations in Hong Kong. To outsiders, it appears, sadly, in the words of a senior member of the church, "as if dividedness is the most important characteristic of the local Assemblies of God."

The history of the second-largest local Pentecostal denomination, the *Pentecostal Holiness Church* (PHC), began in 1909 with the arrival of Anna M. Deane and T.J. McIntosh and his family, the latter staying only a few months.[44] Remarkably, the first long-term PHC missionaries in Hong Kong were all female, with Deane joined by her niece Anna Dean Cole and Jane A. Schermerhorne.[45] Initially, Deane, together with Meng Xiuling from Guangxi and Li Kun, a local fisherman, reached out to the fishing community in Shaukiwan, where they established the first PHC church. In the following decades, the PHC's mission continued to preach the gospel among the fishing communities, and it established several more churches in seaside villages. The Tanka, a local ethnic minority group traditionally living on junks in coastal waters were particularly receptive to Pentecostal preaching. As social outcasts, they had little to gain from the established social order of China, and Christianity offered new possibilities to them.[46] Since the 1920s, the PHC had used a gospel boat to reach out to the Tanka and this sea-based mission continued to reach communities in less accessible parts of the territory's coast. After the war, in 1952, the PHC Hong Kong was registered locally and began ministry among the growing numbers of refugees flocking to the city. Today, 60 percent of the denomination's members are from one congregation, the Wing Kwong Church. Under the leadership of its first Chinese superintendent, Ng Shan Ho, the church has moved from common Pentecostal-charismatic teachings toward a more evangelical direction, emphasizing the gifts of the Spirit as corporate rather than individual. With this teaching, introduced by (among others) the Singapore-based theologian Simon Chan, who calls for an ecclesiology that seeks "to 'corporatize' Pentecostal experience,"[47] the church has moved closer to traditional liturgical churches, which similarly understand the charismata as subsisting in the community.

Another historic Pentecostal church is the local *Foursquare Gospel Church*, which claims to have been founded in 1910 and prides itself on having a longer history than the U.S. Foursquare Gospel Church.[48] Aimee Semple McPherson, the church's founder, had been in Hong Kong already in 1910 and gave birth to her daughter in the territory, but when her husband Robert died of malaria soon after their arrival, she returned to the U.S. where she founded the Foursquare Gospel Church in 1923. However, she never forgot her vision to bring the gospel to China, and Hong Kong always stood, in McPherson's telling, for a sort of "mythical birthplace for her ministerial identity and vocation."[49] In 1936, the church sent Edwin and Beulah Lee, a Chinese pastor and his wife to the city. The war years interrupted the ministry of the church and for the subsequent decades the local church remained a branch of the U.S. church. Only in 1982 did it register locally.

The *True Jesus Church* (TJC) is different from the aforementioned denominations: it is an early independent Chinese church with Pentecostal characteristics that rejects its identification as Pentecostal, and it is debated as to whether or not it actually belongs to Pentecostal Christianity.[50] Its founder, Wei Enbo, who had become a Christian through the London Missionary Society, had a conversion experience in 1917 near Beijing, where he was led by the Spirit to immerse himself, unassisted by any clergy, and receive baptism.[51] In the same year, he established the True Jesus Church, which rapidly spread across China, particularly among Seventh-Day Adventists, from whence it received its Sabbatarianism and its eschatological teachings. The TJC belongs to the Oneness Pentecostals, who baptize only in the name of Jesus and regard Jesus as the New Testament name of God. Locally, the church began in 1929 when Maria Yau, who had become part of the TJC community in Singapore, began her ministry. She was soon joined by another deaconess, Yau Yuk Ying.[52] Their worship, where men and women are seated separately, combines strict orderliness with communal sessions of glossolalic prayer and bodily shaking.

The *Christian Assembly* or *Little Flock*, also known as the *Church Assembly Hall*, is another independent Chinese denomination. Its founder, Watchman Nee (Nee Tuosheng), became one of the best-known Chinese Christian leaders due to his devotional books, among them *The Spiritual Man* (1928). His movement has several Pentecostal characteristics and it influenced global Pentecostalism, but its most important elements are its premillennial dispensationalism[53] and a critical distance from other Christian denominations. Followers of Watchman Nee have been gathering in Hong Kong since 1937. They purchased their first property after 1949 and began to welcome a growing number of refugees from China. In the first decades, the church spread through reading rooms that were set up in poor neighborhoods, where members offered counseling and study support. These rooms were then also used as meeting points for worship.

Slightly younger is the Ling Liang Church, also called the *Bread of Life Christian Church*, a third independent Chinese church, founded by Zhao Shiguang in Shanghai (1942), from whence it spread across Asia.[54] In 1949, Zhao moved to Hong Kong and established several churches.[55] Like the True Jesus Church and the Little Flock, it emphasizes independence from Western mission. Locally, its twenty-one congregations are all overshadowed by the 611 Bread of Life Church, which, within only a few years, grew to one of the city's largest churches. It has a weekend attendance of over 9,000 and has founded three branch churches locally and thirty-five more across Asia and beyond. It was established not by local Bread of Life churches but by Joshua Cheung, a local pastor who was commissioned by the church in Taiwan; on his return to Hong Kong—at the airport, in fact—the Holy Spirit directed him to Isaiah 61:1, hence the name of the church. In this congregation, charismatic practices flourish: ecstatic worship, glossolalic prayers, and spiritual healing. Like other large-scale churches, it grew through a rigorous cell group ministry, modelled on the "G12" strategy of Colombian pastor César Castellanos, with more than 100 cell group leaders who train group members to establish their own cells. The strong relationships experienced in these cell groups are the backbone for the strong grassroots growth of this church. Significantly though, the church also successfully attracts professionals and highly educated Christians. The original Bread of Life Churches maintain an identity separate from and critical of 611 and have, like other historic Pentecostal churches, turned to more broadly evangelical practices.

Among the major charismatic churches of the "third wave" that entered Hong Kong in 1990 with large-scale evangelical meetings conducted by John Wimber and John White,[56] the *Praise Assembly* offers the most intensely charismatic experience, with ecstatic dancing and worshippers falling to the ground or rolling on the floor, an energetic exuberance that stands in contrast to the restrictions and repressions experienced in daily urban life. Its congregations operate largely independently, but leading figures move among them. After starting in 1986 in a believer's home, Praise Assembly's first church was established one year later and has grown continuously, attracting many grassroots people.

Whether to list the *Seventh-day Adventists* (SDA) as Pentecostal-charismatic may be debated. The church grew out of the millennialist teachings of William Miller (1782–1849) and the prophecies of Ellen White (1827–1915), who is still highly honored. While the SDA exhibits a resemblance to Pentecostalism in some teachings, such as millennialism, it rejects typical Pentecostal practices such as speaking in tongues. The Seventh-day Adventist Church in Hong Kong claims a history as far back as 1888, when former miner and seaman Abram La Rue opened a seaman's mission in the territory and sold Adventist tracts, but an actual church was not established until 1902.[57] Since then, the church has grown through its educational and social ministry.

Several other churches belong to Pentecostal-charismatic Christianity, among them the historic *United Pentecostal Church of Hong Kong*, the *Kowloon Pentecostal Church*, and the *Pentecostal Tabernacle*. In addition, some congregations of otherwise evangelical denominations—for instance the Shaukiwan Baptist Church or the Evangelical Free Church of China's Tung

Fook Church—belong to charismatic Christianity; or rather, belonged at some point, at least in the case of the SKW Baptist Church: The congregation did eventually not further support the leading pastor Eddie Ma's charismatic leanings. Ma moved on and established the Incubator Ministry (IM), which is influential among the younger generation—a charismatic body with constant overseas contacts, organizing conferences and publishing music that other charismatic local churches use. On the Catholic side, the Catholic Charismatic Services Committee gathers charismatic believers. Finally, as we will see in the next chapter, many international Christian congregations tend toward charismatic practices.

Independent Churches

Around one-fifth of local churches (264 or 20.2 percent)[58] are independent of denominational networks and founded by individual leaders. They cover the whole field of theologies and spiritual orientations, with the majority conservative evangelical. Some of these churches have planted daughter churches and gradually developed into small networks. Their origins usually lie in leaders who preferred administrative independence, theological flexibility and spiritual freedom from denominational restrictions and historical baggage.

Some of these churches were founded by Western missionaries. The *Hope Mission Church*, with meanwhile three local churches, is a fruit of the ministry of Gladys Aylward (1902–70), a well-known missionary to China, made famous by the movie *The Inn of the Sixth Happiness*, which starred Ingrid Bergman and was loosely based on Aylward's story. The *St Stephen's Society* grew out of the ministry of Jackie Pullinger, who arrived in the 1960s and worked among drug addicts in the infamous Walled City in Kowloon, a territory outside local jurisdiction. The *Revival Christian Church*, with meanwhile three churches, was established by Dennis Balcombe, an independent Pentecostal missionary who received his calling within the Foursquare tradition, came to the city in 1969 and worked initially with local AG churches. Balcombe played an important role in bringing Pentecostal-charismatic beliefs and practices to house churches in China.

Other churches have been started by charismatic local individuals. One of them is the *Fuk Lam Church in Temple Street* (also called "Jesus in Temple Street" and formerly called the Shepherd Community Fuk Lam Church), located in Yaumatei, a poor and densely populated area with a rampant sex and drug trade. It was founded by charismatic Samuel Lai. As a young man, he was a gangster belonging to the triads, as the criminal gangs are locally called, and a drug addict, firmly at home in the criminal milieu of downtown Kowloon

FIGURE 2.4 *Jesus in the Temple Street: The Fuk Lam Church and Community Center, with entertainment venues, restaurants, and trade unions as neighbors (copyright Tobias Brandner).*

and serving several prison terms. In 1973, he joined the police force, without breaking with drugs or the triads, a common path at the time for uneducated young men, who could continue their criminal practices in the corrupt police force. Finally, a conversion experience during drug rehabilitation brought about radical change. Sent by *Youth with a Mission* (YWAM) and inspired by the missionary theories of Ray Bakke, Lai began to reach out to drug addicts, triad members, and sex workers in his former stomping grounds, eventually setting up the Fuk Lam Church (1988). They commonly conduct outdoor worship in an area that evangelical Christians would regard as firmly in the hand of demonic forces, with gambling and prostitution dens, and with the nearby Tin Hau temple surrounded by booths for fortune tellers, and they socialize with the people in the neighborhood.[59] In the early days, the church followed a strongly charismatic path, with power evangelism and healing prayers among the drifting poor. Gradually—reflecting the upward social mobility of converts from among the social margins—Fuk Lam Church became more evangelical, more learned, more orderly and, like other Pentecostal-charismatic churches, began to deemphasize charismatic practices. Meanwhile, it has planted two churches in other grassroots districts of Hong Kong. The church in Temple

Street is related to the ministry of another independent charismatic church, the *Shepherd Community Church*, formerly known as Shepherd Community Grace Church, founded in the industrial district of Kwun Tong by Pastors Benjamin Wong and Anthony Chan (1987).[60]

Several independent churches theologically follow the conservative Calvinist-Westminster tradition, among them the *Reformed Evangelical Christian Church*, which started in 2015, and the *Grace Reformed Evangelical Church*. Others have grown from a simple fellowship into a church with a particular focus group in mind, such as groups of released prisoners or rehabilitated drug addicts. In recent years, several ecumenical and progressive independent churches have sprung up. A pioneer was the *Sen Lok Christian Church*, started by Timothy Lam in 1997 and famous for its music ministry. In response to many churches' rejection of sexual minorities, two churches for the LGBTQ-community emerged: The Blessed Ministry Community Church, the first LGBT church in Asia, founded in 1992; and, more recently, the One Body in Christ Church, which is theologically more progressive and also emphasizes issues of ecology and social justice.

TABLE 2.1 List of major denominations[61]

Denomination	Name in Chinese	Year founded	Number of parishes/ congregations	Members (2020)
Catholic Diocese of Hong Kong	天主教香港教區	1841	52	580,000
Anglican Church (Hong Kong Sheng Kung Hui)	香港聖公會	1843	46	30,000
Tsung Tsin Mission of Hong Kong	基督教香港崇真會	1847	28	10,000
Baptist Convention of Hong Kong	香港浸信會聯會	1880 (1842)	108	102,600
Methodist Church Hong Kong	香港基督教循道衛理聯合教會	1882 (1851)	26	13,000
Chinese Rhenish Church Hong Kong Synod	中華基督教禮賢會香港區會	1898 (1847)	19	14,000

(*continued*)

Table 2.1 Continued

Denomination	Name in Chinese	Year founded	Number of parishes/ congregations	Members (2020)
Hong Kong-Macao Conference of Seventh-day Adventists	基督復臨安息日會港澳區會	1902 (1888)	21	4,823
Union of the Swatow Christian Churches	基督教潮人生命堂聯會	1909	14	10,000
Pentecostal Holiness Church Hong Kong	香港五旬節聖潔會	1909	15	10,000
Hong Kong Council of the Church of Christ in China (CCC)	中華基督教會香港區會	1927 (1843)	73	20,000
Assemblies of God Hong Kong	香港神召會	1928 (1912)	Around 50	18,000
Salvation Army	香港救世軍	1930	15	2,500
True Jesus Church	真耶穌教會(香港教會)	1932	8	1,500
Foursquare Gospel Church	國際四方福音會香港教區	1936 (1910)	7	1,000
Evangelical Free Church of China	中國基督教播道會	1937	60	27,000
Church Assembly Hall (Christian Stewards)	香港教會 – 教會聚會所 (基督徒管家)	1937	12	3,000
Christian and Missionary Alliance	基督教宣道會香港區聯會	1940	120	51,355
Lock Tao Christian Association	基督教樂道會	1948	8	1,000
Hong Kong and Macau Lutheran Church	港澳信義會	1949	9	2,400
Lutheran Church Hong Kong Synod	香港路德會	1949	35	12,000
Mission Covenant Church	香港聖約教會	1949	13	775

CNEC (Christian Nationals' Evangelism Commission)	中華傳道會	1949	21	3,535
Bread of Life Christian Church	靈糧堂	1949	21	5,493
611 Bread of Life Christian Church	611 靈糧堂	2001	1+3	9,000
Association of Baptists for World Evangelism (HK)	香港萬國宣道浸信會	1951	29	4,000
Cumberland Presbyterian Church	金巴崙長老會香港區會	1952	10	2,800
Evangelical Lutheran Church Hong Kong	基督教香港信義會	1954	50	17,800
Peace Church (Ping An Fu Yin Tang)	平安福音堂	1962	33	6,000 (2012)
Conservative Baptist Church Association	香港浸信宣道會	1963	13	1,500
The Church of God in HK	香港神的教會	1968	16	5,000[62]
Mennonites	基督教門諾會	1969[63]	3	100
South Asian Lutheran Evangelical Mission	南亞路德會	1977	10	2,500
Praise Assembly	基督教敬拜會	1987	11	No information

Notes: "Year founded" refers to the actual beginning of local ministry. In some cases, the additional year in brackets refers to earlier ministry by a mission agency that later developed into a church (e.g., the LMS starting in 1843 and then merging with others to form the CCC) or to the earliest missionaries arriving but without local ministry (e.g., the Rhenish Church). The number of congregations is relatively reliable, though different calculation methods may lead to different results, e.g., depending on whether branch churches of other congregations are counted. Membership numbers should be read with much caution, as they depend on widely different forms of calculation and estimation. Some churches include all baptized members even if they have migrated elsewhere, while others only count regular participants, which remain on the electoral roll of a congregation. This may explain the difference between, e.g., the TTM and the Rhenish Church, or between the CCC and the Anglican Church, with the former in both cases probably larger than the latter. The information regarding membership numbers is from various sources: mostly from churches' general secretariats, in other cases from senior church leaders, annual reports, or denominational websites. The information gained from these sources did not yet take into account the 2019 social movement, the Covid pandemic and the major wave of migration since 2020, all of which have a significant impact on church membership numbers.

Trends

Overlooking the whole landscape of Protestant churches and denominations in Hong Kong, a few observations stand out.

First, significant church growth has happened since the 1950s, caused by several factors: When the CPC's religious policies caused the departure of many church leaders from mainland China, many of them moved to the city and began to reach out to locals.[64] At the same time, many refugees flocking to the city were receptive not only to the diaconal ministry of the churches but also to the Christian message. They were poor and uprooted from their communities of origin, and they were eager to establish new belonging. Many of them found a new home in a Christian church. Furthermore, churches played a crucial role in the process of Hongkongers developing their unique identity since the 1970s. Churches contributed to this local identity-building through their social and educational ministries, through their presence in the cultural realm, or through their critical participation in society, as the next chapters will show. Another important growth factor is that in a city where people live in extremely crowded conditions and where all space is commercialized, churches are one of the few places where people can find space for individual and communal development, for creative activities, and where they are freed from the pressure of consumption.

Second, although Hong Kong does have a few larger churches with several thousand members, so-called mega-churches, they are less important locally than similar churches in places like Seoul or Singapore. One would think that large churches offer a better allocation of resources with potentially better "returns" for a believer: by concentrating the offerings of many members, one gains access to better infrastructure and services. Yet only thirty local congregations have over 1,000 members, and they account for less than 20 percent of all worshippers. Three-quarters (74.7 percent) of the churches have fewer than 200 members, accounting for 36 percent of Sunday worshippers, and 15 percent have less than 50 members.[65] Why, then, do Christians in Hong Kong, compared to other major Asian cities, tend less towards mega-churches? When local believers explain their preference for smaller churches, one answer dominates: deeper and more meaningful relationships. Churches' closely-knit communities resemble family relations. This is so even in the case of the mega-churches, whose growth is equally based on the strong personal links built up in cell groups. In fact, "family" is local Christians' most common image of their congregations. "We need a father, not an executive" was the advice that a local elder of an international church gave to a new pastor from the U.S., introducing him to local culture.[66]

Building church communities in the likeness of families has both strengths and weaknesses. The strong relationships offer a warmth that is lacking in the anonymity and individualization of urban life. It allows people to experience genuine care and mutual support within the church. The traditional Chinese emphasis on the family, which has been undermined by modern Hong Kong life, with tiny flats at horrendous prices, finds a substitute in the family-like church community. On the other side, family-like churches tend to be rather inward-looking, and they deemphasize the church's trans-congregational dimension. A focus on one's own "family" is a major obstacle to stronger ecumenical relations. Furthermore, in a context where a Confucian culture shapes the family-image, the church (or cell group) leader's parental role easily assumes hierarchical and patriarchal traits. This is particularly the case in churches with less organizational structure and more charismatic leadership, such as Pentecostal-charismatic churches. Although female church leadership is common, men still dominate senior positions. An interesting female role is the pastor's wife who, in local Christian culture, has high status and significant authority. Yet, her authority is always clearly subject to her husband's. Family-like churches can also be rather confining, with (intra-family) relationships closely regulated. Separation from a church appears disloyal—lacking filial piety—and can leave a person traumatized. The family-like character of many churches is also a cause of division. Junior leaders may prefer to establish their own independent "households," rather than being endlessly subject to the father-like authority of a senior pastor; this is seen particularly in Pentecostal denominations but also among independent churches. Competition between lay leaders and pastors is indeed a common cause of tension, and large churches find it commonly difficult to transition from an iconic founding pastor to the next generation.

Third, while the rise of Pentecostalism as a global phenomenon can also be witnessed in Hong Kong, the *largest local denominations* are not Pentecostal-charismatic but evangelical: the Baptist Church, the Alliance Church, and the Evangelical Free Church of China. Equally, the largest *congregations* are rather evangelical: the EFCC's Yan Fook Church, the North Point Alliance Church, and the Kowloon City Baptist Church. Even the Wing Kwong Pentecostal Holiness Church, which is nominally part of the Pentecostal tradition, as well as some of the AG churches, have gone through a process of de-pentecostalization and belong instead to evangelical Christianity. The only large Pentecostal-charismatic churches, which show charismatic practices, are the 611 Bread of Life Church in Tsuen Wan, the AG's Kam Kwong Church in Yuen Long, and the EFCC's Tung Fook Church in Causeway Bay. (We will see that the situation is slightly different among the international churches.) A significant growth factor for Pentecostal Christianity across the Asia-Pacific rim has been local societies' this-worldly spirituality and their receptiveness toward Pentecostal faith, a worldview of spirits and miracles,[67] yet this seems not to equally apply to Hong Kong.

Why, then, are evangelical churches in Hong Kong thriving more than Pentecostal-charismatic ones? The question may be partially explained by a comparison with Singapore, where Pentecostal-charismatic Christianity has grown dramatically in the past forty years: Several mega-churches have sprung up, each with well over 10,000 worshippers.[68] Singapore is ethnically a much more global city and uses English as a common language much more than Hong Kong. Pentecostal churches blend the ethnically diverse population in a politically unproblematic way into a cosmopolitan and tech-savvy religion and thus align with the government's developmental aim for a post-colonial Singapore. Joining a Pentecostal church gives Singaporeans a taste of being a global citizen and a sense of belonging. Pentecostalism's rise has followed the government's pressure against a liberal, capitalism-critical, and socially engaged Christianity, which has subsequently declined. While global citizenship is also an aim of people in Hong Kong, the city is more Chinese in both ethnicity and language. There is less need for harmonizing multiple ethnicities. Instead, Hong Kong's prevalent Confucian culture shows a stronger affinity to evangelical Christianity, with its emphasis on learning rather than experience, cognitive apprehension rather than emotional expression. The church is foremost a place to learn about God and godly life. Even local Pentecostal churches reflect openness to education and a more cognitive approach to faith compared to the anti-intellectualism of Pentecostal Christians observed elsewhere.[69] Another important factor in the local affinity to evangelical Christianity is that many local people are critical of "uncontrolled" emotions and "chaotic" forms of spirituality—they favor orderliness. This has partly to do with the impression that individual spiritual gifts may be related to superstition and irrationality. It has also to do with historical experiences such as the traumatic chaos of the Cultural Revolution that still lingers in the collective consciousness. A controlled and more rational faith appears safer and a better guarantee for a good life. A third factor mentioned in discussions with local Christians, which may also explain the limited success of mega-churches in Hong Kong compared to their Singaporean and Korean counterparts, is that locals are less obedient compared to people in Singapore and Seoul. For instance, the early morning prayer gathering that some local churches tried to introduce imitating their Korean counterparts had little success, even among those who regularly attend prayer mountain retreats in Korea. Hongkongers show pragmatism and a dislike of extremes, also in matters of faith.

Emerging Churches: Cyber, Slow, and Flow Christians

Finally, the demographic findings show that Christianity is much larger than what happens in the churches. In other words, many Christians are firmly outside the church.[70] Of course, Christianity without church attendance is not unique to Hong Kong, but here it seems to correlate with a still clear affirmation of Christian identity. It appears not to be an expression of only half-hearted identification with the Christian faith. So, where are these self-declared Christians? In recent years, a new form of Christian participation emerged, partly taking place in the virtual world. This is a vibrant expression of local Christianity and a fruit of Christian social media that has attracted many de-churched Christians. They are alienated by what they regard as the churches' lack of participation in the political protest movement, critical of most churches' focus on constant church growth to the detriment of the simplicity of the gospel, and critical of the rigidity and social control they have experienced in some local churches. "Cyber-Christianity" is a typical form of Christian faith in the global city—fluid, tech-based, and avoiding expensive space. One example of such an emerging church with a strong social media presence is the *Umbrella Cyber Church*, which emerged in the context of the 2014 democracy protests. Another emerging church is the *Slow Church*, its name reflecting critical distance from the city's speed and growth culture. The Slow Church began in the early 2010s, parallel to the emergence of social media, and gradually formed into a church. Yet, it still maintains a strong presence on social media. More recently emerging churches are Aspire Church, Simplychurch, and the Roundtable Church. They emphasize simplicity and flexibility in their place of worship, a fellowship character of the church, an interactive form of ministry and communication, and some even practice a communal life that integrates devotion, mission, and service to the community.[71]

The Reformation Continues: The Flow Church

The largest of these emerging churches is the *Flow Church*. Its founder, John Chan, followed a typical young theologian's path—conversion in his late teens, membership in a traditional evangelical church, admission to a bible seminary, and doctoral studies in Germany. At the age of thirty-three, he returned to a city where the call for democratic progress had gained steam and was about to turn into large and peaceful protests, the Umbrella Movement of 2014. Like other young people in Hong Kong, Chan felt dissatisfied by the reluctance of many churches to address the burning political and social issues of the city and by their preoccupation with church growth and inner-church activities. Gifted with a sharp mind and an ability for public speaking and writing, he began to use social media to comment on public issues from a Christian perspective. His public comments brought political theology to a broader audience, i.e., beyond the small circle of theological experts. In 2017, when Protestant churches worldwide commemorated the 500-year anniversary of the Reformation, Chan asked: What does the Reformation mean today, and what reformation do today's Hong Kong Christians need? From there, it was a small step to setting up a new group to gather the many who had turned away from the church. In May 2018, the church began with worship live-streamed through social media. For the first large-scale meeting, Chan chose an auspicious day, the local Ghost Festival, when, according to tradition, the dead return to visit the living. It was a powerful metaphor, as Chan was inviting dead Christians to become alive again. The name Flow Church was inspired by the famous words of Bruce Lee—"Be water, my friend"—pointing to a different kind of church, with less structure and fewer redundant meetings, more fluid and more experiential. A simple organization with no permanent property, it committed itself to being a "pilgrim church" in order to avoid the petrification of institutional churches. Within only three years, it attracted several hundred regular worshippers and an even larger audience through social media, 90 percent of them young people. The future will show whether the church is able to realize the Reformation principle of a church that must always be reformed (ecclesia semper reformanda)—the principle of fluidity against petrification—or whether it will go the path of all institutions. In any case, the Flow Church touched a nerve: only one year later, Bruce Lee's proverb would become young locals' strategic motto in their creative protest against an increasingly repressive government: "be water," avoid identification, and maintain vagueness.

Many of these emerging churches were active on social media through blogs and videos long before gathering their followers into a church, and they have in common a clear political position, in contrast to most churches' ambiguity in matters of politics, perhaps to avoid church splits. Yet virtual Christianity is not restricted to young, theologically inclusive and politically progressive Christians. Led by charismatic Christianity's emphasis on high-tech communication and global connectedness, many churches' active use of social media prepared the ground for their expansion into cyberspace. Already in 2001, local pastors and church leaders established the *Chinese Church Network*, which became an app—a platform for a range of well-known Chinese preachers from the city and the wider international Chinese community. Since then, traditional churches have increasingly used social media for faster and more direct communication with their members, with the recent pandemic further accelerating this trend. New platforms and networks are continuously emerging, among them the #DeltaΔMovement,[72] a hashtag used by different Christian content creators on Instagram and Facebook, where more than twenty individual pages form a decentralized and organic Christian resource center with creative media, new songs, devotional material, personal testimonies and discussions on politics, faith, theology, and the Bible. Cyber-Christianity overcomes ecclesial and geographical boundaries and, although strongly based on local Hong Kong preachers, brings Chinese Christians around the world closer together. It shows the global city at its best, offering high mobility and connecting global space while being grounded in local reality and physical fellowship. It blurs traditional forms of church life, as visitors to these networks may not even be members of local churches. They may offer their donations anonymously and hide their identities. As the city's freedoms are increasingly under threat, such anonymity is an obvious advantage.

3

All the Nations Worship
the Lord

Christian Migrant Workers and Expats

Sunday morning in the central business district: among the thousands of domestic workers who gather here every Sunday to enjoy their holiday stands a group of Filipinas singing, worshipping, and reaching out to their countrywomen. They are from the evangelical *Jesus Is Lord Church*, a global mega-church from the Philippines. At the same time, just ten minutes' walk up the hill, in the St. Joseph's Church, hundreds of Filipinas follow a Catholic mass. The two groups are just a small part of the vibrant and multi-colored international Christian community in Hong Kong.

As we turn to the city's international churches, we find the same diversity of denominational traditions and spiritual directions as among local churches, yet with a stronger penchant for Pentecostal-charismatic spirituality. Among the estimated 150 international Protestant churches,[1] some are non-Chinese congregations of traditional mainline or newer evangelical and Pentecostal denominations: St. John's Cathedral and St. Andrew's Anglican Church, International Baptist Church, Methodist International Church (MIC), Church of All Nations of the Lutheran Church Missouri Synod, and the Assemblies of God Tai Po Church, to name a few. The Roman-Catholic Church conducts regular worship services in English and other languages. The Eastern Orthodox Church has a metropolitan seat for Hong Kong and Southeast Asia in the city and conducts regular worship in English. Some congregations are attached to or established by major local churches who hope to reach out to unevangelized socio-cultural groups using other languages. A few are local branches of international mega-churches; a few other congregations are national churches abroad. Many, though, are independent of denominational affiliation. These churches cater to expatriates working in the financial industry, traders from Africa, migrant workers from South or Southeast Asia, descendants of the Nepalese Gurkhas, and, most importantly, to the many Chinese locals or returnees from abroad who simply feel more at home in an English-speaking church.

What is an international church? This question leads to the core issue of residents' identity in this global city: Is it a church whose members are mainly non-locals? But who is a local? Or is it a church founded by people from outside the city? If so, how long does it take for an outsider to become local? Is it a branch of a church from outside the city? But is not the mix of local and global, the presence of global religious brands and their local appropriation, at the heart of a global city? Or is it simply a church that uses a language other than Cantonese in its worship? But are Putonghua and English not equally official languages in Hong Kong?

For the sake of convenience, this chapter uses this last understanding of international churches to introduce the manifold expressions of Christian worship, life, and ministry that happen in Hong Kong in non-Chinese languages. The chapter surveys this variegated landscape of international Christianity in the global city and examines how migrant identity and religious identity strengthen each other, and how Christians from around the world contribute in unique ways to the city.

Filipino Migrant Workers' Churches

With nearly one-third of the city's non-Chinese population—and representing half of local migrant workers[2]—the over 200,000 Filipinas[3] are the most important group of foreigners in the city. Most of them work as low-paid domestic workers at a prescribed monthly minimum salary of around US$600. While this is double the average salary that most of them would receive at home, it comes at the price of a painful separation from their families. Many of them live in slave-like conditions, legally required to live in the same household as their employer, some forced to share their room with a member of the employer's family, regularly exposed to physical and verbal abuse,[4] and without protection from excessive working hours. They are the first to get up in the morning and the last to go to bed, even preparing late-evening meals for their ever-hungry employers. They are not only discriminated against by strict live-in rules and a lack of legal protection, but also by a residential status that never translates into the right for permanent residency, no matter how long they have been working in the city. In many ways, they may be regarded as the city's most vulnerable social group, persons whom government policies keep in officially sanctioned disadvantage, yet persons without whom the city's families and, by extension, the city's economy, could not function.

Sunday is their only day off, a day of freedom, though most local employers, ignoring that a day lasts 24 hours, define it as from around daybreak until early or late evening. Yet, within Filipinas' meagre free time, religious life is important. In the absence of a private home, the church is, most simply, a free space to gather, to eat, and to celebrate, far better than the scorching heat of the open square in the Central Business District where many Filipinas meet. More than just a convenience, church is also a break from isolation, a place to establish crucial networks, experience bonding, and remember that life is worth living.[5] Often lonely, emotionally burdened with guilt for being absent mothers, anxious about their husbands' faithfulness in their absence, threatened by a breakdown of family relations due to the long separation, struggling with homesickness, and facing daily hardship—Filipinas can find comfort and a sympathetic community at church.[6] It is a place that brings them a feeling of being back home. Expressing their faith and participating in religious life is a public reaffirmation of their dignity that is so often denied them.

Among Filipinas, St. Joseph's Church is the most popular parish, due to its central location. On a Sunday, starting at 7 a.m. and ending at 6 p.m., it conducts non-stop mass, nine services throughout the day, in English or in Tagalog, to cater to this large and mainly Catholic workforce. Particularly when attending a Tagalog service, being in the church is just like being back home, but religious belonging among migrant workers is typically fluid: many are open to new religious experiences. In numerous Protestant international churches, Filipinas are among the most regular and active members. While their tight work schedule makes it difficult for them to join church activities during the week—and while only a few more progressive churches invite them to take up leading roles such as membership in the church council—they find empowerment and respect in other activities, serving in such positions as small group leaders, Sunday school teachers, liturgists, lead singers, or choir members. Some engage in pastoral work and outreach activities where they visit the sick and those in prison and thus experience a sense of dignity.

Sunday Worship in the Jesus Is Lord Center in Shek Kip Mei

One of the churches where migrant workers' agency is strongly visible is the *Jesus Is Lord Church* (JIL). Founded by Eddie Villanueva, a professor of economics and finance, as a small Bible study group at a university in Manila in 1978, it grew within only a decade to a mega-church that today has around 5 million members worldwide and churches all over the Philippines and in nearly every country that hosts Filipino domestic workers.[7] While charismatic churches have been criticized for a use of religion that rationalizes or justifies multifarious oppression,[8] JIL differs from other megachurches by being less consumerist and related more closely to the working class and to the historical and social contexts of Filipinos.[9] It is a place where women take up leadership roles. More than St. Joseph's Church or any of the mainline Protestant churches welcoming Filipinas, JIL contributes to at least partial empowerment by offering women leadership positions—as lead singers, liturgists, preachers—that stand in contrast to their daily experience of heteronomy, so completely at the whim of employers who pass on the pressure and heteronomy of their own harsh work lives to their domestic helpers. However, this comes at a price: JIL, like other neo-evangelical Protestant churches, encourages members to tithe. For migrant workers with low salaries, high family burdens, and overstretched budgets, such a regular expense can be difficult to bear.

The JIL Center in Hong Kong is a large theater-turned-church in the heart of Shek Kip Mei, an old working-class district. Several hundred Filipinas gather in each of the three Sunday services, with only a handful of men sprinkled in. Music plays a central role, with a young lead singer, a dozen support singers, and a band preparing for the one-hour long sermons of the female pastor. As the band plays, the Filipinas stand up, raise their arms and sway their bodies to the rhythm of the music. Worshipping, they come alive. The community helps alleviate the accumulated pain of their hard work and their separation from home.

The sermon on this particular Sunday, a Father's Day, is on Jairus, who is both a good leader and a good father. "If your family prays together, it stays together," proclaims the guest preacher, Pastora Ligaya, triggering loud applause and calls of amen. The end of the worship is marked by final songs, gifts to the eight fathers present in the audience, and a message from Joel Villanueva, politician and son of the church founder.

In charge of the congregation in Shek Kip Mei is Pastora Fina, who has been in Hong Kong for thirty years. Being modest, she hesitates to give an interview. She is not an official representative of the church, feels uncomfortable in a conspicuous role, and defers to her male superiors. Behind her reluctance stands the reality of a patriarchal system, which pervades even this women's church. Yet Pastora Fina shares how virtually all the people in the church are, like her, female domestic workers. They prepare their sermons and teachings during their few free evening hours before going to sleep and spend their sole weekly day off immersed in church ministry. Like all the other female co-workers, Pastora Fina receives no payment for her service. "I do it voluntarily for the service of my God," she calmly expresses. For her role as head pastor of this large church, she did not receive formal theological training but attended internal leadership courses run by the church. Yet, she brings along a firm faith, natural authority, and the skills of a manager of a large household. As the third worship service of the day ends, a group of nearly a hundred Filipinas are already queueing at the entrance: they had been in an earlier worship service, went out for lunch and to meet friends, and now return to attend one of the church's leadership courses that will equip them to be small group leaders in the future.

International Megachurch Branches

JIL is not the only church that caters to migrants from the Global South. Another important church from the Philippines is the Iglesia Ni Cristo, with its non-trinitarian teaching outside of orthodox Christianity, which gathers several thousand domestic helpers in fourteen congregations across the city. More than a dozen mostly small churches gather African migrants, often with some Southeast Asian migrant workers among them. One of these African churches is the *Redeemed Christian Church of God* (RCCG), which established its Hong Kong Mission in the 1990s. A Nigerian megachurch with a vision of planting churches around the globe, RCCG has established three congregations in the city's working-class neighborhoods, one of them in downtown Jordan. Located in a small commercial unit, several dozen participants of African backgrounds—families, postgraduate students from local universities, businesspeople, and asylum seekers—and a few Southeast Asian migrant workers gather for two hours of praise, preaching, and prayer. The service concludes in a passionate prayer, where the pastor, in a style derived from Nigerian fire-ministry churches, enters an intense and powerful spiritual battle, condemns satanic plans in a loud voice, and invokes the fire of the Holy Spirit to scatter and kill all evil spirits and other enemies.

Very different in tone, but similar in its global outreach strategy, the North American *Saddleback Church* established a local branch in 2013 as part of its grand vision of opening churches in twelve major global cities, called "Gateway Cities" for their "proximity to the final 3,800 people groups that still do not have a church."[10] When Saddleback chose Hong Kong for its first overseas campus, critics derided it as simply another example of the McDonaldization of Christianity and pointed to the oddity of the Hong Kong Saddleback church simply replaying the sermon of Saddleback's US senior pastor on a large screen with Chinese sub-titles, thus mocking all attempts at contextual faith expression. Indeed, the local church, although financially fully self-supporting, is simply another "campus" of the church in California and does not have its own church council; the senior pastor is employed by and accountable to the US church. Yet, the fast growth of the local Saddleback church—to well over one thousand members within only a few years, over 90 percent of them locals—shows that it has touched a nerve. The success confirms again that Hongkongers easily embrace popular global products, not just in the shopping mall but also in the religious marketplace: from the Billy Graham Crusades in the 1950s, 1970s, and in 1990; to the Alpha courses that were first introduced to the city in the late 1990s (with Hong Kong the first overseas location of Alpha's global outreach), and that have been running since then; to the Benny Hinn shows in the early 2000s and the Rick Warren products. Yet, more than just due to a receptivity towards global products, the success of the local Saddleback church also points to a core concern of local identity: to connect the local with the global; to be not just Chinese but— linguistically and culturally—bilingual, a quality practiced perfectly by the local Saddleback worship leaders, who alternate effortlessly between English and Cantonese. However, the foremost reason for the success of the local Saddleback Church, as we will see in other international churches, is that it attracts many local believers who have turned their backs on local churches.

That Hong Kong also plays a strategic role for the world's largest megachurch, the South Korean *Yoido Full Gospel Church*, should be no surprise. Yoido has over 700 missionaries in all parts of the world, around 3 percent of South Korea's overall global mission force.[11] In the past, China was a core concern of Korean missionaries; Yoido would purchase properties in good urban locations, start a church, and attract people. But with religious repression reaching a breaking point and with the Chinese government even terminating some churches' property rights, many Korean missionaries decided to leave the mainland. As a result, the Hong Kong Yoido church, which had already been founded in the late 1980s, has assumed more strategic importance. Around 40 percent of her around 250 members are ethnic Koreans; the rest are locals or believers from the Philippines and from other parts of the world. Here, Korean linguistic and cultural elements dominate, with prayers and robed choirs; English and Cantonese appear only as simultaneous translation. In 2019, reflecting Hong Kong's strategic role, the church even started its own seminary, the *Full Gospel Hong Kong Seminary*, with two dozen students from Hong Kong and the Philippines who train, tuition-free, for the mission of the church.

Hong Kong is a favorite target for several other megachurches as well. The influential Pentecostal *Hillsong Church*, a global megachurch network from Australia, became known locally first through its worship songs, popular in many international churches. Hillsong has also found entry into the city through the *Lifehouse International Church Hong Kong*, planted by a network of churches located mostly in Japan and other places around the Asia Pacific Rim. Here, the emphasis is on dynamic and youthful worship. The liturgists are MCs who bilingually lead through what is essentially an entertainment program, and the preacher addresses the audience in chatty dialogue with his Cantonese translator. Also linked to Australia is the *C3 Church Hong Kong* (C3 referring to the three Cs in "Christian City Church"), one of the nearly 600 C3 congregations worldwide, which worships in the basement of a commercial building in the heart of the entertainment district in Eastern Tsimshatsui; in contrast, the *Sky City Church*, part of the iSee church group, which has a smaller number of churches in Australia and Asia, meets on the top floor of Hong Kong's third-highest skyscraper.

The local branches of global megachurches offer multiple ways of internationalization and of connecting local and global. Some offer a home-far-from-home experience for ethnic minority groups who look for religious life in a familiar cultural and linguistic context. This is the case with the *Redeemed Christian Church of God*, which offers a space for a clearly African religious expression, not much different from a church in Nigeria. Likewise, Yoido does not hide its close connection to Korean religious culture and offers a familiar religious space for Korean Christians in the city. Others, such as Saddleback and Hillsong, offer a global religious experience in the local context, benefitting from the view that sees cultural products from the West and the English language as global and normative. The bilingual worship, with English and Cantonese balanced and alternating, supports this impression even though, in the case of Saddleback, the sermon's allusions to Californian life reveal it as simply a religious import. These churches are a node in a transnational religious network[12] linked through popular media—Rick Warren books here and Hillsong worship songs there.

National Churches Abroad and Independent International Churches

Among the highly movable expatriate workforce in global cities, some choose to adopt the lifestyle of a global citizen, easily and multilingually moving between different cultures and at home in all of them; others, especially mono-national families and expats on short contracts, prefer to maintain their distinct home culture and find togetherness in national communities. For the latter, national churches offer a space in which they can experience something of the normality of home while abroad. An obvious example is the small *German-speaking Evangelical-Lutheran congregation*, which is initiated and partly supported by the Evangelical-Lutheran Church in Germany. It offers a spiritual home and pastoral care in a familiar environment, and keeps German expats connected to Christian home traditions such as autumn thanksgiving or Advent wreaths. Numerically more significant are around a dozen Korean churches for the estimated 1,200 Protestant *Korean Christians*,[13] many of whom worship only in the Korean language. They practice their religious home culture in the foreign land with morning worship before work and with early morning prayers on the hills of Hong Kong Island.[14]

A growing group of churches are *Nepali churches*, the oldest founded only in 1993. The growth to fifteen churches in less than thirty years reflects an amazing growth of Christianity within the local Nepali community, a trend also observed in Nepal, which, according to some reports, is the country with the strongest Christian growth rate worldwide, nearly 11 percent annually since 1970.[15] These churches worship in the Nepali language, sing Nepali hymns (some composed by Nepali Christians), and use traditional instruments such as the *madal*, a Nepali drum, or the *tabala*, a drum originating in India. Most of their churches are in the downtown areas of southern Kowloon or near Yuen Long and Kam Tin in the Northwest of the territory, where many descendants of the Gurkhas have settled. One reason for the growth of the Nepali community is that they are strongly evangelistic and that the Nepali in the city maintain a close-knit community emphasizing familial togetherness even more than the Chinese community does—the Nepali, in fact, see the Chinese as rather individualistic. The local Nepali community is not affluent; yet, with many Nepali men working in the well-paid construction industry and many women also working, they are financially strong enough to rent premises for their churches. Most pastors, though, are serving their churches as unpaid volunteers. The city's Nepali Christians have even established a Nepali Christian Council, which not only fosters communal relations in the city but also connects them with Christians in Nepal.

While Germans, Koreans and Japanese (with three churches) benefit from the relative economic strength of their home churches and of their expatriate workforce, some churches catering to ethnically homogenous groups depend on local or international churches for worship space or other support. The *International Christian Assembly* (ICA), a church founded in North Point in the early 1970s through Assemblies of God missionaries, stands out for offering separate services in Indonesian, Nepali, Sinhala (Sri Lanka), and Thai besides its regular English and Cantonese services. Some international (and local) churches engage with ethnic minority groups as their mission outreach and help them establish their own independent churches. A fruit of such a project, to name one example, is an international church aimed at ethnic minorities (especially Nepali), the *Hope for All Church*, planted by the Community Church Hong Kong.

More widely known within the community are the many international churches that are inter-denominational and draw people from different nations. Historically the oldest are the *Union Church Hong Kong*, whose roots reach back to the early ministry of James Legge (London Missionary Society), and her younger sister church, the *Kowloon Union Church*, both independent and ecumenical. Some international churches have grown to large congregations with over 1,000 members. Most famous are *The Vine*, a moderately charismatic international church that grew out of the Repulse Bay Baptist Church in the 1980s and that today has around 2,500 members worshipping in a cinema-turned church in downtown Wanchai; the *Evangelical Community Church* (ECC) and its meanwhile much larger sister church, *Island ECC*, which gathers more than 3,000 on an average Sunday; and the *International Christian Assembly* in North Point. There are several other international churches, mostly on the island, among them the *Community Church Hong Kong*, a solidly evangelical yet spiritually progressive and inclusive church; *Solomon's Porch*, which planted not only an Indonesian congregation in Causeway Bay but also churches in Singapore, Tokyo, and New York; and the *Ambassador International Church*, which worships in the Conrad Hotel in Admiralty.

A study conducted by the Hong Kong Church Renewal Movement, the organization that also surveyed the local churches, found seventy-three English-speaking international churches in the city, up from sixty five years earlier.[16] This number does, however, not include the many international churches who worship in other languages than English—Filipinos, Koreans, Japanese, Indonesians, Germans, Nepali, and others. It also does not include many lesser-known English-speaking churches such as the more than a dozen African-founded ones, some of them operating under expressive names: *God Said It I Believe It Ministries, Mountain of Fire, Christ Jesus Healing Miracles Ministries Worldwide*, or *Resurrection Power Christian Church International*. Taking all these churches into account, Hong Kong may have as many as 150 international congregations.

International Christians and Local Society

All these international churches, whether denominationally affiliated or independent ones, contribute to local society in multiple ways. Many are affluent upper-class churches, yet they offer significant financial support to local ministries. But more important for their members is that they offer opportunities for involvement in the local community: through outreach to street sleepers, prisoners, refugees, migrant workers, and other people in need. Among them, The Vine is noteworthy for not only engaging in charitable ministry but moving on to a deeper quest for social justice. Its statement of faith explains: "We believe in a God of justice whose heart beats for the poor and marginalized . . . We see social justice as inseparable from authentic Christian witness. We seek to meet the needs and alleviate the suffering of the most disadvantaged and forgotten people within the church and society."[17]

Driven by this concern, The Vine has developed the city's largest church-based ministry to refugees and asylum seekers, serving over 200 people with pastoral care and material assistance.[18] More recently, it has supported regular justice conferences with a focus on marginal and disadvantaged social groups in global cities. While a concern for social justice has long been a core focus of spiritually progressive ecumenical churches such as the Kowloon Union Church or the

Methodist International Church, The Vine is a rare example of an evangelical or charismatic church that not only engages with vulnerable social groups but is also willing to address the root causes of these groups' social marginality.

The international churches' involvement in social and communal ministry offers a chance for their members to connect more deeply with urban society and to be individually and socially transformed. A pastor of The Vine concluded that "They [i.e., the refugees and asylum seekers] completely changed the church."[19] A recent study on the international churches' refugee ministry by Judy Chan concluded that,

> [i]nternational congregations in Hong Kong were strategically positioned to befriend this group not only because of their use of [the] English language, but even more so because of their openness to people of all races, ethnicities, and backgrounds as children of God. International churches that were founded to take care of the foreigners in the days of privilege have evolved into multicultural congregations of all social classes and many nationalities, including a large Asian membership and some local Hong Kong Chinese.[20]

Urban ministry has a transforming impact on locals and foreigners alike, but for many expats, who always risk being stuck in a bubble of privilege and foreignness, it provides a precious opportunity: connecting more deeply with the local community and learning about the social reality of the city and some of its more vulnerable residents. In this encounter with vulnerable strangers, expat members of international churches reconnect with their own repressed vulnerability as strangers in a foreign world. In a context where the language and writing system are so radically different from those of most expats' mother tongues, the sense of foreignness is felt in Hong Kong more intensely than in other global cities. Urban ministry helps expatriates understand their presence in Hong Kong as not just a time to advance economically but as a time of purpose and of giving back to the local community.

This sense of contribution to local society is also reflected in the testimonies of Christian migrant workers, who are socially in a very different situation from that of many expats. Participating in outreach activities allows migrant workers to assume agency, to experience strength and to reaffirm their subject status against the heteronomy of their daily lives. This is most obvious when they visit prisons to support foreign inmates, who experience a kind of heteronomy that is even more complete and painful than what migrant workers experience. Urban ministry adds a meaningful and comforting additional layer to their life in the city, a dimension beyond the overarching and all-dominating concern of sending money home. Often reduced in their identity and in their family ties to being merely breadwinners, migrant workers see urban ministry as significant enrichment, a cause for which it is worth sacrificing their scarce free time.

Some Filipina migrant workers understand their work as a chance to serve simultaneously as modern-day missionaries. Their intimate presence in the lives of locals offers them unique opportunities to reach out to their employers, to support them in times of difficulties, to pray with the children, or even to discreetly intervene in conflicts. They draw gratification from being able to have a religious impact on atheist or folk-religious families for whom they work.[21] This self-understanding as a missionary parallels the testimonies of leaders in the African community, some of whom came as businessmen and discovered new callings as pastors and missionaries to the city. One of them recalled how his calling was triggered by the encounter with the thriving developments across the border in Southern China, where he witnessed the spiritual drought in which people lived, caught in state-sponsored atheism and a consumerist lifestyle. Differing from how they see spiritual needs in Western countries, which some African church leaders in Europe reframe as "reverse mission,"[22] here they see people's spiritual needs as yet unanswered.

Local Christians in International Churches

Invited to participate in a survey on international churches, one pastor of an international church politely declined even to fill out the form, insisting that his church is a local church, that he is critical of such distinctions and that, anyway, most of his church members are local Chinese who simply happen to attend a church that uses English in its worship and ministry.[23] The distinction between local and international churches is obviously problematic, and, considering that most members of international churches are in fact Hong Kong Chinese—more than two thirds[24] and in some churches up to 90 percent—the pastor has a point. Indeed, statistics show a trend, particularly among younger people, of leaving local churches for international ones, a trend that has significantly increased in past years: since 2014, worship attendance has declined by 2.5 percent annually in local churches while growing by 6 percent in international churches.[25] This has caused a larger percentage of international churches (21.9 percent – based on the seventy-three churches identified in the report) than local churches (6.7 percent) to grow into large or mega churches.[26]

Why are there so many local people in international churches? This has first to do with the high mobility of local people, many of them spending years abroad for secondary and/or tertiary education. Some become Christian while studying abroad and, as they return to the city, are naturally drawn to church cultures similar to those in which they first encountered the Christian faith. While their mother tongue is Cantonese, their "faith tongue" is English.[27] Some are ethnic Chinese from Southeast Asia with limited knowledge of

Cantonese. Many are young locals, particularly from middle- and upper-class families, who attend(-ed) international schools in Hong Kong and feel linguistically more naturally at home in English. These young people see themselves as de-localized and belonging to a global community. The choice of international churches also receives support from their families for being in safe distance from local politics and from pressures that second-generation Christians experience in the congregations in which they had grown up. Yet, international churches are also attractive to young people from the grassroots. In the past, one could hear stories of parents sending their kids to English-speaking churches for "free tutoring" in English via Sunday School classes. The participation of many younger de-churched or un-churched locals is one factor in the growth of the local Saddleback campus, and other international church pastors say they have seen the same thing, but there are deeper reasons for the strong presence of local Chinese in international churches.

A study by John Snelgrove, a founding pastor of The Vine, sheds light on some of the backgrounds and the factors in this trend.[28] His study identified several reasons why millennials transfer to international churches. First, many of them found that local churches feel more like an extension of school, where teaching happens by rote learning. The pastor appears not as a community leader or as a friend, but as a teacher or scholar. While many participants gratefully acknowledged the importance of solid Bible teaching, they found that personal relationships with the pastor were weak. Another point of criticism was that local churches were dominated by rules and that formality was the order of the day. Several respondents observed that the dominant habit in Chinese culture of addressing people by their title builds walls between the leader and the people. The pastor is always addressed as "Pastor," always remains an authority figure, and never becomes simply "John" or "Peter."

But more than just for the emphasis on formal interaction, millennials criticized local churches for being legalistic and performance driven. Many churches demand a strict discipline on time commitment or tithing, expectations that members, in the long term, find suffocating. They were taught to be good in order to be accepted, thus forfeiting the message of grace. Good behavior expresses itself in church attendance, attentiveness, dress and, of course, properly managed relationships, particularly with the opposite sex. Some respondents said all this gave them the impression that works were of paramount importance and that church was foremost concerned with control. The church's strong concern with social control is particularly manifest in matters of sexuality, where most churches claim authority. Although most international churches' *teaching* would be similar to that of local churches—against pre-marital sex and against homosexuality—there is, according to the study's respondents, more of an emphasis on grace in international churches. Topics of sexuality are often acknowledged as simply difficult. Participants in the study further found actual church life not sufficiently relevant. Many had witnessed internal politics that stood in contrast to Christian teaching.

Finally, and positively, several participants expressed that they discovered dimensions of faith life in international churches that they had previously missed: most importantly, an emphasis not on teaching but on experience; leaders who are vulnerable, admitting weaknesses and not remaining aloof; transparency; an open-mindedness to accept critical questions; and an absence of a performance culture. Several respondents also said they were attracted by the worship style in international churches, where they felt a joy and freedom they had missed in local worship.

It should be noted that this is not an issue of evangelical local vs. charismatic international churches—young people from both evangelical and charismatic local backgrounds transfer to both kinds of international churches. However, there is an obvious affinity with the charismatic worship culture in international churches, often simply expressed in informal architectural settings, dress codes, and social interactions. Pentecostal-charismatic forms of Christianity contribute more to melting a multi-ethnic community together (as seen in the comparison of Hong Kong and Singapore in Chapter 2). While local churches tend towards an evangelical faith often paired with more formal relationships and more emphasis on orderliness, international churches are more open to charismatic Christianity and are more informal in their relationships and more casual in their worship style. It thus comes as no surprise that only a few—the Korean national churches, and one or two of the English-speaking Anglican congregations—celebrate with a strong liturgical order.

Snelgrove explains further that it is not an issue of language but of culture. While his study focuses on those who have transferred to international churches and not on the many young people who continue to find meaning and purpose in local churches, the statements of the millennials in his study are significant, and not just because they represent a statistically evident trend. They point to a tension of identity, which affects many millennials negotiating their Chinese culture and more liberal Western perspectives and practices. While, in the past years, dominant parts of society have been shifting more towards authoritarian patterns, a growing number of millennials seem to be countering this trend by choosing places for worship where they experience informality, equality, and empowerment, and where they will not feel preached at. They regard many local churches as under the influence of values—correct relationships, learning, and formality—that keep them from growing. Although the most popular image of the local church, i.e., as a family, underlines the relational more than the cognitive aspect of faith, it is still under the influence of the Confucian concept of family, constructed in a patriarchal mode, and with a dominance of formal relationships and clear obedience structures.

In a nutshell, too much education, too much formality, too much emphasis on work, too much a performance mentality—local churches are in danger of mirroring a society that many, not just young people, find suffocating. The 2019 protest movement and the subsequent accelerated erosion of civil liberties in the city have further exacerbated the trend, as it led many young people to identify oppressive elements in their Chinese background more critically and disassociate from them. Joining an international church implicitly signifies young people's sense of belonging to a global rather than a narrowly Chinese community. Positively speaking, international churches show more affinity with democratic models of society. Members of international churches are not rejecting their Chinese identity as such, but they understand it as balanced by alternative perspectives. Participation in an international church strengthens the global aspect of their identity.

Glocalization

These thoughts also respond to the question of the international churches' contextualization. Are they simply a copy of churches elsewhere, an import of products from the global religious marketplace, with global brands such as Saddleback, Hillsong, and Alpha dominating the market? Or is there something like a glocalization, a contextual appropriation? What makes an international church in Hong Kong different from one in the United States or Australia? On the surface, contextualization of global religious products happens when people speak the local language, follow local forms of interaction, and broadly share the values of society. For example, when it comes to the much-treasured meal fellowship around the large round table, or when it comes to a strong sense of obligation and responsibility for one's family, Christians in local and international churches are the same.

Secondly, the question about the contextuality of international churches may be all too theoretical. Crucial in the local context is that it works. I remember once, in a class on contextual theology, critically asking a group of students whether local Christianity should consider developing its own creed, as the commonly recited Nicene Creed is steeped in Hellenist metaphysical thought to an extent that makes only limited sense in a Chinese context. The students' response was unanimous: Why? The Nicene Creed has worked until now, so why rock the boat? Developing a new creed would only create conflicts that are better avoided. In short, local people are pragmatic regarding products from the global marketplace. This focus on what works and what sells may appear as intellectual laziness. Indeed, a similar criticism was voiced when, in the early 2000s, Hong Kong decided to build a local Disneyland rather than developing a park based on Asian tales. Yet, it is exactly this business-mindedness that is open to successful global products, this pragmatism that focuses on what works, and this humility not to reject foreign things as a matter of principle, that is a proper expression of local contextuality.

More important is another point: while Hong Kong is surely a receptive market that readily absorbs global products, the crucial question is where the agency lies. Joining an international church is for locals an active choice, regardless of their English proficiency,[29] a choice that expresses a certain defiance toward the community in which they grew up. For many, it is the result of a process of breaking with a previous church, going through a period of alienation and being part of the large group of de-churched Christians who still treasure their faith until they find a new sense of belonging in an international church. Hong Kong's international churches are thriving because of their culture. Some even start Cantonese and Mandarin services and keep growing because they maintain the international culture even in Chinese-language services. Vice versa, some local churches have started English-language services, but without a change in culture and with formality and control held high; they are not growing. International churches grow because they appeal to a core concern of young people whose lives combine East and West and who feel increasingly alienated by what they experience as Chinese culture. This hybridity of local and international, of East and West, is what most aptly reflects the contextual character of international churches.

To conclude, international churches and their ministries all offer *a dimension beyond*—for expats beyond their relentless drive for financial success; for foreign domestic workers, for South Asians in the construction and logistics industry, and for asylum seekers beyond their marginalized existence, to experience strength and to enjoy a break from their isolation; for young locals turning to international churches beyond the performance-driven culture of their home churches.

4

Movies, Media, and Popular Culture

Christian Presence in the Cultural Realm

Kong Duen Yee (1923–66), popularly known as Mui Yee, was a famous Cantonese opera singer and local actress who appeared in more than 140 movies during the early days of the Hong Kong film industry.[1] At the age of forty, she fell seriously ill and, facing death, turned to the Christian faith. For the remaining three years of her life, she used her fame and her stage experience to preach the Christian faith and to call believers to receive the baptism of the Spirit. Invited by the Assemblies of God, she visited Singapore and Malaysia where she caused a stir in local Chinese communities by attacking the traditional Chinese gods. In response, some spiritual mediums and gangsters attended her gospel and healing meetings to challenge her. They had "protective charms (needles) on them, which reportedly fell off during the meeting, leaving them powerless."[2] While the AOG later withdrew support, critical of her increasingly extreme spiritual claims and her decision to organize her own church, the New Testament Church, her preaching had a long-lasting impact on Pentecostal-charismatic Christianity in Singapore and Malaysia.

Half a century later, another famous singer and actress, Sammi Cheng Sau Man, was at the peak of her career. Dubbed the "Cantopop Queen," she was in her early thirties, and everything seemed perfect: she won countless awards, sold millions of music albums, and appeared in several box-office hits. Yet, the more material wealth and worldly success she gained, the more she felt something missing. She went through a long period of depression that forced her to radically reconsider her values, and she eventually discovered the Christian faith. She understood that life needs a higher calling and purpose, and she found direction and hope in God's word, gaining a peace and assurance which money could never have bought. She described the long period of depression as God's way to fix her through pain and tears—finding her way back to her real self rather than pleasing man, living out higher values and not conforming to this world.[3]

Mui Yee and Sammi Cheng are just two of several stars who adopted the Christian faith and became passionate promoters of it. In this chapter, we look at some of the avenues through which the Christian faith enters local culture and engages with it. While demographics do not identify any specific social group that has a higher affinity for Christianity, and while the spread of the Christian faith has been driven by passionate peers sharing their faith in all social groups—bankers with their peers in the financial industry, businesspeople with their co-workers, social workers with their colleagues, prisoners with their fellow inmates, and most importantly children with their parents and parents with their children—these stars, admired across different social groups, have played a unique role in localizing and popularizing the Christian faith. They express their faith in the local language, in local images, through local music, movies, TV programs, and sport.

Yet, this chapter is not just about the glittering world of the entertainment industry. It is about both the contribution of *all* facets of cultural production to the spread of the Christian faith and the connection of Christian faith to local culture. It describes how Christians embraced the entertainment industry, how they contributed to a distinctive local identity and how this brought some of them into tension with economic and political realities.

Christians in Showbiz

Barbara Yung Mei Ling was a young and successful actress when, in 1985, she experienced relationship problems. In her distress, she called Cheng Ming Ming, a friend who ran a celebrity beauty salon. As it was late at night and Cheng wanted to go to sleep to be rested for the next day's work, she advised her friend to do the same, assuring her that they would talk again the next day. Waking up to the radio the next morning, Cheng was shocked to hear that Yung, aged only twenty-six, had committed suicide by gas poisoning.[4] Realizing her failure to stand by her friend in distress, she felt deeply remorseful and went to her fellow Christian friends Roy Chiao and his wife Otilia Liu Yen Ping, suggesting that they establish a Christian fellowship for those in the entertainment industry. This was the beginning of the *Home of Artists*, also called the Hong Kong Artistes [sic] Christian Fellowship (Hong Kong ACF), which today gathers around forty mostly Protestant Christians, among them

Sheren Tang, Sammi Cheng, Wong Cho Lam, Ada Choi, Hins Cheung King Hin, and Alfred Cheung Kin Ting, along with Lau Chung Yan, a Catholic.

The fellowship is a place for Christian entertainers to grow in their faith as they share their experiences with others who are familiar with the temptations and the emotional stress in this line of work. Yet the intention was not just to create a space for mutual support but equally to spread the Christian faith among artists by offering a model of Christian life within the world of entertainment. Members are encouraged to attend ordinary worship services in local churches, and some choose the Tung Fook Church or Kong Fok Church (both of the EFCC), known among locals as celebrity churches. However, participation in a church is of course more public than joining a fellowship for celebrities, who need time out of the limelight. While there have long been Christians working as actors or directors—among them the actors Lung To (1910–86) and Chow Kit-Lin, better known as Tsi Law-Lin (1924–2015), who dedicated themselves to Christian ministry after their retirement, and Lung Kong, a film director in the 1960s and 70s—the ACF intended to have a longer-lasting, albeit subtle, impact on the perception of Christianity in wider society, on Christians themselves, and on the Christian approach to the world of entertainment.

The founding of the Home of Artists occurred at a time when, parallel to the city's economic boom and reflecting a growing sense of identity, the local TV and film industries flourished. With TV heavily commercialized and dominated by a few channels, Christians began to critically discuss the film industry and make inroads into this yet closed territory, as in a regular column in *Breakthrough Magazine*, a Christian monthly; a television awareness campaign initiated by the Hong Kong Christian Council; and concern groups monitoring the moral values manifested in TV programs.[5] Traditionally seen as rather inward-looking, morally narrow, opposed to mundane pleasures, and as cultivating an escapist and other-worldly spirituality, Christian artists changed the public image of Christians, showing that they were engaged in all parts of society, reaching the successful as much as the broken. Christian actors and singers publicly confessing their faith played an important role in bridging the gap between the entertainment industry and the Christian community, an arrangement that benefitted both sides. Churches gained an excellent channel to promote the Christian faith, and these singers and actors presented themselves as transcending the superficiality of showbiz, showing spiritual depth, standing against the showbiz mainstream, and serving a higher purpose. Besides, their faith brought them liberation from the merciless expectations of the entertainment industry and anchored them in a sustainable spiritual ground beyond the fickleness of stardom. Christian artists also gained by making inroads into the Christian market without losing their secular market share.

Soon enough, they reached beyond their own circle and attended large-scale evangelistic shows in Hong Kong, in Greater China, and in overseas Chinese communities, giving testimonies of their faith and spreading God's love and joy. Members of the fellowship shared about their emptiness and pride before coming to know Christ, about God saving them from emotional turmoil or even the brink of suicide, and about their faith helping them overcome relationship problems. Along the way, they admitted a vulnerability that made them more human and more accessible. Leading Christian artists such as Sammi Cheng (*Faith*, in 2009) and Jade Kwan (*Shine*, in 2009) released musical albums with Christian content. Some of their gospel songs continue to be popular among Christians and non-Christians alike. Cheng's album, published by a secular production company, broke five years of artistic silence after her turn to the Christian faith and was an overwhelming success. The question remains whether such success is Christians' successful use of commercial instruments to spread the Christian faith or merely reflects the market's appropriation of the Christian message.[6] Theologically speaking, although these artists' faith does grow out of their experiences of suffering and emotional breakdown, their actual ministry is commonly pulled back into the world of glitz and glamour that emphasizes the glory of God's victory and leaves little space for a theology of the cross.

Increasing adaptation to the world, decreasing countercultural strength—this formula may also describe how the artists' fellowship historically developed. It had its peak between the late 1980s and 2000s[7] when it had around eighty members, with nearly half regularly attending.[8] This was the time when, in 2000, pastor-turned-entertainer Enoch Lam, initiated a stand-up comedy show inviting Christian artists to perform on stage and give testimonies. It was the time when the fellowship established contacts with artists' fellowships in Taipei and in New York and organized joint gospel concerts in Singapore and Malaysia, thus radiating into Southeast Asia. And it was the time when the fellowship conducted large-scale local evangelistic meetings such as the *Red, Black, Royal Evangelistic Meeting*, jointly organized by the artists' fellowship, the Christian Wu Oi Christian Center, and the police force's Christian Enoch Fellowship. The colors refer to the three unique groups: red for the artists' pursuit of success and a hot (or "red") artistic life; black for the underworld of triads and drug consumers who find transformation through faith in the Wu Oi Christian Center; and royal, a Cantonese homonym of "yellow," for the underworld's name for the police force. The evangelistic meetings conducted in 1989 and again in 2010 by the three groups—entertainers, converted gangsters, and police—attracted an in-person audience in the ten-thousands and was broadcast in over one hundred churches.

However, since then, things have changed, as many Christian artists were commercially drawn into the rapidly developing mainland Chinese market. The price for commercial success in China is to accept alignment with the Communist Party. In charge of such ideological integration is the United Front Work Department (UFWD), a party department that aims at integrating social groups (in mainland China and beyond) into the overall direction of the party. Its strategies include inviting socially significant people to join the Chinese People's Political Consultative Conference (CPPCC), a second chamber of parliament that has only an advisory function; urging celebrities to publicly support China's policies; and, of course, sanctioning those who are "unfriendly" to China, for instance by supporting Taiwan's independence or Hong Kong's protest movement. An example of alignment with Beijing is local artist Wong Cho Lam's membership in the Guangxi provincial CPPCC and his public support for the National Security Law, which was introduced in July 2020 and led to a massive erosion of civil and political rights in Hong Kong. Whether forced by commercial interest or based on genuine conviction, such public support for repressive policies alienates artists from their young supporters back home, most of whom support calls for more democracy. These fans see such affiliation with the government as a betrayal of the Christian faith. A contrary example is Hins Cheung King Hin, who publicly stated his opposition to the central government's interference in the city and was subsequently forced out of the mainland market.

The increased importance of the mainland market and the all-permeating Party-centrism have affected the artists' fellowship in still other ways. Traditionally, members of the fellowship had a strong evangelistic zeal, but this outspokenness is not welcome in today's China because it clashes with Party ideology. Christian artists who want continued access to the mainland market therefore have no choice but to downplay their faith.

Christian TV and Movie Production

From individual Christian entertainers it is a small step to the production of TV programs and movies communicating the Christian message. Locally the earliest form of Christian TV production was a series of half-hour shows, *Melody of Happiness*, produced by local Christians in 1974 and broadcast on early Saturday evenings.[9] A more subtle promotion of the Christian faith was the approach of *Breakthrough*, a local NGO that supports young people, which, commissioned by a local TV station, produced a mini-series in 1989 addressing contemporary social issues from a Christian perspective without explicitly propagating the Christian faith. The series, *Generation 21: Young Spirits of Asia*, was broadcast in primetime, on three consecutive Sunday evenings. It combined music video with social documentary and gained high rankings.[10] Most Christian TV productions, though, promote the Christian faith more directly, among them global religious broadcasters such as: the *Showers of Blessing Evangelistic Ministry*, established in 1987 in Canada and aimed at the worldwide Chinese community, producing content in Mandarin and Cantonese and offering local programs since 2001; the *Christian Broadcasting Network* (CBN), which was founded by the conservative American evangelist Pat Robertson in 1960 and has had a local base with local ministry since 2004; and the *Trinity Broadcasting Network* (TBN), founded in 1973 in California, which has been airing Christian programs twenty-four hours a day on a local pay TV channel since 2014. English TV stations in Hong Kong also broadcast a number of imported Christian programs, such as the sermons of Singaporean pastor Joseph Prince and the long-running American show *Hour of Power*.

Locally, the Media Evangelism Group (ME) went a step further. Established in 1991, it began as a small audio-visual team producing gospel dramas for local churches. In the late 1990s, it turned to the production of large-screen movies that reached well beyond the Christian circle, with some gaining much cinematic acclaim. Among them, *The Boss Up There* (1999), telling the story of four rebellious teenagers drifting through violence, drug addiction, crime, and prison and eventually finding release through their faith, won both a local and an international film award. The same year saw the release of *Sometimes, Miracles Do Happen* (the Chinese title translates as *City of Angels*), with Roy Chiao in his final acting role as Uncle Wang. The movie describes a city embroiled in depression and rampant suicide until a strange elderly man (Uncle Wang) appears in the city's hospitals, bringing the patients good news of hope and joy and, miraculously, even healing. The movie was promoted as Chiao's farewell appearance, and its release was supported by a massive media campaign with advertisements in every subway station and with churches flooded with promotional material.[11] When the first SARS epidemic hit the city only four years later, many people saw the movie as amazing, both for predicting the ensuing suffering and for offering hope during a dark period. Many Hongkongers who were worried about the direction of the city were receptive to the clearly Christian message of the movie. The SARS epidemic was also the background for another ME production, *The Miracle Box* (2004), which became the city's top-grossing Christian film.[12] It tells the story of Tse Yuen-man, a devout Christian doctor who had died during the SARS epidemic in 2003. Tse's selfless and ultimately self-sacrificial service in the high-risk SARS ward gained her admiration far beyond the Christian community. Although ME promoted the movie as a true story, the plot was in fact largely fictional and focused on Tse's supposed romantic relationship with a doctor suffering and ultimately dying of leukaemia, who went around offering a folded paper box to whomever he met, urging them to put all troubles and difficulties into this box so that God could sort it out for them (thus the movie's title). This message of hope against all odds was inspiring to some, but many found it simplistic. One critic pointed out that "there are only good films and bad films but no such things as evangelistic films or secular films; a so called 'secular film' may do a better job in glorifying the divine."[13] Indeed, the movie's simplicity revealed a problem of many evangelistic films (and of much evangelistic proclamation), namely that they approach their subject too directly, ignoring the subtlety of reality. Still, ME had more ambitious goals. It wanted to establish its own TV channel and, despite significant criticism by major Christian denominations and media organizations for being too expensive and too exclusively Christian, did so with Creation TV in 2003.[14] As it turned out, it seems both sides were right: ME and its TV channel have survived, yet ME has repeatedly had to issue urgent appeals for large donations and, with its limited budget, produces a thin program, instead relying more and more on reruns.[15]

Yam Chi Keung, a local scholar who analyzes how Hong Kong Christians interact with media culture, distinguishes three different forms how Christians use media, namely (1) for Christian formation, (2) for evangelism, and (3) as socio-cultural involvement.[16] Yam sees most Christian media production as belonging to the first two categories, with a rare case of socio-cultural involvement the *Breakthrough* series of the late 1980s. A more recent example of this approach was the movie *Ten Years* (2015), a low-budget independent film and the most discussed cinematic work of the last decade. It won an award as the Best Film in the annual local film award ceremony and was received enthusiastically. The film consists of five separate short films, directed by different young filmmakers, that portray an imagined Hong Kong ten years in the future, under tightened political control and with local culture increasingly displaced by mainland Chinese dominance. On the surface, the movie is not a Christian movie at all and has no connection to Christianity except for the epilogue's quotation of Amos 5:13–14 ("For the times are evil; seek good, not evil, that you may live"), though its executive producer Andrew Choi is a Christian with a close connection to Breakthrough and several key members of the production team are also Christians. The movie is significant due to its reception history and its sharp prophetic voice, which penetratingly envisioned the city's future and converged with the voices of many Christians in subsequent years. Many church groups arranged screenings and used the movie as a basis for discussion, which in turn sharpened the socio-political awareness of young Christians. The movie played a crucial role in moving a traditionally inward-looking faith community towards a critical engagement with the socio-political realities of the city. The movie profoundly reflected the mood of many in the city who felt hopeless and frustrated after the government crackdown that brought an end to seventy-nine days of peaceful protest for more democracy in the fall of 2014.

Ten Years was preceded by an earlier movie that portended Christians' changing socio-political role. Vincent Chui's *3 Narrow Gates* (2009) tells the story of corporate corruption, a sinister police force, and violation of press freedom. The crime thriller connects several unrelated persons—a former policeman with a gambling addiction, a political-minded pastor who speaks out for the marginalized via a radio show, a sex worker from China supporting her sick mother back home, and a young and idealistic journalist—all trying to uncover the truth behind the murder of a corporate lawyer on a yacht. A recurring motif in the film is a reference to Matthew 7:14: "Because strait is the gate, and narrow is the way, which leadeth unto life, and few there be that find it," which explains the film's title. The film offers a dark portrait of a city entangled in corrupt and bad governance, with a morally degenerate middle class, and with universal values such as human rights, rule of law, and moral integrity eroding under Chinese rule.[17] Christians appear on both sides of the moral divide. The outspoken Pastor Ma stands on the side of the poor and marginalized, while the lay leaders of his church, typically leaders in society and successful in business, ask him to focus on spiritual matters and remind him of the potentially negative impact on the church of his quest for justice and his outspokenness. While these examples of a subtler engagement of Christians in cultural production may not be the majority and may have been ignored by many media consumers, they had a lasting impact on the perception of Christianity as engaging in and with society.

Publishing

A typical forum for Christianity to present itself in the public sphere is newspapers and magazines. Hongkongers have access to a broad range of Christian publications, some locally produced, and others backed by overseas ministries. The oldest local Christian newspaper is the Roman Catholic diocese's weekly *Kung Kao Po*, tracing its history back to 1928. The paper still publishes every Friday along with a supplement aimed at young people, and it continues to comment on affairs concerning both church and society. A major locally produced Protestant periodical is the *Christian Weekly*, founded in 1964 by the Hong Kong Chinese Christian Church Union, which also manages the city's Christian cemeteries. This organization is, in contrast to the Hong Kong Christian Council, less driven by an ecumenical vision than born out of the pragmatic need to deal jointly with matters of concern for Christian congregations. The *Christian Weekly* offers news and broad spiritual and theological support for Christian life by discussing faith-related topics. It is thus rather inward-looking and reflects local Christians' traditional abstinence from critical involvement in society. In contrast, the other major weekly

Christian newspaper, the *Christian Times*, founded in 1987, has a more public-theological vision. It understands itself as a forum for different voices to engage in dialogue and thus help Christians understand the times and appropriately respond (thus its Chinese name, meaning "forum of the time"). Although the newspaper's backers and regular writers represent more the progressive and socially engaged wing of Christianity, the weekly is well received among a wide range of Christians. Another Christian medium, the *Gospel Herald*, is a non-denominational provider of news for Chinese Christians. Headquartered in San Francisco and with a branch office in Hong Kong, it focuses on a broad range of stories related to worldwide Christianity with an obvious focus on news related to the global Chinese community. On the other side of the theological spectrum stands the Pentecostal-charismatic *Kingdom Revival Times*, published fortnightly by Kingdom Ministries. One of its characteristics is a strong concern for Israel, visible not only in a special section on news related to Israel but also in adding the Jewish calendar to the Gregorian. This concern is rooted in the organization's passionately premillennial theology that regards the modern state of Israel as a sign of the imminent premillennial return of Christ.

Aside from these publications, most local ministries promote their cause through some form of electronic or printed publication. One of the more elaborate magazines is the glossy *Angel's Heart* magazine, published by Media Evangelism, with moving testimonies of the famous and meaningful stories of the less famous. A remarkable magazine is *Breakazine*, a trimonthly magazine published by Breakthrough aimed at young people and displaying a progressive, socially engaged, and critical mindset. Many theological schools publish a newsletter, often with substantial theological essays, and Christian NGOs use their publications for both fundraising and updating donors. Around thirty Christian book publishers produce a broad range of locally written or translated books; and seventy Christian bookstores care for their distribution.[18] Historically significant is the *Chinese Christian Literature Council*, an ecumenical publisher, who began in 1887, when missionaries in Shanghai established (at the time) the largest Chinese publishing house in the world, hoping to promote Chinese and Western culture and introducing books on Western politics and science. After 1949, several of the publishing house's staff relocated to Hong Kong, where they set up a similar publishing company.

The city's enormous Christian print output obviously overwhelms the actual number of Christians in the city and reflects the city's status as a hub for the wider Chinese community. In the past, Hong Kong received over forty million visitors per year from mainland China, some of whom would stock up on Christian and other literature not available on the other side of the border. At the same time, most of the Christian publishers and NGOs have some dimension of their work relating to China and the overseas Chinese community.

Music

The study of local Christian music production offers significant insights of how local Christianity amalgamates elements from local culture, broader Chinese Christianity, the global Chinese diaspora, and the global marketplace. It is thus an area that pointedly reflects the hybridity of local Christianity and local culture. At the beginning of Christian singing in the city stands a traditional hymn book, the *Hymns of Universal Praise* (HUP), that was, until the 1970s, the only hymn book used.[19] Published in 1936 by Western missionaries, it was used all over China. Local Christians enjoyed its classical songs—many from the British and American evangelical tradition such as those of Fanny Cosby, Isaac Watts, and Charles Wesley, connecting Christians across different traditions—and they still do so today, thus expressing respect and gratitude for the missionaries' work.[20] However, since the 1950s, many local Christians have begun to seek new forms of worship expression. They bemoaned that, first, more than 85 percent of HUP's songs were translations from Western hymns; second, the song translations had been made into Mandarin and did not fit Cantonese tones; third, the few Chinese songs included in HUP were likewise produced for Mandarin-speaking Christians and did not reflect the different tonality of Cantonese; and fourth, the contents reflected an outdated theology and spirituality that did not appeal to young people. Gradually, Christian songs of a more youthful and revivalist style emerged, yet the first among them, three volumes of *Youth Hymns*, still largely relied on translations from English, and its hymns were often sung in English.

A significant shift towards local—that is, Cantonese—song production happened only in the late 1970s. Several factors influenced this shift, among them a stronger sense of local identity that can similarly be observed in other areas; the emergence of Cantopop, a unique and highly successful local music style; the movement for Contemporary Christian music (CCM) emerging in the 1960s in the West; and the city folk-music movement, which had its roots in the U.S. folk-music revival and in Taiwanese campus folk songs, which produced contextual songs that often included references to social issues. Social and theological developments in Taiwan, which played a crucial role in promoting contextualization, further encouraged young Hongkongers to turn towards local songs. The 1980s thus saw the emergence of multiple initiatives for local Cantonese song productions, among them *Breakthrough's* release of the audiotapes *Song for the City* and the first tape of the series *Let's Sing a New Song* (1982), the Cantonese hymnals *"Come and Sing*,*"* and the establishment of the Hong Kong Association of Christian Musicians (ACM) with pioneers of local contemporary Christian music such as Vivian Yung Wai Wun, Benjamin Ng Ping-kin, Edwin Tanner (Chan Fong Wing), and Ruth Tsang Lo Tak. In subsequent decades, the ACM was, in the words of a younger musician, "a father figure" for the Contemporary Christian Music movement in the city.

Since then, local music production has benefitted from global cross-fertilization, with Chinese Christians in Hong Kong, Taiwan, North America (particularly California), and elsewhere in the diaspora composing praise-and-worship songs that easily spread across the global Chinese community. An important player was the charismatic *Stream of Praise* (SOP) ministry of Taiwanese Americans in California,[21] founded in 1993. Many of their songs became popular in revivalist local worship, and their music style also impacted churches used to worshipping in more traditional ways. Besides SOP's songs (which are in Mandarin), global revivalist trends from Asia, Australia, and the U.S. were also absorbed by local Christians. Important inspiration came from South Korea—the Yoido Full Gospel Church developed into a global brand and "prayer mountains" attracted local believers, many from traditional evangelical churches, which contributed to a Third Wave kind of Pentecostal-charismatic spirituality. Other popular sources of local praise and worship are Hillsong and the Planetshakers from Australia, the International House of Prayer in Kansas, USA (IHOPKC), Bethel Church (Redding, California), and the City Harvest Church in Singapore. A very important source of influence is the Taipei Bread of Life Church's *Joshua Band*. This group translated many songs into Chinese and produced their own songs and also organized worship and "prophecy" camps for young local Christians. These charismatic worship styles have been transmitted through local ministries such as the youth groups of Shaukiwan Baptist Church and of Tung Fook Church, the meanwhile closed Elim Christian Bookstore, the Kingdom Revival Times, U-Fire (a youth revival ministry), and Incubator Ministries, led by Eddie Ma, the former pastor of the charismatic SKW Baptist Church. Interestingly, Lü Xiaomin, maybe the most important mainland Chinese Christian composer of the twenty-first century (her Canaan Hymns are famous in mainland China), had little impact on local worship. Her lyrics, reflecting life in the rural heartland of China's Henan Province and expressing her hope for a revival in China, and her melodic style, which bears resemblance to Chinese patriotic songs,[22] do not resonate with the city's cultural context.

The absorption of music trends from the global Chinese community initially led to an increase in Mandarin songs, some composed in Mandarin, others translated. This openness to Mandarin songs peaked towards 2010, a time when Hongkongers became more confident about the city's future under Chinese rule and even developed a sense of pride in being part of China. Since then, however, the mood has dramatically changed. Many locals are disappointed with the lack of democratic progress and, more recently, a rapid decline in civil rights. With Mandarin increasingly perceived as part of the mainland's domination of local life, singing in Cantonese has experienced a revival.[23] A music group standing at the beginning of this new development are the *Chung Brothers*, Henry and Roger Chung, who brought out their first album, *The Chimes*, in 2009. They composed and performed a new style of Christian music drawing from a variety of music styles such as traditional gospel music, jazz, bossa nova, hip-hop and rap. Their lyrics combine more traditional and explicit Christian themes with themes of social justice, as in the song "To Do Justly, To Love Mercy." One of their sources of inspiration was a Christian music group of the 1980s, *Equator*, which stripped out all Christian references from their lyrics but offered a secularized Christian message through their songs. While some Christians found the Chung Brothers' music too experimental and less soothing than, for example, the traditional songs of Stream of Praise, many appreciated the two brothers' unorthodox and progressive engagement with new music styles. They reflected the spirit of the 2010s, as local Christians experimented with new forms of Christian expression and developed more critical attitudes towards traditions and authorities. Extending the path taken by the Chung brothers, recent years saw the emergence of new groups such as the popular *Worship Nation, Milk and Honey*, and *Raw Harmony*. They promote Cantonese Christian music, whose songs are sung by many younger Christians across the denominations and include themes such as justice and freedom. Their music appeals to young Christians who have been disappointed with traditional church life or to those who are critical of what they see as a me-centered spirituality in some of the contemporary praise and worship hymns. These groups reach large audiences through social media. Other trends are the reharmonizing of traditional hymns, as shown in cantonhymn.net; the gradual adoption of Taizé, especially among young people who used to follow the music culture of charismatic groups such as IHOP; and the composition of new lyrics for traditional hymns, reflecting the original messages but with more sensitivity to Cantonese tonality, an approach taken by Timothy Lam Kwok Cheung from Sen Lok Church.

Christian Athletes and Sport Ministries

Much of what we observed regarding Christians in showbiz applies also to Christian athletes: they are influential channels to promote the Christian faith; they bridge the gap between the secular world of sport and the spiritual world of faith; and they benefit not only the Christian community but also themselves, portraying themselves as more than bodies and muscles but as persons with spiritual depth. Although many athletes are reticent about their faith, there are some who are known for public witness. Arguably the first major Chinese sportsman who made his Christian faith known was Michael Chang, an

American tennis player whose parents had migrated from Taiwan. Although not directly related to the city, he is well respected among local Christians. Locally, Tam Wai Kwok, who played for the HK national football team, and Sarah Lee Wai-sze, bronze medallist at the 2012 London Olympics and the 2020 (2021) Tokyo Olympics, publicly shared about how their faith helped them in moments of crisis, as when facing career-endangering injuries.[24] Many regard these Christian athletes, who proved themselves in competition and who had to work hard for reaching such high levels of athletic achievement, as ideal witnesses for and role models of the Christian faith.

Local sports ministry[25] first emerged in 1985 from the ministry of *Breakthrough*, when Johnny Yiu Yuk Hing, a young graduate working with the organization, initiated a basketball summer camp. The success of the program led to a regular basketball team that combined sport with youth outreach and evangelism. Encouraged by the director of the International Sports Coalition, Yiu attended the Asian Games in 1986 and the Olympic Games in 1988 in Seoul as chaplain to serve and evangelize Chinese athletes. In 1991, Yiu, together with Chin Yan Pui and Stephen Chung, a local pastor, established the *Sports Ministry Coalition* (SMC) with the aim of reaching out to professional athletes in Hong Kong and the mainland and assisting local churches in ministering to young locals through sport. SMC regularly attended major international and local sport events for evangelism among Chinese athletes. Since then, other organizations with similar aims, such as *Soccer in Christ* (SIC) and the *Basketball Sports Ministry*, have emerged. Both of them share SMC's aim of connecting with non-believers through communal activities and school ministries. SIC was founded in 2001 and has been conducting activities in poor inner-city areas, inviting young people to participate in football and learn about Jesus. In 2008, the group went a step further and established the *Gospel Football Club*, which joined the local amateur football league. For these young athletes, participating in sport offers an opportunity to build healthy relationships, to share and exercise their faith, and to witness it by fair play and humility. For them, faith corrects the inherent self- or group-centredness that is commonly connected with competitive sport.

While Christian artists and Christian top athletes both use their fame to promote their faith, sports ministry has a broader focus with two main aims. First, it uses sport as a channel to reach young people. For those who are financially disadvantaged and living in cramped, sub-standard housing, the sports ground is an important meeting point and the place they spend much of their leisure time. This is also the place where the triad gangs recruit new members. Sports ministry can thus have a significant social impact, by keeping young people from drifting into a criminal career. But sports ministry aims not just at the marginalized but also at young people in general, who often find church boring and irrelevant. Jointly engaging in sports and living the gospel through sport activities is an alternative form of encountering the gospel. A second aim is Christian character building: team-based sport activities cultivate personal qualities of respect, cooperation, and humility. Indeed, core values for athletic success are not much different from central Christian values—passion, focus, self-motivation, self-discipline, and mutual encouragement.[26] Regular debriefings on what athletes can spiritually learn from their sports experiences build an important part of Christian engagement in sports.

On another level, sports ministry changes the image of Christianity and of typical believers. It stands in contrast to the stereotype of Chinese churches as influenced by a fundamentalist physical/spiritual dualism that neglects the body.[27] Sports ministries present Christianity as muscular, promoting "the idea that the physical condition of a man's [sic!] body ha[s] religious significance" and that "meeting the physical demands of godly behavior require[s] good health and physical conditioning."[28] Such muscular Christianity rejects the usual devaluation of the physical—in many religions, not just Christianity—as well as the widespread view of the body as a source of temptation and sin. Instead, it offers a positive view of the physical world and gives positive significance to the body. As elsewhere, it is mainly Protestants who are involved in sports ministry, thus confirming the affinity between Protestant Christianity and sport.[29]

Observations

Several features of Christians' connection with the cultural realm stand out: First, historically, the emergence of independent and localized forms of Christian expression in the cultural realm began in the 1970s. The years from the late 1970s to the early 2000s were the heyday of Christian engagement in popular culture, a period that witnessed amazing creativity in faith expressions and in interactions between Christianity and culture. This was the golden age of local cinema production and a time when the city's economy and culture boomed, and it was in these decades that Hong Kong acquired its unique local identity. Before the 1970s, Christians were too absorbed in caring for the needs of the fast-growing immigrant population from mainland China to develop contextual faith expressions, and they remained largely within the theological framework provided by Western missionaries. Since the early 2000s, Christians have remained actively involved in the cultural realm, but the atmosphere has markedly changed: much of the confident interaction has given way to a more defensive and subdued engagement that tries to skilfully navigate the limits imposed by a state that increasingly controls and encroaches on local cultural life.

Second, the Christian presence in the cultural realm clearly shows the hybridity of local Christianity: its combination of global and local, Eastern and

Western cultural elements woven into a unique expression of religious identity. Many Hongkongers have a "flexible citizenship,"[30] that is, not just two passports, but also a sense of being at home in Hong Kong *and* overseas. They easily move along Chinese linguistic lines, passing ideas and cultural expressions via networks that also function as transnational business and family relationships. Ideas and cultural expressions that emerge from one part of the Chinese cultural realm easily find roots in another one. This hybridity and permeability of local culture enable the exchange of Christian ideas, practices, and faith expressions. While in the past, the absorption of ideas and products from global Chinese networks also happened across the border, socio-cultural changes since the early 2010s have greatly reduced the free flow of Christian ideas and expressions to and from mainland China.

Third, we can recognize two main modes of Christian engagement with culture, which may be called *instrumental* and *incarnational*. The two modes should not, however, be understood as mutually exclusive but rather as different emphases. The former has always been the dominant mode, using the cultural realm and public figures as channels to promote the Christian faith. Christian movies, TV programs, and songs, and Christian engagement on sports grounds served to communicate the gospel. This changed the perception of Christianity into a faith at home not just in church or among religious people but equally on the football pitch, the film set, or the stage. Yet, the instrumentalization of culture and its subordination to the "primary" goal of evangelistic proclamation easily led to a shallowness that undermined the depth and credibility of this approach. Artistic products that served religious communication became predictable and superficial. Still, there has always been an alternative, an incarnational mode where faith finds expression in worldly terms and in independent cultural expressions. An example of this mode is *Breakthrough*, which has played a unique role in the socio-cultural realm with its early socially engaged TV program, its promotion of local song production, its publication *Breakazine*, and its role in the emergence of a local sports ministry. Breakthrough "embodied the call for social concern among young evangelicals in the earlier part of the 1970s. More importantly, it was in fact a collective of culturally minded and media-sensitive young evangelicals."[31] Its faith-based socio-cultural engagement understood the cultural and social realm not simply as a target to be evangelized or as a channel to reach out to the world but as an arena in which faith could be lived out. Co-founded and for many years led by Philemon Choi Yun-wan, a major figure among Chinese evangelicals, Breakthrough connects socially engaged evangelical and ecumenical Christians, thus demonstrating that these different spiritual and theological orientations can converge in a joint concern for the local context. The most intriguing example of this incarnational mode was of course discussed above—the movie *Ten Years*.

Finally, the most compelling feature of local Christians' socio-cultural engagement is its flexibility, its ease in crossing religious-secular boundaries and its light-footed appropriation of elements from the cultural realm; vice versa, local culture shows a relaxed receptivity towards Christian cultural expressions. A good example of how easily Christian expressions move beyond the original Christian circle was Stream of Praise's popular song *The Covenant Under the Rainbow*, the favorite song of Tse Yuen-man, the Christian doctor who died during the SARS epidemic: the song was frequently played in secular radio stations and on public transport. Other examples are Sammi Cheng's and Jade Kwan's Christian albums, produced by secular music companies, or artistic expressions in the 2014 and 2019 social movements, where Jesus appeared adorned with typical protest insignia—yellow umbrella, goggles, and a protective helmet. Local Christians' agility in entering the secular realm and the secular market's absorption of religious products are an expression of the youthfulness of local Christianity, which appears unconstrained by the usual reverence toward tradition, and which tolerates contradictions rather than seeing them as mutually exclusive. Without the burden of a centuries-old local Christian tradition and the obligations deriving from it, local Christians are free to playfully engage with the foreign elements of transmitted tradition, to creatively explore new paths in contextualizing these elements, and to constructively engage with local society and culture. While most people *do* have a deep respect for tradition, they engage with it in pragmatic ways and do not hesitate to introduce new practices if this attracts new people. In Hong Kong, what counts (as always) is not tradition *per se* but whether it works.

5

Serving the People

Christianity at the Forefront of Social Change

Born in 1953, Uncle Gutt grew up in the poor neighborhood of Kowloon City as one of six children raised by his early-widowed mother, who ran a small tofu factory for the shops in the neighborhood. Like many of his peers, he spent much time in the streets, and at the age of sixteen, began to follow the triads, a local criminal gang. He helped run an illegal gambling den, lending money to gamblers and recovering debts. He also took up occasional jobs such as driving a taxi, and in his late thirties, he was asked to drive a friend on an errand. It turned out to be a robbery that ended in the killing of a shopkeeper. Uncle Gutt was arrested and sentenced to life in prison as an accessory. After a few years in prison, out of curiosity and lacking any other meaningful activity, he joined a worship service in prison and felt surprised by what he experienced, an atmosphere much different to what he had known. He was particularly moved that the chaplain and the volunteers continued their regular monthly visits even during Chinese New Year, the time when people typically go to see their *own* family members. Uncle Gutt became a regular participant in worship and, after a few years, radically broke with all triad affiliations and applied for baptism. After around twenty-four years in prison, Uncle Gutt was eventually released, having gained the respect of inmates and staff alike. He had always kept a low profile but was a steadfast and solid friend to many. Back in society and already in his sixties, he set up a cleaning company specializing in pest control. He understood that outside society looked with much suspicion on people like him, and he didn't mind cleaning the dirtiest parts of apartments and restaurants. It was his own form of testimony to his faith, in his words: "If even Jesus cleaned the disciples' feet, why should I mind cleaning other people's toilets?" He regularly attends a Lutheran church and leads a fellowship of former inmates. The Christian faith is not a precondition to join the fellowship, but a clear break with the triads is.

The life of Elder David Lam has been much more orderly, but similarly reflects the significant role of Christian social ministry in local citizens' lives. Born in the 1950s to parents who had escaped the economic and political hardship of Mao-ruled China by migrating to Hong Kong, David spent his early childhood in one of the temporary shacks dotting the city's slopes. While his parents barely made a living by working in a nearby soy sauce factory, he remained in the care of his older sister and the close-knit community of the settlement, with neighbors from the same Chaozhou-speaking area in China. The settlement, in Shau Kei Wan on the eastern part of the island, stood next to a church of the Tsung Tsin Mission. His parents did not like the church much and were critical of the many new immigrants who relied on the churches' food handouts and subsequently turned to the Christian faith, so-called "milk powder believers," but they felt it was surely not a bad thing for the older sister to be admitted to the church's primary school. And taking her two-year-old brother with her to Sunday school and other church activities was certainly better than risking the children being alone at home. This is how little David joined a church and grew up in it. A few years later, he was admitted to the same primary school, a popular choice for many parents. At ten years of age, he began to confess the Christian faith and actively joined the youth fellowship. At seventeen, he received baptism and has remained faithful to the congregation to this day, serving in various positions and finally being ordained as a church elder. His professional career similarly reflects a solid social upward movement shaped by faithfulness and constant blessing. After graduation from secondary school, he wished to continue to university, but his family could not afford it. Instead, David entered the work force and saved money for further studies. After a few years, he was admitted to a university in Canada, but Canadian immigration rejected him because all his funds had gone toward tuition, and he couldn't prove that he would be able to support himself. This disappointment, however, did not undermine his resolve, and he vowed that he would enable his children to study in his place. He worked the next thirty-seven years in the same insurance company, gradually moving up to a senior position and supporting his two children through school and into successful careers, all along remaining steadfast in his commitment to the church.

Uncle Gutt and Elder Lam are just two among the innumerable people impacted by the churches' social ministry. While the last chapter described Christianity's connections with the cultural realm, this chapter shows Christians' participation in society, most significantly through schools and social services. This has been a feature of local Christianity since the earliest times, and it has remained so until now. Today, around half of all schools and between one-quarter and one-third of all social services in the city are run by Christian churches or NGOs.

Facts and Figures

Of the city's 508 *secondary schools*, 240 (47.2 percent), are run by Christian churches and organizations (152 Protestant and 88 Catholic). In contrast, only 21 secondary schools are run by Buddhists, 6 by Daoist organizations, 5 by Sik Sik Yuen (a religious charity founded in 1921 that manages the famous Wong Tai Sin Temple and follows the teachings of Buddhism, Daoism, and Confucianism), and 1 by a Muslim organization. Among the city's 591 *primary schools*, 292 (49.4 percent) are run by Christian bodies (183 Protestant and 109 Catholic) while only 16 by Buddhists, 8 by Daoists, 4 by Sik Sik Yuen, and 2 by Muslims.[1] Most active among the Protestant churches are the Anglican Church and the Church of Christ in China, which have more than 80 and 50 schools, respectively.[2] Additionally, three universities or parts thereof and two other tertiary institutions grew out of Christian educational ministry and still cultivate, to varying degrees, this Christian heritage: the Chinese University of Hong Kong's Chung Chi College, the Hong Kong Baptist University and the Lingnan University, as well as the Caritas Institute of Higher Education and the Seventh-day Adventists' Hong Kong Adventist College.

The situation in social services is similar:[3] The Christian community runs 13 (7 Protestant and 6 Catholic) of the city's 55 hospitals, along with 30 clinics (17 Protestant and 13 Catholic). Protestant churches manage around 110 welfare organizations providing services to over 100 centers for families and youths, as well as 11 children's homes, 170 elderly centers and nursing homes, and about 60 rehabilitation centers for drug addicts and the disabled. They further offer services through chaplaincies in hospitals, prisons, the airport, and even campsites. The government's yearbook mentions 730 para-church agencies attending to the community's needs. The Catholic Church serves the community mainly through the diocese's official social welfare arm, *Caritas Hong Kong*. Besides its support of hospitals and clinics, it oversees 42 social and family service centers, 23 hostels, 19 homes for the aged, 35 rehabilitation service centers, and other social care agencies. According to various estimates, Christians operate one-quarter to one-third of all the social services in the city.[4]

The first section of this chapter summarizes developments from the 1840s until the 1960s, from the establishment of the first medical facilities, social services, and schools, to early concerns for justice and poverty alleviation, and the misery of the post-war years; it explains why faith-based organizations have played such a central role in the city's educational and social services. The following sections survey the vast landscape of Christian NGOs—from ecumenical justice initiatives to conservative evangelical and charismatic ministries—that have emerged in more recent decades and review the social footprint of these ministries. The variegated Christian ministries in the social realm testify to the enormous vibrancy of Christian engagement in Hong Kong society. Understanding them leads us to the heart of Christians' participation in and relationship with society.

Active Christians and Disinterested Governors (Nineteenth-Century Hong Kong)

What are the reasons for Christians playing such an eminent role in the city's educational, social, and medical services? To answer this question, we need to consider the British colonial rulers' original intentions: they were not actually interested in establishing a colony for settlement but instead needed a coastal base to secure their trade with China. In the words of Ernst Johann Eitel, an administrator in charge of Hong Kong's education system in the 1880s and among the first to write about the city's history, "the settlement on Hongkong must be treated rather as a station for the protection of British trade in the Far East in general [rather] than as a Colony in the ordinary sense of the word."[5] The historian John Carroll described the nineteenth-century colonial government as determined "to run its colony as cheaply as possible and taking so little interest in its Chinese subjects, that these people had to rely on themselves and on personal networks."[6] In shortest form: It was about trade, not about people. Until the late 1800s, the colonial government regarded the local Chinese population rather as an unavoidable nuisance. It viewed them mostly as criminals needing to be controlled rather than understood, and blithely imposed severe and discriminatory restrictions and punishments on local people.[7] It was more than willing to leave a broad range of responsibilities for the local population to voluntary organizations: neighborhood and mutual help committees linked to a temple like the old Man Mo Temple or based on kinship, ancestral origin, or language.

An important such voluntary organization in the early time was the *Tung Wah Hospital*, initiated by local elites in 1869.[8] Another local organization, the *Po Leung Kuk*, was founded in 1878 as "Society for the Protection of Women and Children," as many women and young girls were kidnapped and sold for adoption and for work in domestic service in Hong Kong and overseas.

Like these Chinese social networks, Western missionaries were happy to fill the gap left by a detached and disinterested government. Yet, more than that, the government, lacking sufficient understanding of the local population, relied on the cultural and linguistic skills of several missionaries to build bridges to the local population: In 1845, Karl Gützlaff from Germany, the first Lutheran missionary to China and Hong Kong, became Chinese secretary, the government's officer in charge of relations with the local community; Wilhelm Lobscheid, who had worked with the Rhenish Mission and the Chinese Evangelization Society, became Inspector of Government Schools in 1857;[9] and Ernst Johann Eitel, who had served with the Basel Mission and later the London Mission, became Inspector of Schools in 1879.

A second reason for Christians' engagement in society was that nineteenth-century missionaries saw social care as naturally complementing the propagation of the gospel, the "two hands of the gospel." They believed they had been chosen to bring not only the gospel but also the blessings of their civilization to the whole world and to witness the life-transforming power of their faith. They understood their educational, social, and medical support as a testimony of Christian love and as an expression of the superior knowledge of Christian civilization.[10] Schools, medical facilities, and social services offered a platform to prove the usefulness of Western knowledge; they served as a bridge to reach out to the local population and remove suspicion about foreigners, and they provided opportunities to evangelize local people. The educational ministry further aimed at training a native clergy and Christian teachers for the propagation of the gospel in China and at raising a generation of well-equipped local leaders who could communicate and cooperate with the colonial administration.[11] In all these ministries, a sense of condescendence was deeply intertwined with emancipatory motifs. The former was a hardly avoidable result of a relationship of superior-inferior, of colonially backed missionaries who had something to give and followers who were expected to receive;[12] the latter resulted from ministries such as Christian education for girls or the empowerment of those at the margins of society.

Earliest Schools and Social Services

Christian social ministry began with the arrival of the first missionaries in the city. *Henrietta Shuck* (1817–44), an American Baptist who reached Hong Kong in 1842 and was one of the first Western women in Hong Kong, established a school for Chinese children and ran it until her death (in childbirth) in 1844. Her original intention was to focus on girls' education, yet such plans were frustrated, as she had to accept boys so that she could also teach girls.[13] Early missionary schools still operating today are the London

Missionary Society's *Ying Wa College*, founded in 1818 in Malaysia before moving to Hong Kong in 1843, or the Anglican *St. Paul's College*, which opened in 1849. The LMS also established Hong Kong's first Western clinic in 1843. Other early Christian social ministries are: on the Catholic side the Diocese's first school for Chinese boys in 1843; a home for orphans and abandoned girls established by the French Sisters of St. Paul de Chartres in 1848; the Catholic St. Francis Mission Hospital in 1852; a school of the Canossian Daughters of Charity in 1860, which later became the Sacred Heart Canossian College; on the Protestant side a school of the Basel Mission in 1851 and a boarding school for girls in 1862; and the Anglican Diocesan Girls' and Boys' Schools, in 1860 and 1869 respectively. Other important organizations and agencies that started in the colony's first century were the German Hildesheimer Blindenmission's *Ebenezer School for the Blind* (now Ebenezer School & Home for the Visually Impaired), founded in 1897; the *YMCA* in 1901; and the *YWCA* in 1920.

However, these early endeavors encountered various difficulties. First, many locals initially distrusted Western education and, even more, Western medicine.[14] Because of this, most missionary hospitals in the early period (1842–1859) served the non-Chinese population. The earliest LMS hospital, in fact, moved to Canton in 1848 due to insufficient numbers of Chinese patients in Hong Kong. A Catholic hospital, established in 1852, served mainly non-local people. It took a major outbreak of the bubonic plague in 1894, with a death toll of more than 20,000, to lead locals to a greater acceptance of Western science and technology.[15] Another difficulty was that locals were attracted to mission schools for utilitarian rather than for spiritual reasons. The missionaries' plan to raise Christian clergy did not materialize, as the advantage these students had gained by studying in a mission school did not naturally translate into spiritual change, much less full-time church work.[16] Many graduates aimed at more lucrative employment and moved on to settle elsewhere or returned to their home villages.[17] Third, the mission schools did not have enough money. While the government introduced some subsidies through a school grant scheme in 1873, this came with strings attached: a more balanced curriculum less geared towards evangelism.[18] Fourth, the mission schools regularly faced a shortage of missionaries for teaching.[19] Subsequent decades brought growing professionalization and secularization, a reduced role of religion in education, and the outsourcing of clergy training to specialized seminaries. Yet, the disinterest the colonial government showed towards the concerns of the local population combined with close supervision of local affairs—i.e., leaving care for local people to voluntary organizations while maintaining control through strict funding conditions—remained the pattern for decades to come.

The root problem also remained: a social welfare system based on voluntary bodies alone cannot bring long-term social improvement.[20]

Social Impacts and Concerns for Social Justice (1840s until 1930s)

The missionaries' care for local society through educational, social, and medical facilities had a profound impact on society—not only through school graduates and service recipients, who gained political and economic influence and benefitted society, but also through female education and through the care of orphans, delinquents, and the disabled, which gradually transformed the fabric of society and fostered new moral values. This is shown particularly well in the opening of girls' schools by several early female missionaries: Henrietta Shuck (see above); Mary Isabella Morison (1815–53), wife of James Legge; and Marie Lechler, wife of Rudolph Lechler of the Basel Mission. To be clear, girls' education was for a long time driven by a conservative spirit that taught moral values such as faithfulness, purity, and neatness as ideals of womanhood, with the aim of educating "good Christian wives" who would be subordinate to their husbands, serve humbly in the church, lead a Christian household and master the language to read the Bible to their children.[21] Yet it sowed seeds that eventually led to the empowerment of women. The missionaries in charge of girls' education offered an unintentional but powerful role model of female autonomy; and female education prepared women to move beyond the traditional roles of mother and wife, contributing significantly to women's social upward mobility.[22]

But social change came not only through the direct recipients of such services. Christians soon began to address more fundamental issues, bringing deep change to local and even overseas societies. One was the role of Christianity in migration. During the 1850s and 1860s, some missionaries in Hong Kong actively supported Chinese migration to the West Indies, Guyana, Hawaii, and East Malaysia.[23] This migration was part of a global movement after the abolition of slavery, with migrants from the British Empire and even mainland China finding employment in a system of indentured labor, typically a five-year commitment of work at low wages on a colonial plantation. While Chinese migrants under this scheme were not as numerous as those from India, many came from poor parts of southern China and migrated through Hong Kong. The missionaries who helped them hoped to mitigate their exploitation by encouraging the migrants to establish Christian communities for better adjustment to their new contexts. However, critics saw the indenture system as an extension of slavery by other means and worried that it undermined the local success of their mission.[24]

A mong the missionaries, the strongest promoter of the indenture system was Wilhelm Lobscheid of the Rhenish Mission. Philip Winnes from the Basel Mission criticized him as being driven more by monetary concerns than by the welfare of the migrants. Agreeing with Lobscheid was Winnes' senior colleague and fellow missionary Rudolf Lechler. He saw the hardship of many Hakka Christians who had gone through the Taiping Wars (1851–64) and the Punti Wars, a series of wars between Hakka- and Cantonese-speaking locals in the Pearl River Delta (1855–67) and wanted to help them.[25] He remained in contact with many of the overseas Hakka communities that grew out of these migratory movements and witnessed their social progress in far-away lands.

Whether the missionaries' support for migration under the indenture system benefitted the workers or rather gave legitimacy to an exploitative labor system may be debated. Undoubtedly, the long-term social impact was that Chinese migrants moved on to more profitable positions after completing their terms of indenture, set roots in their new homes, and grew into vibrant and economically successful Chinese overseas communities. A further effect of this migration was the spread of Chinese Christianity around the world: to Sabah in East Malaysia and to Latin America, the Caribbean, and Hawaii. Many of the descendants of these migrants, most importantly the Hakka in Sabah, have remained connected to their places of origin in South China and to the origins of their religious community. The Hakka people in Sabah are a significant group among Malaysia's 23-percent Chinese minority and have been able to preserve more of their Hakka heritage than the Hakka in Guangdong, who have had to adapt to China's one-language policy suppressing Chinese languages other than the official Putonghua. They have also remained in close contact with the Basel Mission, which supported them in their migration to Sabah.

Other pressing social and political issues that Christians addressed were the sale of opium in the early years of the twentieth century; patriarchal customs such as foot-binding, polygamy, prostitution and arranged marriages; and the political future of China, with local Christians such as Ho Kai, son of the first locally ordained Chinese pastor Ho Fuk Tong (see Chapter 1),[26] Sun Yat-sen and others involved in the political-reform movement. Their political visions combined Chinese nationalism with an appreciation of British free trade and liberal government.[27]

The most important example of Christians engaging in justice and social change in the colony's first century, and the first time Chinese Christians worked together on a social issue, was the *Anti Mui Tsai Campaign* to ban female child-servants.[28] Mui Tsai, literally "little sisters," were young girls sold by their poor parents to many of the city's more affluent households in exchange for these girls being fed and clothed and, when grown up, married to a suitable husband. Defenders of the system maintained that by being sold as domestic servants, the young girls escaped starvation or even being killed as infants by parents unable to afford their care. As with other social issues, the government preferred not to intervene in the internal matters of the colony's Chinese population, referring to the British proclamation in 1841 that religious rites and social customs of the Chinese would be respected. The (male) defenders of the *mui tsai* system were prestigious local elites from the Po Leung Kuk, ironically an organization established to protect women and children, and from the chambers of Chinese commerce; they appealed to the public with a nationalist defense of Chinese culture.[29] Opposition to the plight of these vulnerable girls, many of them living in slave-like conditions and often sexually exploited by the male members of the house, was shaped by the atmosphere of the 1910s. After the Chinese Revolution of 1911, a wave of liberal ideas permeated society, influencing the emergence of labor unions and women's groups advocating changes to the social status of workers and women. Other opponents were liberal expatriates supported by anti-slavery groups back in England. British women continued to play a role in the expansion of social services through the empire with, as some suggest, a hint of racism, believing that only British women and not Chinese could care for the *mui tsai*.[30] Soon enough, though, the question of the female child-servants triggered a debate in the local Chinese community. Many of those who opposed the *mui tsai* system were members of Protestant churches, the YMCA, and the YWCA, and were spurred on by the moral values of the Christian faith, while others were from labor unions. They toured churches and schools, set up the *Anti Mui Tsai Society* (1921) and, by campaigning in both England and Hong Kong, eventually succeeded in convincing the government to abolish the system. The story of this campaign is remarkable for several reasons: It was the first time that the Chinese Christian community, often described as conservative, rose in opposition to the city's commercial and social establishment and successfully effected socio-political change. It is also an early example of Christians cooperating with labor unions for social reform, equality for all, and the rights of women and children. Furthermore, it is a story in which Christian women played a major role in transforming society and, most importantly, it is a case of Christians opposing both the Christian colonizer and Chinese nationalist sentiment, which argued in favor of the status quo by reference to alleged Chinese cultural values.

Christian Ministries in the Post-War Years

The period from the 1930s to the early 1960s, with the Second World War, civil war on the mainland, and the turmoil of the early Communist years, brought an unprecedented wave of refugees to Hong Kong. The strong growth of the

TABLE 5.1 Hong Kong population growth 1931 to 1965[31]

1931	840,473
1940	1,800,000
May 1945	650,000
1950	2,237,000
1955	2,490,400
1960	3,075,300
1965	3,692,300

city's population in the 1930s had been reversed during the Japanese occupation (December 1941–August 1945), when many inhabitants left the territory and when deportations and a high mortality rate further reduced the city's population to around 650,000. Yet, after Japan's surrender, every month brought 100,000 new refugees from the civil war in China to Hong Kong, and by 1950, the population had more than tripled.

During this period, overseas relief agencies played an important role as social-service providers.[32] In response to immediate needs, they offered food, housing support, health care, and other services. For longer-term development and community reconstruction, they opened clinics, schools, and youth centers in squatter areas, simultaneously juggling the needs of the steadily arriving refugees and fending off the never-ending demands of corrupt government officials. The situation of that time is vividly described in the autobiographies of *Elsie Tu (Elliott)*, a former missionary, who lived among the immigrants and became an activist against government misconduct.[33]

Many of the overseas charities that helped new immigrants in those years were of Christian backgrounds—important among them the Catholic Relief Services, World Council of Churches, Church World Service, and Lutheran World Service. Mission agencies forced to leave mainland China decided to use their resources in support of Chinese refugees' needs in Hong Kong, and traditional mainline churches already involved in social ministries intensified their efforts. The Catholic Diocese established a local branch of Caritas in 1953 (until 1961 under the name of Catholic Social Welfare Conference) to offer relief and rehabilitation. From 1946 to 1969, the Catholic Church opened over fifty secondary schools, primary schools, and kindergartens.[34] Other denominations established similar social ministries: the Methodists in 1953, the Church of Christ in China in 1957, and the Tsung Tsin Mission in 1960. Younger churches and individual congregations also entered the field: the Salvation Army, with a girls' home (1948); the Assemblies of God, with roof-top schools for poor children in the 1950s; the Christian and Missionary Alliance, with seven rooftop schools (from 1958 to 1966); and the Pentecostal-Holiness Church, with a rooftop school in the Shek Kip Mei resettlement area (1958) and a medical service center in the 1960s. Initially, much of the initiative came from Western clergy and missionaries. By the 1960s, the localization of social services had begun, and in 1967, several of the major ecumenical agencies merged to form the *Hong Kong Christian Service* (HKCS), now the social-service arm of the HKCC.

Among the many who contributed significantly to society during this period, four deserve special mention. *Rev. Karl L. Stumpf* arrived in Hong Kong in 1952 from Shanghai.[35] Heading the Lutheran World Service, he played a leading role in raising funds for the construction of an ecumenical center, which still houses the HKCC, the HKCS, and other Christian social service agencies; a hospital in Fanling, in the north of Hong Kong; and a vocational training center in Kwun Tong. Elsie Tu (see above) came to Hong Kong in 1951 after having served in China as a missionary of the Plymouth Brethren since 1947. She soon became annoyed by the otherworldliness of fundamentalist Christians around her, leading her to leave the mission and eventually divorce her husband, who remained bound to his fundamentalist faith. For the rest of her life, she remained dedicated to the defense of the city's underprivileged and was possibly the staunchest critic of the colonial government. Approaching the handover in 1997, her anti-colonialism and her frequent criticism of the city's democratic forces gained her much sympathy with Beijing, and she was rewarded with a seat in the provisional (and not democratically elected) legislative council.

Undoubtedly the person who played the most significant role in Christian social ministry was the Anglican bishop *Ronald Hall*, under whose leadership the Anglican Church established nineteen new primary schools and eight secondary schools in the period between 1950 and 1966.[36] He was particularly moved by the plight of orphans roaming the streets and trying to make a living by polishing shoes, but also by the poverty of families living in crowded tenements. In response to this, he initiated or contributed to the establishment of several new welfare agencies in the post-war years, among them the *Hong Kong Juvenile Care Centre* (1948), offering residential care and educational services for needy juveniles; *St. James' Settlement* (1949), providing services for children, teenagers, families, the elderly, and people with disabilities; the *Hong Kong Family Welfare Society* (1949) to help families in need; and the *Hong Kong Sea School* (1952) for orphans and young delinquents. He also established the *Hong Kong Council for Social Service* (1946), which was designed to coordinate the work of voluntary social agencies and has been a crucial partner of the government in supporting the needy. Another important contribution Bishop Hall made was to housing: A present-day visitor to Hong Kong would find it hard to imagine the poverty of the post-war years, when one-quarter of the population was homeless and when there was an endless influx of refugees. People were sleeping in doorways or in narrow alleys and setting up shacks wherever they could find a suitable place.[37] Facing such needs, Bishop Hall initiated the *Hong Kong Housing Society* (1948) long before the government began its public-housing program. Many high government officials called him the "Red Bishop" for his compassion for the poor and the homeless, for his harsh criticism of the governor, and for what they saw as his friendly ties with mainland China.[38] A close colleague of Bishop Hall was the Irish Jesuit *Thomas F. Ryan*,[39] who had been in Hong Kong since the 1930s. He shared Hall's passion for the marginalized and joined him in some of the social initiatives. During his time in the city, he served in various positions, teaching at the famous Wah Yan College of the Jesuits, leading the Jesuits as their superior, presenting radio broadcasts of music and arts, and even serving in the post-war government in roles related to agriculture and the reforestation of the city's hills, which had been stripped during the war. Many of the beautiful trees in today's Hong Kong were planted under his leadership.

Christian social ministry in the post-war years was affected by global political shifts, as Hong Kong was walking a tightrope trying to not provoke mainland China while at the same time becoming a major base for the U.S. during the Korean War and the Cold War. Tensions were also ripe within the local population, with hostility between Nationalist refugees and supporters of the CPC. The government considered the huge influx of refugees only a temporary problem and was reluctant to take responsibility for responding to the tremendous humanitarian needs.[40] Its Social Welfare Office, set up within a larger department in 1948, remained weak. Only in 1958 would it become the Social Welfare Department, which gradually began to plan social services more proactively, entered into partnership with voluntary agencies, and offered partial funding for their services.

A former general secretary of the Hong Kong Council of Social Service, Paul R. Webb, described the immediate years before the late 1950s as an emergency period dominated by basic humanitarian aid. The following years, the late 1950s to the 1960s, were, according to him, the "golden decade," a period when churches and NGOs could provide services that had a lasting impact on development and reconstruction of the community.[41] Both periods were important in Christianity's social role and the public's perception of it in subsequent decades. While the government was partly overwhelmed by the needs of the arriving refugees, partly simply uninterested and ignoring them, churches and NGOs welcomed them without hesitation. As these refugees settled down, prospered, and helped transform Hong Kong into a city with a successful economy and a vibrant civil society, they remembered with gratitude the support they had received. The Ma Tso Lung New Lutheran Village, next to the border with Shenzhen, is an example of this gratitude: In the 1960s, it was affected by the flooding of the Shenzhen River, and the village's houses were submerged. With donations from the Lutheran World Federation, they were able to rebuild it and, in gratitude for the LWF's support, have called it by its new name ever since. Similarly, the names of several Methodist villages, built in the 1950s and 60s to accommodate the large number of refugees who were then absorbed into the expanding city—Wesley Village in Tai Hang (Happy Valley), Asbury Village in Kwai Chung, Epworth Village in Chai Wan, and St. Andrew's by the Sea Village on the waterfront in Tai Po—bear witness to the help received from the worldwide Methodist community.[42]

Advocacy for Industrial Workers and Community Organization: The Story of the Christian Industrial Committee

The period from the 1960s to the 1990s brought significant new developments in Christian social ministry, as in local society overall: a move towards independence, localization, and growing self-confidence. This period was the city's heyday, when Hong Kong flourished, when locals began to enjoy continuous economic growth, when a growing number of Hongkongers were locally born and saw themselves as permanent residents of the city, unlike their parents who had treated Hong Kong as a transitional place—in short, it was the time when Hongkongers acquired a unique identity. Several Christian initiatives and agencies contributed to social change during this period, but the story of one organization stands out—the *Christian Industrial Committee*, CIC for short. The CIC was a response to the miserable working conditions of workers in the many industrial plants and sweatshops; a reaction to a form of suffering that could not be healed by simple charity, and a result of Christians' transnational connectedness. The story is recounted in a beautiful little book, *The Gospel is Not for Sale*, written by Raymond Fung, CIC's director in its early years, who would move on to become the city's only ever executive staff member of the World Council of Churches in Geneva. His writings and the work of the CIC may be regarded as one of the earliest forms of a local theology and it reflected, though largely independent from and at a critical distance from liberation theology, a similar movement of thought and practice.

The story of the CIC begins in the late 1960s,[43] at a critical time in the city when it was straining under the continual influx of refugees from China while trying to stave off the turmoil of the Cultural Revolution, which had gripped the mainland since 1966 and had attracted a following among local trade unionists and industrial workers. When, in 1967, striking workers at a plastic flower factory were locked out by the factory owner, three months of unprecedented riots broke out. Most locals were grateful for the government standing firm, preventing the territory from sliding into the chaos that raged on the other side of the border. Yet even the government, which had for so many decades ignored local needs, realized that underlying problems needed to be addressed. The situation was not much different among Christians: while they had begun in the late 1950s to study ways of engaging with the industrial world, and while a concern for workers had reached Hong Kong through some missionaries, the local church now realized that it had been too detached and had no idea what was happening in the factories. This was the situation in 1968 when the CIC was established.

The founding of the CIC received significant inspiration from the worldwide ecumenical mission movement, which in the post-war years had embarked on an unprecedented engagement with the world. Key themes were: *missio Dei*, the understanding that mission is rooted in God's will for not only transformed individuals but also transformed societies and that God is at work through Christians and non-Christians alike; a *salvation-historical approach* to theology that sees God revealed not only in the inner-biblical history culminating in the person of Jesus Christ but also in the history of the church and the world, wherever people move towards peace, towards liberation from enslaving conditions, and towards relationships of justice; and Bonhoeffer's idea that the church is only the church if it exists *for others*. Based on these theological developments, sometimes called "secular ecumenism,"[44] the WCC had set up a desk for *Urban and Rural Mission* (URM) within its mission department, coordinating Christian engagement in social change across the world. Parallel to this, industrial chaplains and worker priests had emerged in the West: pastors who lived and worked among the workers and embodied the gospel in the industrial world. The connection to the worldwide mission movement proved crucial for the work of the CIC, for several reasons: it brought them into a supportive network of progressive missionaries from across the world; it gave them a level of independence from sponsoring churches; it fostered a missionary spirit that was interested not in institutional growth but in constantly moving on to new shores; and it kept them from becoming simply another social-service agency that delivered services to its clients. In short, the CIC always regarded the industrial world as a place where the transforming power of the gospel needed to enter and be experienced. The connection between local concerns and worldwide mission was reflected in the make-up of the staff, which included missionaries such as Margaret Kane from the UK and Hans Lutz from Switzerland as well as locals such as Lau Chin Shek and two young graduates on placements, Yeung Sum and Rosanna Wong, all three of whom would become influential figures in local politics.

At a time when industrial workers had only three annual days off (at Chinese New Year) and otherwise worked seven days a week, when women had no maternity leave, when victims of industrial accidents received no compensation, the CIC successfully campaigned for changes in labor laws and educated workers in labor rights. In the 1980s, Lau Chin Shek led the CIC to establish the *Association for the Rights of Industrial Accident Victims* and the *Trade Union Education Centre*, a predecessor to the *Confederation of Trade Unions* (CTU), which would play an important and independent political role representing workers' interests, in contrast to the pro-Beijing Federation of Trade Unions. Lee Cheuk Yan, later a major political leader and democracy activist, joined the CIC in 1980 and helped establish the CTU, which he would lead for the next few decades. The spirit of the CIC was best reflected in a declaration adopted in 1970 that expressed beliefs such as an option for the workers that, independent of Latin American liberation theology, paralleled some of its basic thoughts:

"We do not think that workers are always right. Neither do we think that workers are saints or that they have superior morals because of their poverty. No, workers are human, and they are sinners just as we and others are. And, we do not think for a moment that workers are beautiful, for they can be very ugly and corrupt. But we have chosen to be on their side because in our society they are the powerless and the poor and too often, justice is not available to them. As Christians, we believe we belong on their side. We want to stand close to them so that we can hear their sighs and feel their pulse and perhaps there and then find a gospel word that speaks to them."[45]

To be clear, the CIC was a marginal group within the larger Christian landscape of the 1970s and 80s, but it was a widely recognized Christian voice—loud, creative, and often disturbing—and it paved the way for much of the later local Christian advocacy. In 1971 it helped found an independent and non-faith-based sister organization, the *Society for Community Organization* (SoCO), which, encouraged by Masao Takenaka and Oh Jae Shik, visiting staff from the Christian Conference of Asia's Urban and Rural Mission office and inspired by Saul Alinsky's *Rules for Radicals* (1971), aimed at organizing residents of low-cost housing estates around livelihood issues. The *Tsuen Wan Ecumenical Social Service Centre*,[46] founded in 1973, followed the same community-organization approach and was linked to the CIC and SoCO through the person of Hans Lutz.

Christian Social Activism since the 1970s: Livelihood, Social Security, Gender, and Politics

The 1970s brought significant change to Christian engagement in the social realm. In 1973, the government adopted a policy of funding social work done by voluntary organizations, thus effectively outsourcing large parts of its social work.[47] Many of the agencies receiving public funding were Christian churches and NGOs. A parallel partnership had developed in the field of education, with Christian schools. This private–public cooperation has shaped social and educational work in the city, to mutual benefit. The government relied on charities to do much of the work for the needy while simply offering funding, setting the parameters for the work to be done, and assuming a supervisory role. It enjoyed the flexibility, the manpower and the additional financial resources that churches and charitable organizations contributed. A side effect was that Christian schools helped the government counterbalance the influence of communism in Hong Kong.[48] The private partners, on the other hand, benefitted from the prestige they gained by offering social and

FIGURE 5.1 *The Church of Christ in China's Leung Faat Memorial Church, in the heart of the industrial Kwun Tong area; for several years, the church offered support to the ministry of the CIC (copyright Gabi Baumgartner).*

educational services; they used schools and social-service centers as platforms to reach out to the community, and they could use the facilities for Sunday worship, a significant advantage in a city with astronomically high property prices. As a result, churches were able to develop huge educational and social services by receiving land and subsidies from the government. For example, the Anglican church alone has today more than ninety social welfare units.[49] A danger in this patron–client relationship, of course, was that churches might shrink back from speaking prophetically against the government, for fear of losing funding.[50]

That did happen, but only in part. Outside of government-funded social ministries, many initiatives continued to thrive. Without deliberately planning it, Christians benefitted from a division of labor: while their social-welfare agencies were largely tamed by their role as government contractors, Christian NGOs continued to flourish in great numbers, engaging with various needs. Organizationally separated from churches, yet spiritually and financially supported by them and by individual Christians, these groups remained untamed and independent. We may distinguish two major forms of engagement: ecumenical and spiritually progressive groups that critically engaged with social issues, and evangelical groups that focused on evangelism.

The ecumenical and spiritually progressive form largely followed the CIC and community organization approach, taking up livelihood issues neglected by the colonial government. Their story is thus intertwined with that of the CIC. Strong support came from Catholic priests and nuns, who had been serving the poor for many years. Now, Catholic groups such as the *Young Christian Workers*, the *Maryknoll Labour Advisory Team*, and the *Industrial Relations Institute*, headed by *Fr. Patrick McGovern*, an Irish Jesuit, joined the social movement.[51] Their concern for social justice was further strengthened when, in 1977, the diocese established a local *Justice and Peace Commission*, following the Second Vatican Council's call for attending to the needs of the world and Pope Paul VI's establishment of a Pontifical Commission for Justice and Peace; in 1991, it further set up the Catholic Commission for Labour Affairs (HKCCLA).[52] The story of these groups is one in which the boundary between Christians and non-Christians blurs, congruent with the theology of *missio Dei*, the belief that God is at work in the world, through both Christians and non-Christians, and that the mission of Christians is simply to follow wherever God is transforming society. Whether it was for Vietnamese refugees who arrived in large numbers starting in the mid-1970s, for people living in sub-standard housing, for workers laboring without social security, or for poor people in general, Christians and non-Christians campaigned hand in hand to improve their situation. An early galvanizing event was the struggle of the boat people for housing on land when, in 1976, they were driven out of their traditional livelihood by government policy but denied public housing.[53] One fruit of these concerns was the *Hong Kong People's Council on Public Housing Policy*,[54] a pressure group established in 1978 campaigning against rent increases. Two years later, when two bus companies planned to double their bus fares, protests came from a broad swath of Christianity, not just activist groups. It began with the CIC's Raymond Fung convincing the HKCC to conduct a broad-based consultation on the churches' concern for the poor. At the end of the consultation, full of heavy presentations and faithful commitments, a young and freshly graduated Methodist pastor, *Lo Lung-kwong*, stood up and asked: "We have all affirmed our concern for the poor, but what about the bus fare increase? Should we not say something about it?" This critical intervention triggered a strong response and led the HKCC to issue a statement calling for a public consultation and to form a coalition (consisting of more than 300 groups) against higher fares.[55] The aftermath of this campaign saw a continuous emergence of new committees and coalitions monitoring government policies, promoting grassroots improvements, and advocating legislative change. Clearly, the emerging middle-class had adopted Hong Kong as their home, and they wanted to make sure that citizens would jointly enjoy the fruits of progress. The prominent involvement of the HKCC in the bus fare campaign did, however, not mean that mainline churches broadly supported such activism; rather, it was driven by a few progressives who knew how to establish coalitions without alienating the majority of Christians. Lo Lung-kwong, who had played such a critical role in the campaign against the bus fares, would move into denominational leadership, yet, in his heart and in his actions, he retained progressive Christians' concern for justice.

An important development in the 1980s was the strong voice of women striving for social change and an end to patriarchal domination. Christian feminism in Hong Kong built on the work of earlier women leaders such as *Ma Fok Hin Tong*, who was one of the leaders of the anti-mui tsai campaign in the 1930s and the founder of the local YWCA, and *Ellen Li*, a member of the Church of Christ in China (CCC) and the city's first woman legislative councilor (1966–73). Both were vocal in their opposition to discrimination against women.[56] In the 1970s, a growing group of Christian elite women campaigned for gender justice. Feminism found organizational expression in the *Hong Kong Women Christian Council*, which was founded in 1988 as local Christians' response to the World Council of Churches' (WCC) Ecumenical Decade of Churches in Solidarity with Women (1988–1998). A dominant theme in the early years was the topic of the ordination of women, which many churches had been resisting. While the Anglicans had played a pioneering role, other local churches agreed only reluctantly. An important reason for this resistance (against ordination and equal treatment of women in church and society) is a Confucian undercurrent that influences much of local society. Confucianism sees social and familial relations in strictly hierarchical terms, and women as subject to the patriarchal head of the family.[57] But opposition to the ordination of women came not only from Chinese Christians, but equally from conservative Westerners, as *Angela Wong Wai Ching*, a leading feminist theologian since the 1990s, has pointed out. Indeed, some of the Hong Kong churches resisting ordination of women have simply been following their U.S. mother churches' lead. Such is the case of the Lutheran churches affiliated with the Missouri and Wisconsin Synods. Wong argues that Christianity is a place with a firm patriarchal ideology, yet also a space where women can experiment with new social relations and acquire alternative social values. Early female converts in Hong Kong, far from their home villages in mainland China and benefitting from education offered to girls, felt free to move beyond the boundaries of traditional society and culture, to participate in new social organizations, and to adopt modern views on gender. At the same time, those who had migrated to the city since the 1930s increasingly benefitted from the post-war economic boom. This rising middle class has, since the 1970s, increasingly adopted egalitarian values as part of its distinct identity. While many women in today's Hong Kong work in senior political and economic positions, Christian feminists still see much unfinished business: traditional views on gender roles are tenacious and, while women pastors are in no way unusual, senior and lay church leadership is still predominantly male.

With women's ordination increasingly adopted, the Women Christian Council and other groups advocating gender justice turned to new themes, among them the rights of sexual minorities or, more recently, responding to the worldwide MeToo movement, sexual violence in the church. Advocacy for inclusiveness towards sexual minorities has become a major theme for many progressive Christians since the early 2000s, and it is the single most controversial issue between progressive and conservative Christians in the city. A leading voice calling for inclusion has been *Rose Wu*, a former general secretary of the council.[58] Campaigns by these Christian social activists have targeted discrimination in both church and society. One of the groups established by these LGBTQI+ activists was a *Queer Theology Academy* (2013) that aimed at the publication of feminist and queer theologies, promotion of inclusive theological education, and advocacy. Together with other organizations and churches, they campaigned for anti-discrimination legislation and encouraged churches to create an inclusive environment that allows sexual minorities to fully participate in church life. Benefitting from Hong Kong's relatively liberal context, local activists have networked with others in Southeast Asia and elsewhere to support sexual minorities in more repressive contexts and to affirm an inclusive and sexually diverse Christianity.

An organization that developed parallel to the Women Christian Council is the *Hong Kong Christian Institute* (HKCI). Founded in 1988 by a local pastor of the CCC and former general secretary of the Hong Kong Christian Council, *Kwok Nai Wang*, it was born out of a sense of frustration with the politically tame mainline churches and their more conservative and less prophetic positions. With the HKCI, Kwok wished to stand outside the institutional constraints of the church and to regain a prophetic voice and independence for social and political action, "to be a sign of promoting human rights, democracy and justice."[59] The HKCI may be described first as a progressive Christian thinktank and second as an activist group for human rights, for gender and ecological justice, and for democratic development. Towards the late 1980s, with Hong Kong's handover moving closer, human rights became a central issue for many other progressive Christian NGOs as well. Cooperating with Christian and secular groups, their approach was solidly ecumenical. A typical fruit of this effort was the *Hong Kong Human Rights Commission*, founded in 1988, which has eleven member organizations, eight of whom are Christian.

With many groups focused on constitutional progress and human rights, the more grassroots concerns—housing and social security—were left to groups such as the CIC and SoCO. Close to workers, the homeless, people in sub-standard housing, new immigrants, refugees, drug addicts and released offenders, they offered para-legal counseling, campaigned for social support, and gave important inspiration to the founding of new and specialized NGOs. Some of these NGOs offer hospitality to refugees (see also Chapter 3); others address migrant workers' struggles for better working conditions and offer concrete help such as shelters for dismissed domestic workers.

Evangelicals and Charismatics in the Social Realm

The detailed description of ecumenical Christians' social involvement is not because this form of engagement is the dominant mode but because, due to the public nature of its campaigns, it is more visible. However, with most local Christians belonging to evangelical and, to a lesser degree, charismatic churches, these groups also shaped social services, with evangelicals and charismatics sharing much commonality in their approach to society. Their various ministries engage with all kinds of people in need: the homeless, the disabled, marginalized youth, those in prison, ex-inmates, drug and gambling addicts, sex workers, new immigrants, industrial workers, the unemployed, the working poor, and many others. Evangelical and charismatic Christians' social ministries naturally combine faith proclamation and social care, always with a strong focus on the individual who needs support, transformation, and foremost salvation, which comes only from God. They share several characteristics:

First, conscious of possible structural factors impeding behavioral change, they emphasize that true transformation starts in a person's heart, and this transformation will happen only through faith. This is what holds the various ministries of evangelicals and charismatics together. If a person truly believes, his or her behavior will change, and he or she will find liberation. Integration into a loving Christian community will further support the process of regeneration and healing that started with a person's conversion.

Second, and a direct consequence of the first point, conservative Christians are primarily concerned with the individual in his or her spiritual growth and with the traditional family. They do not deny the importance of social factors and political contexts, but they see it as the primordial task of Christians to bring hope and transformation to individuals and their families within a given context, while political affairs should be left to politicians. Within the Chinese context, this *focus on the individual and the family* converges with the classical Confucian view that good governance builds on good familial care, which depends on individual moral self-cultivation, as expressed in the famous Chinese saying, "cultivate yourself, put family in order, govern the state, and pacify the world."[60] This quote shows well the affinity between conservative Christianity and Confucianism in their joint concern for individual self-cultivation and familial care, to which could be added the traditional patriarchal family image and the importance of moral education. This apparently apolitical and surely less activist approach to social matters has long shaped local evangelicals' and charismatics' social ministry.

Third, only since the 1980s have conservative Christians moved towards political activism, yet the focus was, until very recently, largely restricted to questions of sexuality and the family. Several NGOs have been established that passionately and successfully advocated traditional family values and campaigned against equal rights for sexual minorities. Among them, as a leading group in this field, is the *Society for Light and Truth* (1997), the *City of David Cultural Centre* (1998), which brought the 'chastity movement' and the 'purity covenant' to Hong Kong, and the *Hong Kong Sex Culture Society* (2001), which targets pornography in the public realm. These groups argue that homosexuality is a result of moral corruption and an import from the West that stands in contrast to traditional Chinese culture and its family values.[61] Their advocacy is to be seen in the context of the U.S.-led emergence of the Evangelical Right, which has impacted social movements across the globe.

Fourth, evangelicals and charismatics usually give *priority to evangelism over social service*, as famously expressed in the 1974 Lausanne statement: "In the church's mission of sacrificial service, evangelism is primary."[62] Locally, such positions were echoed by evangelical leaders such as Philip Teng.[63] Following the advice of people like Donald McGavran, a U.S. evangelical leader and church-growth specialist in the 1960s and 70s, evangelicals regard the management of institutions like schools and hospitals as surely desirable but never as urgent as preaching the gospel, because institutions can be managed by anyone while the gospel can be shared only by Christians.[64] Recent years have seen a more balanced view of evangelism and social care, as expressed in the 2010 Cape Town Statement.[65] Nevertheless, and against such global evangelical principles, Hong Kong evangelicals and Pentecostal-charismatics have since early times built schools, hospitals, and social service centers, but they did so less than mainline churches, and more with an instrumentalist view of social services, which sees them as a means for evangelism.[66]

Fifth, evangelicals' and charismatics' social ministries show less contextual particularity than ecumenical ministries; in other words, they are not much different than evangelical work in other parts of the world. The major difference

FIGURE 5.2 *Peaceful multireligious togetherness: The Aberdeen Baptist Church and a temple dedicated to Tin Hau, the goddess of the sea (copyright Joel Brandner).*

to other places is that Christians in Hong Kong, with a relatively affluent middle-class base, may be more financially able, more entrepreneurial, and more creative in identifying social needs in a context where the government still maintains a hands-off approach to social welfare. As a result, responses to many social needs are firmly managed by evangelical and charismatic ministries. This is evident, for example, in drug rehabilitation, where fourteen out of sixteen voluntary agencies running rehabilitation centers are related to Christian churches or para-church organizations (twelve Protestant and two Catholic), most of them solidly evangelical.[67]

Ecumenicals, Evangelicals, and Charismatics: Competition, Complementarity, and Cooperation

Conservative Christians' opposition to ecumenical Christians—specifically in their approach to society—was at its peak in the 1970s and 80s. This was a time when people like Philip Teng sharply criticized ecumenical churches and when the Baptist Convention left the HKCC because of the council's affiliation with the WCC.[68] Yet, it would be wrong to divide the two modes dualistically and ignore the converging interests. Yes, there was competition, but it was a competition of different mission theologies, not so much a competition for clients, because the people's needs to be responded to were plentiful; and yes, there was controversy particularly where it came to issues related to sexuality, but in most areas progressive and conservative Christians have complemented each other and have remained connected in many ways. Some of the staff of ecumenical and social activist groups clearly see themselves as evangelicals, like Raymond Fung, who was for many years the general secretary of the CIC.[69] Some agencies connect with both sides, such as *Breakthrough*, founded in 1973 by So Yan Pui and Philemon Choi. The former was the chief editor of *Breakthrough Magazine* and a critical and progressive evangelical; the latter, a medical doctor and the general secretary in charge of developing new ministry fields, is an evangelical Christian, and, as a leader of the 1983 campaign against decriminalization of homosexuality, solidly anti-gay. Breakthrough was possibly the first to call for social concern among young evangelicals.[70] Besides its engagement with the cultural realm (see Chapter 4), it reaches out to young people to offer support through counseling and through community-building activities. The organization is thoroughly rooted in the evangelical tradition yet has inspired much critical engagement with social and cultural issues and nurtured many progressive Christians.

A typical example of this complementarity is the *Industrial Evangelistic Fellowship* (IEF), also founded in 1973, which emerged in response to the

CIC's negligence in evangelism and church planting due to its emphasis on social campaigns—something that the CIC readily acknowledges.[71] Even though the IEF was born out of a more tense rivalry between the ecumenical and the evangelical sides, mutual respect has clearly grown.[72] The IEF offers more individualized care for the working poor, support for gambling addiction, and counseling for the unemployed.

In cases where interests converge, conservative and progressive Christians have had no problem cooperating. An example is the joint campaign against soccer betting in the late 1990s, which brought together the IEF, the evangelical Church Renewal Movement (HKCRM), the HKCC, and even a secular group, the Professional Teachers' Union. All these groups felt that widespread betting was causing harm not only to individuals and families, but also to society as a whole. Another example is the *Hong Kong Church Network for the Poor* (HKCNP): Founded in 2002 by the two ecumenical bodies (see Chapter 2), plus the HKCRM, it is jointly led by ecumenical and evangelical leaders and is a network of several organizations involved in care for the poor. At its outset, it responded to a situation of worsening unemployment, but, as the economic situation improved, a huge disparity between rich and poor remained. The HKCNP serves as a platform for Christian NGOs involved in caring for the poor to engage in joint campaigns, to identify gaps in services, to offer joint training to volunteers, and to jointly engage in advocacy for poverty alleviation.

One of the member organizations of the HKCNP is *Jubilee Ministries* (JM), a group that clearly integrates charismatic practices into its social ministries. It is part of what scholars on Pentecostalism describe as a worldwide Pentecostal-charismatic turn towards social engagement.[73] JM has a strong grassroots orientation, with the Holy Spirit linking personal and communal transformation. Together with partner churches, they befriend people at the margins of society and offer practical help such as distributing hot meals to street sleepers, street sweepers, and garbage collectors, supporting the unemployed as they look for work, offering free medical services to the poor and the refugees, providing medical advice and occupational counseling to sex workers, conducting fun activities with construction workers, and more. As part of their goal of empowering the poor, they even run a theological school, the Jubilee School of Missions, with a strongly practical orientation. Their emphasis on the Holy Spirit finds expression in ministries that clearly transcend the institutional church, as when they conduct outdoor worship on construction sites. All the ministries of JM are undergirded by a strong conversion orientation.

This stands in contrast to another member of the HKCNP, *Christian Action* (CA), which was founded in 1985 as the Hong Kong Christian Aid to Refugees. Its roots lie in the ministry to Vietnamese boat people, from where it gradually shifted to employee retraining, paralegal counseling for migrant domestic workers, and services for new immigrants. This broadening of the scope of their ministry led CA to adopt its present name (1994). Meanwhile, CA extended its service to include other refugees, ethnic minorities, and rehabilitation of differently abled children and orphans in China's Qinghai Province. The organization has strong links to the Anglican Church and to the political establishment. Although having a strong evangelistic passion, CA refrains from explicit evangelism because it is aware of the potential conflict such conversion could trigger in the lives of vulnerable people such as migrant workers and refugees from Islamic backgrounds, particularly in their familial relationships.

Reviewing Christians' Social Footprints

Fast forward to the 2020s: Carrie Lam, the fourth Chief Executive of Hong Kong; Joshua Wong, from 2012 until his imprisonment in 2020 one of the young leaders of the democracy movement; John Lee Ka-chiu, Secretary of Security under Carrie Lam during the 2019 protests and fifth Chief Executive of Hong Kong; and Benny Tai, co-founder of the Occupy Central movement in 2014 and, like Joshua Wong, now in prison—the four have one thing in common: they all studied at a Christian school. After 180 years of engagement in social and educational ministries, Christianity has touched all parts of society and left a deep footprint. The list of high-ranking officials, of politicians, and of business leaders who went to Christian schools could easily be extended, as could the list of those who were homeless, in prison, in hospital, or went through a crisis and encountered someone from the church who brought help. Churches and Christian NGOs were there when, out of a mass of impoverished refugees who fled their homeland, modern Hong Kong was built. The presence at a crucial point in local history has deeply inscribed Christianity in the public mind.

Of course, not all who encounter Christian ministry become Christians, and not all who encounter Christianity have a positive image of it. In fact, the decades of Christian lobbying against the rights of sexual minorities have reinforced an image of Christianity as a morally strict and intolerant community. But the breadth, depth, and length of Christians' social ministries, in contrast to the government's history of negligence or, at best, out-sourcing of social care, have made Christianity a central pillar of society despite its minority status. The many Christian schools and social NGOs are like a conveyor belt that carries Christian values and ideas into society to transform it even where individual Christian school graduates and social service recipients do not adopt the faith.

Local Christianity has benefitted from political privilege granted by a sympathetic government, and, at the same time, connected with culturally marginalized people from China who, after leaving home and settling in Hong Kong, were free from traditional village bonds and thus receptive to new beliefs and forms of communal interaction. While enjoying friendly government policies, Christians have maintained a spiritual independence that has fostered opposition to the government, such as the anti-*mui tsai* campaign, Bishop Hall's criticism of the governor, the CIC's advocacy for workers' rights and the recent social movement for democracy. Christian values have maintained a critical potential even where the explicit teaching is conservative. Equipped with spiritual independence and solidly shaped by ideals of justice, yet pragmatically embedded in a city that is collectively geared towards prosperity and economic advancement, Christians have been at the forefront of social change throughout the city's history (see more in Chapter 7).

There are still a few loose ends to address in our overall picture of Christian social engagement.

First, Christian NGOs involved in social ministries are as divided as (Protestant) churches overall. There is, on one hand, the already described division between ecumenicals and evangelicals, which, undergirded by a deep difference in worldview and beliefs, centers on issues of sexuality and the family. This division has abated in recent years, for various reasons: partly because conservative Christians have been successful in their opposition to the anti-discrimination ordinance; partly because churches have taken a public stand, made a decision, and put aside the conflict; partly because sexuality was an issue more for older and mostly male church leaders while the younger generation is less concerned about different sexual orientations; and most importantly, because the overwhelming and uniting concern to defend basic civil rights in Hong Kong has pushed the divisive issue of sexuality into the background. But there is still another and more common kind of division among Christian NGOs, similar to the divisions between the churches: individual leaders, who prefer independence rather than allegiance to a larger organization and launch new NGOs even though the new ones resemble existing ones. On the negative side, this may undermine Christian unity, for, as these NGOs cooperate with the government, they may be subject to the government's divide-and-rule strategy. Yet, on the positive side, the division may lead to increased vibrancy, with more players raising awareness and funds, with more ministries identifying needs and filling gaps, and with more diverse services being offered. Supporting churches and individuals usually remain loyal to one NGO, to which they have previously committed, or which grew out of their own network.

Second, while Christian NGOs target many social needs, it is noteworthy what they neglect. One area in which Christians have remained largely absent is *ecological justice*. When the Chinese government decided in the 1980s to construct a nuclear power plant in Daya Bay, Shenzhen, only 50km from densely populated Hong Kong, public protests arose. Christians, however, were mostly silent, although Fung Chi Wood, an Anglican priest, played a key role in the protests. Until today, ecological concern in churches and even the global concern for climate change has not resonated among local Christians except for a small ecological concern group connected to the HKCC. More significant is the reticence regarding *economic injustice*. Even groups such as the CIC or SoCO, usually outspoken in matters of social justice, refrain from major anti-capitalist rhetoric. All the while, the city's ever-increasing and government-supported gap between the rich and the poor—economically irrational, as it keeps large parts of the population from meaningful participation in economic life—continues to grow.

A few numbers: in the 2016–17 tax year, the city's five top-listed tycoons received dividends amounting to 23 billion HKD (2.95 billion USD), without the government charging any taxes on this income.[74] Hong Kong's wealth disparity is the worst of any comparable developed economy, with a Gini coefficient of 0.539 based on original household income (2017), and 0.473 after tax and social welfare transfer (Canada 0.318, United Kingdom 0.351, United States 0.391, Singapore 0.356, and Australia 0.337, all post-tax and post-social welfare transfers).[75] The reasons for Christians' lack of attention to these issues are revealing. First, local activists, no matter how passionate about injustice and

FIGURE 5.3 *The Pentecostal Tabernacle in Waterloo Road, Kowloon: church and bank under one roof (copyright Gabi Baumgartner).*

how conscious of economic disparity, are thoroughly disillusioned about socialist experiments after decades of watching mainland China. The theology of the CIC is therefore not so much modeled after the more capitalism-critical liberation theology than after the Korean minjung theology, which focuses on political justice and the struggle against dictatorship, and which emphasizes justice within a broadly capitalist framework. Both the CIC and the Hong Kong Church Network for the Poor refrain from engaging in fundamental criticism of the capitalist system, but instead try to tame it. Second, local activists are pragmatic and results-oriented and want to avoid being drawn into ideological battles to the detriment of their practical concerns. Third, the city's economic boom helped create an attitude of "working hard earns you success"—the so-called "Lionrock Spirit" that describes locals' resilience and willingness to work hard. A person's wealth simply reflects his or her individual efforts. Finally, Hongkongers inherited a largely positive view of prosperity from the popular-religious context (see more about this in Chapter 8) and see wealth not as evil but rather as a fruit of a person's hard work and as a special blessing. Even for social activists, wealth is not something to be ashamed of.

To conclude, the social engagement of Christians in Hong Kong is, first, a story of how Christians stepped into a huge gap left by a government that was not interested in the people's plight, lacked an understanding of them, and was overwhelmed by the sheer size of their needs. This gap is the same since 1997 as it was during colonial times: the pre- and post-handover governments have been chronically disconnected from ordinary people, and politically not accountable to them.

Second, it is a story of how Christians responded to people's needs by combining practical help for survival in moments of hardship with campaigns for social change. The comprehensive response to social needs that this combination of different strategies allowed—from partnership with the government to independent social ministries that fill the gaps in a slow and bureaucratic public welfare system, and to social campaigns calling for new responses to social problems—was a crucial reason for the success of Christians' social ministry.

Third, it is a story of how Christians benefitted from the geographic and social catholicity of the church. The network of the worldwide ecumenical and mission movement played a crucial role in the formation of local Christianity, but so did the wide reach of a church that includes both rich and poor. While Christians in Hong Kong are as socially divided as elsewhere, and while affluent Christians in the city may be as detached from the economic realities of the poor as elsewhere, Christians in the corporate world equally contributed to social change. One of the strengths of Christianity has always been that it could reach across the social divide. Christian social ministries and NGOs bring people from various social backgrounds and ideological orientations together—from grassroots organizers to businesspeople and from conservative establishment members to progressive social activists.

Finally, it is a story of local Christians' pragmatism in transforming society. They brokered alliances between different Christian groups, or between Christian groups and other civic entities, and aimed at change in small and reasonable steps. This pragmatism was a trademark of the CIC and other activist groups and earned them much praise.

Flexibility, diversity, comprehensiveness, and *creativity* are some of the words that summarize this story. Flexible responses by individual Christians and small groups have continuously allowed fast reactions to newly emerging needs. The diversity of responses to social needs, from cooperation with the government to critical distance, has integrated Christians of various ideological orientation in Christian social ministries. This comprehensive social engagement has given considerable strength to local Christianity. In turn, this Christian involvement in society has opened a space for individuals, Christians and non-Christians alike, to creatively redefine traditional roles and identities, as women's campaigns have shown.

Altogether, the Christian sense of responsibility for society has built a crucial training ground for the emergence of a vibrant civil society and has continuously affected church–state relations, as Chapter 7 will further discuss. Whether or not the social space left for Christian ministry will remain, only the coming years will show. Surely, the horizon has darkened, but Hong Kong, this harbor offering protection from typhoons, has witnessed many storms.

6

Moving Beyond Borders

Reaching Out in Worldwide Mission

The simplicity of life in Cambodia and the faithfulness of people living in poverty, in such contrast to her comfortable life in Hong Kong, first moved Almond to become a missionary. That was in 2005, when she visited Phnom Penh for the first time. She had been a Christian for many years, had been attending an evangelical church, the EFCC, had been working in a Christian NGO, and had started to study theology. Yet, she was not sure whether she wanted to work as a pastor in a congregation. She found that there was too much gossip and politics underneath the tidy surface of church life. It took another five years and several visits to Cambodia until her decision ripened and she was ready to move to Phnom Penh on a more permanent basis. Through her visits, she had become acquainted with a small Hong Kong-based mission agency, *Tree of Life*, that had for some years been engaged in Cambodia. Almond joined the organization and, for the first few years, moved back and forth between Phnom Penh and Hong Kong, caring for and teaching the pastoral workers of Tree of Life's rapidly growing church network, helping set up a Bible school, planting churches and, while in Hong Kong, assisting the agency with fundraising and organizational development. After five years, Almond moved on to another small Hong Kong mission agency, *Metta*, which had grown out of an earlier organization, *Beautiful Life*, founded in 2014 by a Christian businesswoman who had gained some wealth in the local beauty industry and wanted to give something back. Combining Almond's experience, the businesswoman's financial resources and the help of a third woman, Almond's former NGO colleague, Metta took on its present direction—offering physical, emotional, social, and spiritual care for children and youth in Cambodia. Today, Almond and fourteen local teammates continue to work in

Phnom Penh, supported by three staff members in Hong Kong. Almond believes that her faith has deepened, as she has experienced God transforming people and communities. "I saw people who had been living in the streets coming to our center and starting to worship God and praying for each other," she said. "This is very moving and powerful. God has become more real."

The journey to becoming a missionary was even longer for Rose (not her real name), who today serves as a missionary in Jordan. Mission had been a concern for Rose ever since she became a Christian in a Baptist Church in the late 1990s—her charismatic pastor was passionate about mission and often preached about it. When Rose joined her first mission trip, to North Thailand, a few years after becoming a Christian, she felt immediately touched. In the following years, whenever the pastor preached about mission, her desire to dedicate herself to full-time mission gradually grew. However, she faced a crucial obstacle: her husband, equally a devout Christian, was not thinking of leaving Hong Kong. Although sharing her passion for mission, he regarded his workplace in Hong Kong as his natural mission field. For several years, Rose felt confused. How could God call her to serve in mission but not call her husband at the same time? God answered her questions by giving her a clear message: she should just prepare herself and simply trust God for all else. When she shared this with her husband, he was supportive, and she decided to stop working and enroll in theological studies. Another message she received soon after was that, if her husband was sent abroad for work, she should simply follow him as a missionary. Not long after, her husband was indeed sent to Turkey as an employee of a Chinese company, and Rose's church sent her along. She began to learn the local language and reach out to her husband's Chinese colleagues. However, after only one year, he was called back to Hong Kong. Again, she couldn't understand: how could God send her out and call her back so soon? As she returned to her previous work as her church's youth minister, she realized that God had given her opportunity to sow the seed for mission in the hearts of young people in her city. Finally, in 2017, the couple attended a conference of the Cell Church Mission Network, where a pastor shared about his ministry among Syrian refugees in Jordan. Meditating over one of the pictures, the pieces of their faith journeys fell into place and both Rose and her husband felt called to dedicate themselves to serve among these refugees. Since then, the two have started their ministry with refugees, running a small tutorial center that offers English classes for young people preparing for final exams. They read Bible stories to teach English and establish contacts with their students' families. Reflecting on her missionary journey, Rose says: "From 2001 until 2012 when I went to Turkey, during those long 11 years, when I realized that my husband was not ready yet, God always kept giving me messages that guided me. I am grateful for God guiding us together on a missionary journey."

These are just two among the hundreds of Hong Kong missionaries serving overseas. And there are more, for countless are those who participate in mission as part of short-term visit teams, offering medical, educational, or social services or simply building faith-based friendship beyond borders. Retired Christians set up second homes across the border in China, discreetly helping local churches; individual pastors tour China and the Chinese diaspora to preach and teach; and business travelers witness their faith on business trips and support schools or orphanages in poor local communities.

While the previous chapter showed how Christians engage in local society, this chapter portrays how local Christians engage in mission outside Hong Kong, particularly in mainland China, and how the city's unique position has shaped their self-understanding: called to spread the gospel in closed contexts. It tells the story of how Hong Kong has been a stepping-stone and safe place for missionaries sent to China; how local Christian pastors and lay people have contributed to the growth of Christianity in China; and how, with increasingly tight religious policies, missionary engagement has moved beyond China. An important emphasis of this chapter will be the notion of *node and network*: the mission movement follows network lines, and important churches and charismatic pastors become nodes connecting the city with China and the worldwide Chinese diaspora.

Sending Missionaries from Hong Kong, Past and Present

On the surface, Hong Kong was, until the 1960s, a *recipient* of missionaries and has, since then, gradually turned into a *source* of missionaries. This view, however, needs to be modified in two respects: First, most missionaries *received* in the past did not aim at mission in Hong Kong proper but regarded the city simply as a stepping-stone to reach the millions in China. The receiving of missionaries thus was mostly for the sake of sending them to the mainland or supporting mission there. Most mission work in Hong Kong itself was, for the first hundred years, rather a side product. Today, the city continues to serve as a base for mission to China and to East and Southeast Asia. Second, Hong Kong has always *sent local* missionaries to China because Western missions, in practice, depended on locals for inland work. It was impossible, in the early days, for foreigners to effectively conduct mission in China.[1] However, those early local missionaries to China remained within the overall Western mission framework.

With these two caveats, then, it is fair to say that mission planned and conducted by Christians from Hong Kong began only in the 1960s, when the first local churches began to send out missionaries. Among the earliest was Kwok Kam Shin, a female missionary sent in 1962 to Vietnam by the Christian and Missionary Alliance North Point Church. Even earlier, some alumni of the Alliance Bible Seminary had made missionary contacts to Southeast Asia.[2] Several factors contributed to Hong Kong's emergence as a missionary-sending territory: First, the economic growth of the city after the post-war years increased the economic strength of local churches. This went together with an atmospheric change—a growing self-confidence not to rely on help but rather to help others. Second, the movement of Chinese overseas Christians to actively support worldwide mission among the diaspora began in the 1960s, with missions and charities such as *Chinese Christian Mission* (CCM), founded in the USA in 1961, *Asian Outreach* (AO), founded in 1966 in Hong Kong by an American missionary, and Christian Mission Overseas (CMO), founded in 1968 in Taiwan. Third, many of the international missions that had flocked to the city after the war saw a declining local need and an ever-growing need in other parts of Asia. These missions began to regard Hong Kong as a base rather than as a mission field in its own right. Fourth, important local Christian leaders began to promote the idea of mission from Hong Kong and established cooperation between churches. An important fruit of these endeavors was the *Hong Kong Association of Christian Mission* (HKACM), founded in 1973, which has remained an important cooperative platform. The association has a broad base within local Christianity and gathers twelve denominations, thirty-nine churches, thirty-two missions, and twenty supporting seminaries or other organizations. Finally, and most important, the Lausanne Congress on World Evangelization (1974) brought new impulse to the worldwide mission movement and inspired the founding of the *Chinese Coordination Centre of World Evangelism* (CCCOWE), established in 1976 after the first Chinese Congress on World Evangelization in Hong Kong. Core figures in this evangelical mission movement were the U.S.-based Chinese Christian leader Thomas Wang, who had founded the CCM; Philip Teng, a leading figure within Hong Kong's Christian and Missionary Alliance; the Indonesian-Chinese evangelist Stephen Tong; Hay Chun Maak, who had grown up in Hong Kong and served in Singapore; and Philemon Choi, a local evangelical leader and one of the founders of Breakthrough, mentioned in previous chapters. CCCOWE is a transnational Chinese organization but with strong links to Hong Kong, as the city has always been a crucial node between Chinese people on the mainland and the worldwide Chinese diaspora. CCCOWE was among the earliest voices promoting mission—both to the Chinese and cross-culturally—and today is known for mobilizing Chinese evangelicals around the world.

Since then, many churches and denominations have set up mission departments, promoted congregations' missionary engagement, and supported them in sending out missionaries; some Western mission agencies have remained and adopted local leadership; and new agencies with new strategies and missionary visions have emerged. The city's strategic location at the intersection between China and Southeast Asia, its convenience and infrastructure, and its traditionally reliable judicial system have made it a natural base for the headquarters or branch offices of many international organizations focusing on local evangelism or coordinating their Chinese and overseas mission programs. Among them are the *Overseas Missionary Fellowship* (OMF), which inherited the tradition of the China Inland Mission (CIM) and focuses on mission in Asia; the locally founded *China Evangelistic Mission*, which began working with overseas Chinese in North Thailand and has since expanded; the local arm of YWAM; *Campus Crusade for Christ*, with local and overseas ministries mobilizing young people for global mission; *Operation Mobilization* (OM), known for its ship ministry; *Wycliffe Bible Translators*, with around fifty overseas missionaries from Hong Kong; *Interserve Hong Kong*, which focuses on mission in Central and South Asia; and the Far East Broadcasting Company.

Hong Kong Mission in Numbers

The HKACM counts 624 Hong Kong missionaries overseas (2019).[3] However, this number refers only to Protestant missionaries and excludes Catholics; it also excludes the many who serve under the radar in mainland China or in other so-called creative-access nations (CANs); and it ignores the many independent missionaries not sent by mission agencies or member churches of HKACM. Based on this obviously too low number of missionaries and the overall Protestant Christian population, Hong Kong sends out one missionary for every around 1,900 Christians (compared to one per 520 from South Korea[4]). The number of missionaries from Hong Kong has grown quickly in recent years, from 511 in 2010 to 624 in 2019, an increase of 20 percent. Among the different denominations, CMA sends out the most missionaries.[5] Nearly two-thirds of all missionaries are female (married male 193; married female 194; single female 213 and single male 24, or a total of 407 female vs 217 male) and nearly 70 percent serve in Asia (up from 65 percent in 2010). Around 11 percent serve in Africa, a declining 8 percent (down from 12 percent) in Europe, and an increasing number of missionaries, 5.6 percent (up from 3.1 percent), go to the Middle East. By far the most favorite destinations are Thailand (66), Japan (61), and Cambodia (46), with Phnom Penh alone hosting around 30 missionaries from Hong Kong. The influx of missionaries from Hong Kong to these three countries has grown over the past ten years, while those going to the UK and to Macao, other popular destinations in the past, has declined. The reasons for the popularity of Thailand and Cambodia are obvious. The two destinations are easy to reach and relatively safe; they have little work restrictions and people in these countries have obvious social and spiritual needs; they are geographically and culturally relatively close; and, particularly in the case of Thailand, there is a long historical connection with the place. In 2010, 42 percent of Hong Kong missionaries said their target group was "only Chinese," but this declined to 25 percent in 2019. On the other hand, mission among only non-Chinese people has grown from 35 percent to 41 percent, with the rest serving mixed groups. This trend is paralleled by another trend—an increasing concern for Muslims, with 220 missionaries serving them (up from 171 in 2010). Local churches are overall strongly engaged in mission: 80 percent make regular financial offerings to mission, and 20 percent of churches offer more than one-tenth of their annual expenses.[6] Two-thirds of the Hong Kong churches surveyed (68 percent) regularly conduct short mission trips, with Northern Thailand and Cambodia the most popular destinations. These numbers reflect the casual impression that almost every church has conducted mission trips to Cambodia.[7]

Mission to China

Although declining in the past decade, a large part of Hong Kong mission happens within the *ethnically Chinese world*: pastors preaching and teaching across China; missionaries serving the Chinese diaspora and Chinese migrant workers in the Middle East or Africa; visiting short-term mission teams supporting churches in the Chinese countryside or in the Chinese diaspora; and, missionary personnel and funds flowing into campus ministries in Europe and North America to reach out to the many exchange students from China.

Still, foremost is Hong Kong's missionary concern for the Chinese *mainland*, which began with the opening of China in the 1980s. It is, for individuals and groups from Hong Kong, convenient to move back and forth across the border. Hongkongers easily blend into the environment when engaging in China, an important advantage for a country with restrictive religious policies. They find themselves linguistically and culturally well-prepared to reach out to their fellow people. They can make use of existing networks to spread the gospel—through family, ancestral origins, joint denominational history, or professional links. Importantly, Chinese people have seen in the growth of the last decades,[8] a high receptivity for the Christian faith, what evangelicals call "a field ready for harvest." One local pastor who visited China monthly for three decades described his calling to the Chinese quite simply: "I do not have a burden for mission to non-Chinese because mission to the Chinese keeps me already fully occupied."

Neighboring Guangdong Province has, since the opening of China, been a focal point for Christian outreach to China, as much as it has been a recreational area for Hongkongers, from food to shopping and more. Many churches have established partnerships with congregations across the border with regular visits for leadership training, joint Bible study, or simply fellowship; invitations to pastoral co-workers from the Chinese countryside to come to Hong Kong for exchange and training; and significant financial support (often hand-carried) for church construction, scholarships, and even living allowances for poorly paid pastoral workers in the countryside. Until the past decade, these activities were largely tolerated as part of the government's effort to encourage broader support from patriotic-minded people for the reconstruction of China and to project a more liberal image to attract foreign investment.[9] With improved mainland infrastructure, increased professional contacts between Hong Kong and the mainland, and more Hongkongers working in all parts of China, these connections have reached gradually deeper into the mainland and contributed substantially to Christian growth. Typical is the story of a young Hong Kong Christian who went to Wuhan to set up a textile factory and, through the help of a pastor of a charismatic church in Hong Kong, connected with a house church and began to serve in the church's music ministry.

Hongkongers engaging in China need to be cautious because legally, they fall under the same category as any foreigner and are banned from engaging in mission. In practice, depending on the macro-political atmosphere and local church–state relations, religious-affairs officials have long tolerated church visits, joint Bible sharing, preaching by pastors from Hong Kong and other activities, at least when they remained low-key and were properly declared (contacts are never called "mission" but always "exchange," and even a one-hour long sermon is simply called "sharing"). Hong Kong Christians had contacts to both the official, state-registered churches and the independent or so-called house churches. As a rule, senior church leaders and official bodies preferred exchanges with China's registered church, while lower-level exchanges happened equally between registered and unregistered churches; mainline Christians tend to have more contact with registered churches while evangelicals and charismatics more with unregistered churches. When China began to open its doors, many mainline denominations reconnected with their mainland sister churches of the same denominational background that had been integrated into the official church structure after 1949. Sometimes, old missionaries who had been expelled after 1949 returned to their old mission fields and were moved by the endurance of old relationships. Those who support only official churches do so not based on ideology or theology but simply for pragmatic reasons. Bob Lo, for many years chief pastor of the Tsung Tsin Mission Church and coordinator of the HKCC's China ministry, strictly adhered to contacts with official churches and throughout the years established solid relations with religious-affairs officials across China. The trust that he had gained allowed him, in his words, to broaden the space for local Christians, explain the Christian faith to skeptical officials and conduct large-scale evangelical meetings that would even be broadcast outside of the church premises.

For many of the city's evangelical and charismatic churches, though, it was a matter of course to support the suffering house churches. Passionate about the freedom of the church from state supervision, they regarded the official church as a wolf in sheep's clothing bowing to the wrong authority. For house churches living under the constant threat of state sanctions, Christians in Hong Kong were an important lifeline and a source of spiritual and financial support. For Hong Kong Christians, it was an opportunity to move beyond the safety of the city and engage a new spiritual frontline. One of the early charismatic leaders reaching out to mainland China was the American missionary and long-time Hong Kong resident Dennis Balcombe who, in the 1980s, brought Pentecostal teachings to house churches such as the Fangcheng Church, a network originating in central Henan Province.[10] Missions such as Asian Outreach International, which aimed at supporting Chinese house churches, used Hong Kong as a base and easily crossed the border to bring in Bibles, literature, and money, and to introduce friends from overseas. The city thus became what it was best at: serving as a node in the exchange between China and the world. For many house church leaders, the city became a safe haven to gather and to connect with the outside world. This was further eased by a new travel scheme, introduced in 2003, that reduced restrictions for mainland Chinese visitors to Hong Kong. As large-scale gatherings on the mainland were too dangerous, Chinese house church leaders opted instead to meet in Hong Kong, where evangelical and charismatic groups organized large-scale conferences to welcome hundreds of Chinese house-church pastors. These conferences were important nodes for the transmission of teachings and products from worldwide evangelical and charismatic Christianity to those in China, where Internet content is strictly censored. They offered opportunities for house church leaders to get to know each other, to discover inner-Christian unity, and to develop joint missionary visions.

Hong Kong missionaries serving in China did so in various capacities: as underground missionaries fully supported by Christians in Hong Kong or by the Chinese diaspora; as tentmaker missionaries, supporting themselves through paid work; as NGO-workers, language teachers or other professionals, in short-term and longer-term engagements. An important local mission organization working in China is the *Jian Hua Foundation* (JHF),[11] which was founded by four local businessmen in 1981 and was one of the first international NGOs to enter China after 1979. JHF has established solid relationships with the government without compromising on its Christian principles. Although refraining from explicit evangelism due to political sensitivities, they share their faith through compassion, evangelical values expressed in their work and lifestyle, and relationships with the local people. JHF benefits from its relationships with a wide network of Western and overseas Chinese NGOs and sends well-qualified missionaries not only from Hong Kong but from around twenty countries who contribute through educational, medical, developmental, and social services.

A less evangelistic mission to China is the scholarly engagement with Chinese Christianity with several local institutions dedicated to the study of Christianity in China, among them the China News Analysis, founded by the Hungarian Jesuit Father Lazlo Ladany (1914–90),[12] which was an important tool explaining what happened to Chinese Catholics when China under Mao was closed to the outside world and which operated from Hong Kong from 1953 until 1994 when it relocated to Taiwan; further the diocese's Holy Spirit Study Center, and, on Protestant side, the Christian Study Centre on Chinese Religion and Culture, both of which regularly publish on Christianity in China. This engagement was part of a bridge-building ministry of local Christians connecting the mainland Chinese church with global Christianity. This has been a particularly central aspect for Catholics, where the local diocese always assumed a double role as a local church and as a bridge of the universal church to the large Catholic community across the border.[13] This bridge-building mission aimed at supporting churches by sending religious literature and teachers, offering financial aid, and assisting both the official and the unofficial church in the mainland.[14]

Hong Kong's concern for Christianity in mainland China was driven by passion and opportunity: Foremost was a sense of calling to share the blessings, received after escaping the hardship of the Mao years, with those who had stayed home. It was a way of making sense of the own personal or family history—psychologically to atone for avoiding difficulties while others stayed, and theologically as God's good provision of bringing some to Hong Kong where they became Christians and could then bring the gospel back to their places of origin. Christians in the city saw themselves in a unique position to contribute to the spread of Christianity in China. They saw the improving infrastructure and communication as God's way of building a path for the gospel and saw themselves as entrusted with God's special mission to support God's amazing revival in China. Many were the pastors who, returning from their visits to the Chinese countryside, reported with a glance in their eyes how the Chinese people hungered for the word of God, how they asked them to preach one hour or more and how they would walk several hours to hear a preacher coming from afar. Large crowds would gather even in mid-sized cities, more than a Hong Kong pastor could ever imagine bringing together back home. For those who had grown up in Hong Kong, visits to churches in China meant immersion in a radically different environment and offered memorable opportunities to experience the life of their forebears in the Chinese countryside (unforgettable, for many of the city's young Christians, were the doorless squat toilets). These visits were the early forms of mission trips that would later lead to North Thailand and Cambodia. In the 1980s and 90s, as China opened to the world and showed some tolerance to Christian activities, there was a sense of excitement and a feeling that God was about to break through the stranglehold of communist atheism. Many locals who had escaped the atrocities of Mao's rule were staunchly anti-communist and saw in what was happening the harbinger of a breakdown of this anti-Christian grip. The illegality of mission in China offered a chance to test one's faith and to find creative ways for engaging in mission. At times, there was a pinch of adventurism, as when Dennis Balcombe entertained audiences with his stories of miraculous salvation from mainland officials who tried in vain to get hold of him. The smuggling of Bibles and Christian literature was so popular that it went on even after China had turned into a Bible-*exporting* country with the world's largest Bible printing press.

The peak of local Christians' missionary engagement in mainland China was around 2008. First, a huge earthquake hit Szechuan Province and brought death and destruction—many victims were caught in poorly built houses. People in Hong Kong (and elsewhere) responded with generous help, financially and as volunteers. For local Christians, it was an opportunity to show patriotism and Christian love and at the same time to serve in a remote part of China. Only a few months later, China hosted the Olympics, and locals were proud to be a part of such a momentous achievement. Since then, the importance of the mainland as missionary destination has gradually declined, as Figure 6.1 shows.

Several factors have played a role in this decline. Christianity in China has grown to an extent that reduces the need for outside support. Many of the resources that visitors used to bring are now locally available or accessible online. The economic gap between Hong Kong and the mainland, which had made China an attractive and affordable destination for missionary trips, gradually shrank. But the two most important reasons are increasingly repressive religious policies since 2012 and a change of attitude among many Hongkongers: Since 2012, Xi Jinping has increasingly strengthened control over all aspects of life, including religion. A cross-demolition campaign in the eastern Zhejiang Province that began in 2014 was a sign of darkening clouds.[15] A series of party declarations since 2016, centered on the idea of a "sinicization" of all religions, have led to an increasingly repressive management of religious affairs, intensifying the pressure on house churches. Many of them have dissolved or withdrawn into smaller, less detectable units. For Christians in Hong Kong who had been regularly visiting and supporting these house

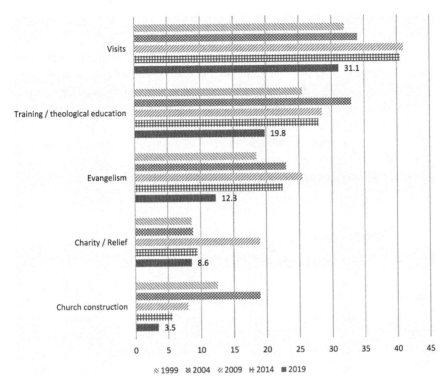

FIGURE 6.1 *The Hong Kong Church Renewal's 2019 report shows changes in the different forms of local Christians' missionary engagement with China since 1999, measured in five-year intervals. The numbers refer to the percentage of Hong Kong churches reporting such activities within the past three years. In 2019, 44.4 percent of churches in Hong Kong reported one or several forms of exchange with mainland Chinese churches, down from 60.1 percent in 2014.* Source: Research Group, *HK Church Census 2019* [Chin.], 57.

churches, contact became more difficult. Even visits to official churches were less welcome because officials would question the visits' necessity and purpose. Developments in China were paralleled by those in Hong Kong, where frustrated calls for democratic development in the 2014 Umbrella Movement and in the 2019 Anti-Extradition Movement led to a growing sense of alienation from China and a perception of China as a threat to civil rights. Young Christians who in the past had been actively involved in visiting Chinese churches turned away in disappointment and shifted their interest to places in Southeast Asia and elsewhere. The strong Christian support for the local democracy movement caused Chinese authorities to view Christians with more suspicion and strengthened their oversight even more. Ironically, it was precisely a concern for mission to China that was one factor in mobilizing Christians against the extradition law in 2019 (see more in Chapter 7). In a widely read interview, Ying

Fuk Tsang, a leading Hong Kong scholar on China's religious policy and state–church relations, warned that the adoption of the extradition law could jeopardize Christians who had been engaged in missionary activities in China. They could face prosecution and a request for extradition to the mainland even after returning to the city.[16] For many local Christians who had been engaging in church-related activities in China, this was a shock. Suddenly, Hong Kong's status as a safe haven seemed to disappear. In sum, Hong Kong's mission to China was squeezed by an increasing political animosity towards Christianity on the side of mainland authorities and, on the other, by Hongkongers' growing sense of alienation from China.

From Mission to the Chinese Diaspora to Cross-Cultural Mission

The 1960s may be regarded as the historical beginning of local Christians' overseas mission, when Hong Kong Christians helped establish migrant churches in North America and other parts of the Chinese diaspora.[17] The two communities, the city and the worldwide Chinese diaspora, are deeply intertwined through family ties, extended periods of stay and, in the case of Christians, church ties. People move back and forth between the city and the U.S., Canada, Europe, or Australia and often prefer to join churches related somehow to those back home. Pastors know each other as seminary classmates; when traveling, they visit Chinese churches overseas, are invited to preach, and further deepen relationships through short mission trips and congregation members' visits. A large church or a charismatic pastor, in Hong Kong or in the diaspora, may thus become a node within the worldwide Chinese Christian community.[18] Hong Kong pastors and churches are particularly suitable for such a function. The city, a place people pass through on their way to their ancestral villages, has always served as a strong node within the overseas Chinese network—"an informational and organizational center of the Chinese diaspora"[19] with a high number of connections to overseas and mainland Chinese churches and organizations. Many Christian leaders within the worldwide Chinese diaspora have grown up in the city and maintain close links to their mother church or seminary. Pastors traveling along these network lines exhibit a highly valued cosmopolitanism that parallels the much sought-after cosmopolitanism of local society: they are as much welcome in Vancouver, Sydney, or Manchester as in Jakarta, Sabah, or Bangkok. With many Hongkongers constantly on the move, if not in reality at least in thought, this sense of being at home across the world is a precious spiritual and psychological asset.

A common activity of early Hong Kong missionaries overseas was outreach to Chinese students in campus ministry. These overseas students, from Hong Kong or the mainland, who live in a new and unfamiliar context, have been highly receptive to the Christian faith. The focus on mission among overseas Chinese, rather than on other ethnic groups, happens first out of convenience, as described above, simply because Chinese missionaries are best equipped to serve this people group. The establishment of ethnically Chinese churches overseas also happens to offer new immigrants a place where they feel at home in a foreign land, a familiar community that helps them adjust. Yet, mission centered on the ethnically Chinese has, perhaps unintentionally, yet another effect, creating a transnational ethno-religious space across the world that in fact keeps Chinese from integrating into the host society. It supports the construction of a pan-Chinese identity, the idea of a transnational "Chinese nation" that is set apart from others, belongs together, and maintains its so-called Chinese-ness.[20] This imaginary construction of one nation of Chinese reaching out to the world finds expression in the self-introduction of CCCOWE:

> The CCCOWE [literally, Hua Fu, Chinese blessing] responds to what God has entrusted to the Chinese, to call upon the whole world's Chinese churches to shoulder the responsibility of spreading the gospel with one mind, beyond cultural, linguistic, or geographical barriers, to all the nations [ethnic groups] that have not yet received the gospel, and thus to respond to the Lord Jesus Christ's Great Commission (cf. Matt 28:18–20).[21]

In the past, many short-mission teams visiting North Thailand or Europe would work with local Chinese churches and support their ministry aimed at overseas Chinese, thus remaining within a culturally Chinese bubble. However, a deeper interest in cross-cultural mission has slowly emerged. Several factors contributed to this shift: increasing repression in mainland China has led to a decline of mission opportunities and set resources free for new endeavors elsewhere; subsequent generations of overseas Chinese have gradually moved beyond the ethno-religious community, don't speak Chinese anymore, identify less with the Chinese culture, and need to be reached through cross-cultural mission;[22] the continuous growth of Hong Kong's overseas mission— in terms of personnel and experience—naturally fostered a hetero-ethnic missionary concern; and finally, younger missionaries felt a sense of alienation from their Chinese identity and moved to other fields for mission. They began to serve in cross-cultural settings and leave the narrow ethno-religious space because they were critical regarding China, critical about repressive elements within Chinese culture, and critical about aligning with a perceived hegemony of the pan-Chinese identity.

Yet, cross-cultural mission developed not only in critical opposition to Sino-centered mission but also as a fruit of it. An example is a small U.S.-based mission with a branch office in Hong Kong, the China Evangelistic Mission (CEM), which began in 1974 with two Hongkongers serving among Chinese refugees in North Thailand. It developed into a mission to reach overseas Chinese and today serves a multitude of people groups. In fact, the vision of Chinese Christians' cross-cultural mission had already been ingrained in the earliest stages of the Chinese mission movement, with CCCOWE stating as their aim to mobilize missionaries from China so that China may evangelize the world. Here, the vision of cross-cultural mission is supported by a sense of a special calling for the Chinese within God's plan of salvation. This is what undergirded the missionary vision of CCCOWE.[23]

The idea of a special calling for the Chinese nation in God's plan of salvation is a common motif in missionaries' narratives. In most simple form it appears as "now it is our turn,"[24] parallel to the political-economic narrative, popular among if not spread by the political elite of China, claiming what it is due and becoming the dominant power of the twenty-first century. For Christians, this means that now is the time for Chinese Christians to lead worldwide mission. Sometimes, the "now it is our turn" goes together with a so-called "gospel debt," as for instance expressed at the Mission China 2030 Conference in 2015, which called for the sending of 20,000 mainland missionaries by 2030, equaling the 20,000 missionaries who originally brought the gospel to China.[25] A stronger and more elaborate expression of this sense of calling is the *Back-to-Jerusalem* movement (BTJ), a missionary vision that has its historical origins in Christian groups in mainland China in the first half of the twentieth century.[26] The BTJ vision, the idea that God has left a unique and important task to Chinese Christians—bringing the gospel back to Jerusalem and thus completing the gospel's westward circumnavigation of the globe—is still the most popular missionary vision among mainland Christians. The vision offers a self-assuring response to many Chinese Christians' question of why a nation with such a rich culture as China received the gospel so late. The BTJ answer is that God kept the most important part of the gospel's journey for the Chinese, namely, to carry the gospel through the world's most resistant parts, and, by bringing it back to Jerusalem, complete what needs to be done for Christ to come again. This missionary vision has equally been inspiring and guiding many missionaries from Hong Kong since the late 1990s. Several motifs in locals' (and more broadly Chinese) missionary visions loosely relate to the narrative of BTJ: a strong "burden for the Islamic world," which goes together with the view that Western missionaries could never reach the hearts of the people in Islamic countries because the West is too negatively perceived (accompanied by the sense that Chinese people are more welcome in the Middle East); a common pre-millennialism that underlines the eschatological significance of Christians' missionary endeavors and that is broadly shared by conservative Chinese Christians; the 10/40 Window, describing the geographical belt between 10 and 40 degrees north, from East Asia to North Africa, that shows the strongest resistance to Christianity and is a focus area for many Hong Kong missionaries; and a passion for Israel that reflects worldwide evangelicals' pro-Israel views. In these missionary motifs, local Christians converge with mission-minded Christians from mainland China.

Whether in response to a special calling and expressing a sense of election, or rather in critical distance from a mission focused on Chinese people, Hong Kong Christians' overseas mission has found manifold expression. While mainline denominations support worldwide missionary endeavors along the lines of their denominational networks or in partnership with their founding missions, other churches have undertaken their own church-planting campaign, setting up churches either for overseas Chinese or for local believers. Among these churches are the one established by the Pentecostal Holiness Wing Kwong Church in Nairobi or the thirty-five overseas churches planted by 611 Bread of Life Church. While much of missionary rhetoric reflects evangelical beliefs and evangelistic goals, what happens on the ground shows a breadth similar to the breadth of Christian ministry in local society (Chapter 5) and is far more than verbal appeals for a "faith decision." Hong Kong Christians show tremendous creativity in developing ministries for all possible needs, flexibility in adjusting to changing contexts, and a surprising ingenuity to turn a difficult situation into an opportunity for evangelism. They serve in cities and villages, care for street children and sex workers, train local church workers, participate in the mobilization of mainland Chinese missionaries, and work in international teams along missionaries from across the world.

The story of Hong Kong's mission beyond its borders, as summarized in this chapter, with its earliest beginnings in overseas mission among the Chinese diaspora, with its long years of focus on China, and with its growing turn towards cross-cultural mission in other parts of the world, has left much unsaid. Unmentioned remain many of the locally funded agencies that follow various mission strategies, from traditional evangelical ones such as *Frontier (HK)*, which aims at the evangelization of Muslims, to developmental and relief agencies such as the *Cedar Fund*. Likewise, many questions remain unanswered—for instance regarding mission and (neo-)colonialism: How far do today's Hong Kong mission endeavors follow the patterns of the nineteenth- and early twentieth-century Western mission movement, i.e., benefitting from economic inequality, arriving with a sense of superiority, and exporting not only the gospel but also one's own culture? Have any lessons been learnt from the criticism of Western mission? Or, regarding missionary strategies and styles: How much are Hong Kong missionaries affected by their cultural backgrounds? How does their style compare to that of Western or Korean missionaries? Regarding short-term mission teams: What are the forms, strategies, and extents of these teams? What is their value for and impact on participants and hosts? Regarding gender issues: What are the reasons for the prevalence of single female missionaries? Does it simply reflect the larger number of female Christians in Hong Kong, the willingness of women to choose alternative career paths, or is it a form of escaping dominant male leadership and finding autonomy from male supervision, or else?

Yet all these questions pale when compared to the one big one that looms in the background—how will Hong Kong's relationship to China and to the wider world look in the future? And what will be the situation of local Christians in the future? The city is undergoing rapid political changes that undermine civil liberties and threaten the past modes of operation of Christian churches. To this topic we now turn.

7

Christians and the State

A Contested Identity

The pictures went around the world: Demonstrators against the extradition law, facing a line of policemen, chant "Sing Hallelujah to the Lord"; a Catholic auxiliary bishop, standing in front of a group of protesters in the heart of the city, explains the Christian belief in God's presence in the social movement; a well-known local Christian scholar, standing on a small podium in front of a wall of heavily armed policemen, addresses a morning prayer meeting of a group of bleary-eyed protesters who had spent the night calling for the withdrawal of the extradition bill; Christian groups with pastors in their midst carry a cross and banners with Christian messages during the political protests that gather two million people, one-fourth of the city's population; churches open their doors and offer protesters rest and refuge from the teargas and turmoil of the streets. Indeed, Christians and Christian symbols were widely visible in Hong Kong's demonstrations during the hot summer of 2019. Long criticized for promoting an other-worldly faith and for being interested only in individual salvation, the church in Hong Kong has assumed an active and critical role in politics.

This chapter asks how all this happened—how it is that Christians, despite being a minority faith, have become so prominent in local politics. Questions about politics and the future of the church in Hong Kong society have loomed large during the writing of this book. The unprecedented changes, particularly after the introduction of the National Security Law, on July 1, 2020, mean that what comes cannot simply be a linear extension of what was. The future role of Christianity in Hong Kong, and of Hong Kong Christians in the social and cultural realm, is unpredictable, but all signs point to something very different—the question is just how much. The first part of this chapter describes the development of church–state relations in recent history. It distinguishes three periods, the period until the handover, as Christians prepared themselves for the end of British colonial rule; the period from 1997 until the early 2010s, as Christians responded in different ways to Beijing's ultimate authority over Hong Kong politics, and the period from the Umbrella movement in 2014 to the present, as Christians have become increasingly involved in social and political movements. The second part of the chapter discusses factors motivating Christians to engage in politics. Methodologically, the chapter draws from interactions with Christians involved in the protest movement of the past decade and with Christian businesspeople and retired government officials critical of Christian engagement in politics, from fellowship with imprisoned political activists, and from scholarly articles discussing the Umbrella and anti-extradition movements and assessing the changing church–state relations.

Church–State Relations in Colonial Times

When Hong Kong was a British colony, church and state existed symbiotically, as described in Chapter 5. The state benefitted from the churches, which took up responsibility for schools and for social and medical services at a fraction of the cost the government would otherwise have incurred. Likewise, the churches benefitted from the state, which paid for the services rendered and offered physical space that could be used for religious purposes. The church also gained prestige through contributing to society and obtained a platform to reach out to the community. It was a relationship of mutual dependence and trust, with the churches as a "contractor" for the government, a role that has been described as "institutional channeling."[1] This close relationship was manifested in various other ways, both formal and informal. Churches and Christian NGOs were, like other religions and charitable organizations, exempt from taxation. Several public holidays were of Christian background. The ceremonial opening of the Legal Year, a tradition of the British legal system, was held alternately in Anglican and Catholic churches. The Anglican and the Catholic bishops ranked fifth in the government's official protocol list (after the Governor, Chief Justice, Chief Secretary, and the Commander of the British Forces). Anglican and Catholic priests, upon application, were given official status as prison chaplains, which gave them unlimited access to those in prison, and Christian churches were the only religious venues licensed to conduct legally valid weddings (until 1997, when the Daoist Wong Tai Sin Temple was given the same right). While the Anglican and Catholic Churches received equal treatment in many formal ways, the Anglican Church, based on its status as the Church of England (headed by the Queen), always played a kind of establishment role. In contrast, colonial officials eyed the Catholic Church and its many Irish and Italian priests with more suspicion.[2] A less formal but more far-reaching influence was exerted by the many prestigious schools of Christian background, whose alumni often moved up to senior administrative and political positions. Although not every graduate of such schools became a Christian, many of Hong Kong's elite were shaped by Christian values and had a sense of familiarity with—if not loyalty to Christianity. In short, church–state relations were solid and mutually supportive of each other, naturally bound together against the threat of communist atheism on the other side of the border.

Yet, as we have seen, this is only part of the picture. Although critics warned that close church–state cooperation would undermine the prophetic role of Christians, this did not happen, at least not completely. Instead, some Christians have always maintained a critical stance towards government policies, campaigning for social change (as seen in Chapter 5). Even though this path was taken only by small groups, they were connected to the broader Christian community. In the late 1980s, as Hongkongers prepared for the city's transition to Chinese sovereignty, constitutional issues such as democratic participation, human rights, and the city's legal and political status under Chinese authority became dominant themes for these NGOs. An important voice was the Hong Kong Christian Institute, led by Kwok Nai Wang, a pastor of the Church of Christ in China, who in 1996 pointed out that the end of the British colonial era might lead to a process of re-colonization rather than de-colonization.[3] A few senior church leaders supported a prophetic role for the church. The Catholic Cardinal John Wu declared in a pastoral letter in 1989 that the church should be both servant and prophet and that, in this latter role, it needed to be concerned about human rights and social justice,[4] and the Catholic Church substantiated its prophetic criticism by keeping a distance from the undemocratic selection process for members of the post-handover legislative council.[5]

While mainline Christians at least partly supported the church's prophetic role, the evangelical majority as well as several important church leaders, most prominently the Anglican Archbishop Peter Kwong, opted for cooperation with the new authorities. Kwong was the Protestant Christian representative in the Basic Law drafting process and in the undemocratic election process for the new government. Evangelicals hoped that by refraining from involvement in constitutional issues, by engaging in politics only when "traditional family values" were at stake, and by otherwise cooperating with the authorities, they could build trust with the Chinese government, which would open doors for evangelism in China.[6] This was the general line followed by evangelical Christians and a line particularly supported by churches with close links to the business establishment, which maintained good relations with the new authorities for their own economic interests. Critics such as Emily Lau, a prominent democratic leader, and Kwok Nai Wang thus talked about an "unholy alliance" between church leaders, business tycoons, and government authorities.[7]

Church–state relations were, of course, shaped not only by churches but also by the government. Colonial officials had a long history of speaking out against Christian criticism, as even prominent and well-established church leaders such as Bishop Hall and the Catholic Bishop Francis Xu experienced.[8] Chinese authorities had their own tradition of managing religious affairs and extended this approach to relations with churches in Hong Kong. They have tended to use a two-pronged approach, rejecting religious groups' political intervention and restricting churches to purely spiritual matters while integrating those they trust into the overall direction of the party. Courted by such a united front and enticed by access to power, many church leaders assumed a more conservative attitude and toned down their prophetic criticism.

Church and State Since the Handover: Continuities and Discontinuities

On the surface, and for the first fifteen years of the post-handover period, church–state relations remained largely unchanged. Churches continued to run schools and social services, and to successfully bid for new ones. Public holidays related to the Christian tradition remained. Churches were (and still are) tax-exempt. The ceremonial opening of the Legal Year is still held in a church, and Christian clergy still serve as prison chaplains, a privilege extended in 1998 to clergy of churches other than Anglican and Catholic, but still not to chaplains from other religions (presumably because they have never applied for it). Government protocol still includes the Anglican and Catholic leaders, though they now rank lower, equal to the leaders of other major religions. The most important area of unchanged *informal* Christian influence in society is through alumni of prestigious Christian schools, who continue to attain high government positions, with three of Hong Kong's five Chief Executives graduating from such schools (Tsang from the Jesuit Wah Yan College on Hong Kong Island, Lam from St Francis' Canossian College, and Lee from Wah Yan in Kowloon). In 1999, around three-quarters of leading government officials were graduates of Christian schools.[9] Throughout the past decades, the number of Christians in the highest government positions has been gradually declining, as Table 7.1 shows, yet it is still higher than the population's average. The representation among members of the Legislative Council has usually not been as high as in senior government positions but it has also been higher than within the overall population. It is noteworthy that Christian members of the Legislative Council include similar numbers of

TABLE 7.1 Christians in politics

Legislative period	Christians/total number of senior government officials	Percentage of Christians
2007–2012	17/20	84%
2012–2017	11/17	65%
2017–2022	10/21	48%
2022–2027	8/29	30%
	Christians/total number of Legislative Council members	
2008–2012	23/60	38%
2012–2016	24/71	34%
2016–2021	27/75	36%
2021–2025	25 (30)/90	27% (33%)

Notes: These statistics include both Catholics and Protestants in the highest government positions of Chief Executive, bureau secretaries, and bureau directors (top) and in the Legislative Council (bottom). The size of the government has been changing throughout the years and some positions were replaced during the term of a Chief Executive. Similarly, some members of LegCo stepped down during the term and had to be replaced. The number in parentheses for the period 2021–25 refers to people who took their oath on the Bible but are not generally known as Christians. The information is based on media references and self-reported data from a government website. The numbers in the table are based on publicly available information and compiled by a colleague, Mimi Tang, to whom I express my sincerest thanks.

democratic and pro-establishment councilors. Of course, the claim of being a Christian does not in itself say much about the quality of a person's faith. Yet, at least some level of absorption of these values, may confidently be assumed.

Within such an environment, churches continued their dual role as "servant and prophet," partnering with the government while critically pointing out failures such as cronyism, policies favoring big business, and neglect of the poor.[10] Catholics and mainline Protestants worked closely together on livelihood and constitutional issues, while Protestants were divided in matters of human rights and the protection of sexual minorities. But soon enough, the dark clouds, which pessimistic Christians had forecast all along, became more conspicuous. The first conflict arose in 1999. The government refused to accept a ruling from Hong Kong's highest court regarding the right of abode of mainland-born children of Hong Kong citizens and decided to appeal to the Chinese National People's Congress, thus actively undermining the principle of "one country, two systems." Many churches, foremost among them the

Catholic, the Methodist, and the Church of Christ in China, criticized this move for constitutional and humanitarian reasons. A second conflict was related to an apparently simple administrative measure, proposed in 2002 and adopted in 2004, that required schools (Christians and others alike) to amend their governing bodies and include elected parents, teachers, alumni, and community representatives. Some churches (Catholic, Anglican, and Methodist) saw it as undermining their granted right to run schools autonomously, as government interference in religious affairs, and as a rollback of religious freedom. When the government in 2002 proposed a new security law under Article 23 of the Basic Law, progressive churches voiced strong opposition and began to organize resistance. Rose Wu, a Christian feminist and social activist played a core role in gathering a coalition of progressive social groups, many of them Christian, to form the Civil Human Rights Front (CHRF), which, until its dissolution in August 2021, organized yearly protest marches on July 1, in some years drawing hundreds of thousands of protesters. The first large-scale protest happened in 2003 in response to the national security law and was energized by broad dissatisfaction with the government's handling of the SARS outbreak earlier that year. Rose Wu's tenure as convener of the CHRF, from 2003–05, reflected the shared trust of the oft-divided pro-democratic political groups that she, as a Christian rather than as a politician, had no political agenda or ambitions. With other Christian members, she successfully introduced Christian values into CHRF campaigns. For example, when several political groups suggested "Down with Tung [the first Chief Executive of Hong Kong]" as the main slogan for the 2004 march, she insisted that the focus should be on political reform rather than personal attack, and the theme was changed to "Return Power to the People."[11]

The all-important topic after China assumed sovereignty over Hong Kong was, of course, democratic progress: the more democratic reforms stalled, the more its pursuit dominated political debates. Progressive churches and Christian NGOs joined local society's broad-based call for the democratic election of the Chief Executive and the legislative council. As they saw it, the problems with the city's governance had to do with the lack of democratic representation.

Meanwhile, the majority of churches emphasized good communication with the government[12] and responded positively to Beijing's outreach. They happily accepted invitations to the *Liaison Office* (the central government's Hong Kong representative), to exchange tours and study classes in China for the younger generation, and to official visits of senior church leaders to Beijing, where they met high government officials and dialogued about Hong Kong's future.[13] They were confident about gradual constitutional progress and saw the churches' role in maintaining positive relationships with the government and contributing to social reconciliation. Participation in such "united-front" activities was broad and included not only most evangelical and charismatic groups, but also mainline churches. Many Christians adopted the idea that faith and patriotism go together, and they embraced China's call for patriotism and for the "sinicization" of religion. They argued that it was natural to love one's country and that it was no different from giving the national flag a place of privilege in church sanctuaries, as is common in the United States or in the United Kingdom. Reflecting a traditional evangelical distance towards politics, they did not find much problem in the concept of "the state leads, the church follows,"[14] a concept that is the basis of religious policy on the mainland. Hong Kong's Anglican archbishop, who had a long history of loyalty to Beijing, even accepted the invitation to be a delegate of the national Chinese People's Political Consultative Conference (CPPCC), a kind of second chamber of parliament without legislative power and an important instrument in China's united-front approach.

Such support of good church–state relations can be seen as a new—or at least extended—strategy on the side of evangelical and charismatic Christians. No longer were they participating in politics only to advocate for moral issues, such as the question of homosexuality, now, they began to have an impact across the board, criticizing fellow Christians who called for democratic progress and joining the election of Christian representatives for the 2007 Chief Executive election committee, which progressive Christians (and, remarkably, the traditionally more conservative Baptist Churches) rejected as giving legitimacy to an undemocratic process. Indeed, the evangelicals' good relations with the government and with pro-government political parties paid off—it was an important factor in convincing the government to abandon legislation that would have outlawed discrimination based on sexual orientation. A largely divided Christianity, with calls for democracy here and calls for patriotism and social reconciliation there—this was, in a nutshell, the situation until the early 2010s.

From the Umbrella Movement to the Anti-Extradition Bill Protests: Christians in the Line of Fire

Since then, church–state relations and the political system overall have gone through profound changes. It shall suffice here to offer a summary of events with an emphasis on the role of Christians. To be clear, the social movements since 2011 have been broad-based and in no way Christian movements. However, Christians did play an important part, and some of the leading activists were Christians.

The events of the period, the political changes, the role of Christianity, and the impact on church–state relations have been widely discussed by local scholars. Ying Fuk Tsang, in an article "Hong Kong Religious Sectors under the Shadow of China's Sharp Power" (2018), analyzes how China, through its United Front strategy, tries to influence Hong Kong churches. In his article "The Entanglement between Religion and Politics" (2021), Ying offers a thorough analysis of how Christians responded to the 2019 movement. An edited volume by Kwok Pui-Lan and Yip Ching Wah, *The Hong Kong Protests and Political Theology* (2021) contains several articles offering interpretations of the 2019 protests and theological reflections on the events. Chan Shun Hing's "Christians and Building Civil Society in Hong Kong" (2021) is one chapter of an edited volume *Citizens of Two Kingdoms: Civil Society and Christian Religion in Greater China* (and one of several related articles by the same author) focusing on the role of Christians during the Umbrella Movement. The article "Almost Democratic: Christian Activism and the Umbrella Movement" (2016) by Christie Chow and Joseph Lee, as well as the latter's *Christian Witness and Resistance in Hong Kong: Faith-Based Activism from the Umbrella Movement to the Anti-Extradition Struggle* (2021), discuss the events in 2014 and up to 2019 respectively. Justin Tse and Jonathan Tan's *Theological Reflections on the Hong Kong Umbrella Movement* (2016) includes articles from four theologians (Mary Yuen, Rose Wu, Kung Lap Yan, and Sam Tsang), telling the story of the Umbrella Movement from different theological perspectives.

What happened and how did the events unfold? The call for democracy was not new—it was rooted in a decades-old call for democratic participation. What had changed was that frustration with the lack of progress towards democracy had reached boiling point; that, since Xi Jinping had become China's undisputed leader, socially repressive tendencies had grown; and that young people were emboldened by their success in a David-and-Goliath-like campaign in 2011–2012, when a group of secondary school students under the name *Scholarism* opposed the government's plan to introduce national education in the local curriculum. "We don't want the next generation of Hong Kong people to be brainwashed," was the rallying cry of the group, one of whose founders was a 1997-born Christian, Joshua Wong, who would become one of the faces of subsequent protests. After more than a year of demonstrations, hunger strikes, and sit-ins, the government under Leung Chun Ying eventually gave in and shelved its plans. The small group of secondary students had successfully rallied large parts of society and wanted to move on to more lasting political changes, calling for the introduction of democratic elections. The protests against national education had awakened political awareness across society and paved the way for what was to come.

What became known as the *Occupy Central Movement*, or the *Umbrella Movement*, began in 2013, when Benny Tai Yiu Ting, a Hong Kong University law professor and member of the Evangelical Free Church of China, Rev. Chu Yiu Ming, a Baptist pastor of a grassroots congregation and organizer of democracy movements since the 1980s, and Chan Kin Man, a Chinese University sociology professor and "non-institutional Protestant,"[15] announced their plan to "Occupy Central with Love and Peace" (OCLP). They aimed at a process of public debates that would end with an act of non-violent civil disobedience and the peaceful occupation of the central business district if Hongkongers' demand for free and fair democratic elections was not met. Cardinal Joseph Zen, a vociferous advocate of democracy and human rights since the handover, encouraged people to support the Occupy Movement, and the Catholic Church and several Protestant churches equally backed it.[16] The central government added fuel to the fire by issuing, in June 2014, a white paper that affirmed its absolute control over the territory. Parallel to the OCLP movement, student groups continued their campaigns for full democracy. On August 31, the central government decided that any candidate for the Chief Executive election in 2017 would need to be pre-screened by a small committee, a move that would have meant that only the nominators but not the electors are controlled by Beijing. While some democratic-minded people saw this as a first step in the democratic progress that should be "bagged first," most rejected this reform, as it would, in their eyes, effectively and for a long-term rule out a proper democratic election. Three weeks later, university and secondary school students began a series of student strikes and class boycotts that culminated, on September 28, in large-scale protests that became the beginning of seventy-nine days of an overwhelmingly peaceful and non-violent occupation of Central and other inner-city parts of Hong Kong (Admiralty, Causeway Bay, Mongkok). Events on the first day, as the police fired several rounds of tear gas at protesters who protected themselves with umbrellas, gave the movement its other name. The peaceful atmosphere at the large downtown protest site—regular open discussion rounds, students gathering in improvised study booths, young pupils in school uniforms collecting rubbish from the site, even cleaning chewing gum from the pavement—won the hearts of many bystanders and inspired visitors from China and further afar.

Christians were visibly and audibly present during the whole period. The official launch of the OCLP movement in March 2013 and the presentation of its manifesto happened at Kowloon Union Church, and the founders and other leading advocates made strong reference to biblical imagery, to Christian practice and to the tradition of civil disobedience. As Benny Tai said in one interview: "For me, this is a religious activity in which I am preaching."[17] Several churches offered their premises for the public debates in the run-up to the occupation. On September 28, 2014, some downtown churches opened their doors when protesters sought refuge from the tear-gas fired by the police; subsequently, they established support groups for the demonstrators, opened small street chapels for intercessory and individual prayer, conducted Bible readings and small worship services, and even celebrated the Eucharist in the street. On the other side, churches and senior church leaders opposed to the protests became equally active and announced their prayerful support for the government and for the police force. Among them were the EFCC's Kong Fok Church, an upper-class church with many government officials, businesspeople, and celebrities among its members; the 611 Bread of Life Church, which organized prayers for the police; and individual leaders like then-Anglican Archbishop Paul Kwong and his general secretary Peter Koon. They were joined by many evangelical and charismatic churches and well-known Christian leaders. Estimates saw the two camps as evenly split.[18]

The eventual crackdown, without any direct political result, left many Hongkongers frustrated but did not quash their struggle for democracy. The unprecedented experience of civic awakening, the friendships grown over the weeks spent together, the solidarity expressed in spontaneous acts of support by strangers—all this transformed many people, young and old, as it empowered them and deepened their resolve to continue the journey towards democracy. Subsequent years were highly politicized, with growing interference by mainland authorities, frequent protests, and even calls for Hong Kong's independence from China, led by Edward Leung, a young Hong Kong University graduate who had grown into a community leader under the auspices of the Jesuits. The question of democracy divided congregations and families. Supporters could be found in all churches; they were rather young and well-educated but were backed by many of the older generation who had been waiting for democratic progress their whole life. Many supporters from evangelical churches stood in opposition to their church leaders; not a few of them, alienated by the leadership's failure to stand by them, left their churches for international congregations or newly emerging faith communities (see Chapters 2 and 3). Opponents, on the other hand, were not only traditional evangelical and charismatic churches and those close to the business elite, but also elderly Christians who felt that the demonstrators were "rocking the boat" too much, as well as grassroots and working-class Christians who were less passionate about democracy, because for them, livelihood issues were more pressing.

The protests erupting on an unprecedented scale in 2019 fundamentally changed the face of Hong Kong and deeply altered church–state and intra-Christian relations.[19] In February 2019, the government introduced a bill enabling the extradition (from Hong Kong) of people charged under mainland law. For the first two months, only democratic lawmakers, some lawyers, journalists, and local and foreign business groups objected. They worried that the new law would dissolve the judicial difference between the mainland and

Hong Kong legal systems. In March, Cardinal Zen was the first Christian leader to voice his concern. In April, Ying Fuk Tsang, a scholar on church–state relations in China, explained in a church magazine the possible consequences of this law for Christians engaged in mission activities in China (see Chapter 6). Throughout May, several churches began to issue statements opposing the bill. Opposition gradually gained steam and attracted growing Christian support. The first large-scale protests happened in late April and in late May, followed by demonstrations of unseen scale on June 9 (more than one million people) and June 16 (two million). From then on, events spiraled rapidly out of control. The suspension of the bill in mid-June and its eventual withdrawal in early September was too little too late—large numbers of Hongkongers, outraged by what they saw as police brutality, had raised further demands, such as an independent inquiry into police use of force, democratic elections, and the resignation of the chief executive, Carrie Lam. While some protesters, disillusioned by decades of peaceful but unproductive demonstrations and angry about police violence, chose increasingly violent forms of protest, the majority remained peaceful, rational, and non-violent. Yet the two sides remained united despite their different approaches, popularly expressed as "brothers climb the mountain each in his own way."[20] It was a leaderless and fluid movement—"be water," a strategy inspired by Bruce Lee's famous advice for Chinese martial arts—with multiple and varied forms of expression, and the longer it went, the more difficult it became to find a peaceful solution.

Public discussions offered a broad range of causes for the extent of the protests. Some pointed to *economic factors*: young people were frustrated about rising housing costs, with ownership of even the tiniest apartment ever more remote; chances for moving socially upwards appeared increasingly slim as the gap between rich and poor deepened; growing economic integration into mainland China heightened pressure in the job market, as locals had to compete with highly educated mainland Chinese job seekers. However, most observers agreed that the protests were not driven by economic but by *political factors*: Hongkongers had been calling for democracy for decades and could no longer accept patronizing arguments that they lacked maturity; approaching the middle-mark of the fifty years promised for "Hong Kong people ruling Hong Kong" (1997–2047), political change appeared unlikely if it did not happen soon; widely bemoaned bad governance and the government's inability to feel the pulse of the people was attributed to the lack of a democratic mandate and proper accountability. The protests in 2019 were a defense of Hong Kong's bedrock identity, as one commentator explained: "The Umbrella Movement five years ago was one with a forward-looking goal. It's a battle for something not yet there—democracy; the anti-extradition bill movement is a struggle to protect our core values—something that is in us— freedom and the rule of law."[21] Some observers saw the events of 2019 as the unavoidable clash between two irreconcilable systems. A retired senior government official, in a private conversation, described the events as the unfolding of a Greek tragedy, with protesters and government forces each following a path of necessity that revealed the fundamental contradiction between authoritarian and democratic models of society.

As in the Umbrella Movement five years earlier, Christians were involved by peaceful means. Media around the world were amazed at how a Christian hymn, "Sing Hallelujah to the Lord," was frequently sung in the early days of the movement and became what some dubbed an unofficial anthem of the protests. Christian participation was visible in symbols carried during the demonstrations, in pastors joining while wearing clerical attire, and in Christian groups positioning themselves, together with other ad-hoc established groups, at the frontlines between protesters and police. Christian care teams, some staffed by elderly church members, assisted those in need of medical or spiritual help. Many churches in the protest areas across the territory opened their premises as rest areas offering protection, care, and counseling to protesters. While some churches preferred to remain silent, partly to avoid alienating the government, partly fearing that the unreconcilable political differences could only divide the congregation, a growing number of church members banded together to issue statements on their own, as members of a church.[22] Churches that were overwhelmingly critical of the extradition bill issued official statements in support of the protesters' demands, criticizing the government for ignoring public opinion, and asking for the withdrawal of the bill and for the establishment of an independent commission of inquiry. The crucial difference from earlier social movements was that this time, it was not just the Catholic Church, the Methodist Church, the Church of Christ, and other mainline churches supporting a prophetic role for Christianity that supported the protest movement, but also many evangelical and charismatic churches, among them the Hong Kong Baptist Convention and the Christian and Missionary Alliance, Hong Kong's two largest denominations. Even church leaders such as Patrick So from the EFCC's Yan Fook Church and Joshua Cheung from the 611 Bread of Life Church, who had traditionally been known for their conservative, pro-establishment stance, called for suspending the bill.[23]

Before the watershed event in the movement, the surrounding of the Legislative Council Building on 12 June 2019 to prevent the council from passing the anti-extradition bill, 69.3 percent of churches had organized activities related to the extradition bill such as prayer meetings, worship, or counseling; in subsequent months, this number rose to 82.5 percent.[24] In comparison, only around 45 percent of the churches had conducted any activities regarding the Umbrella Movement before the occupation started on September 28, 2014, rising to around 68 percent after the start of the occupation. While these numbers show the tremendous interest in the political events of the time, they cannot be translated directly into a measure of support for the movement. However, support was overwhelming, particularly among young people. An online survey of Christian youth revealed that 80 percent had at one point joined the demonstrations.[25]

Eventually, the arrest of over 10,000 people during the protests and in subsequent months, around two-thirds of them younger than twenty-five, as well as the Covid pandemic (which gave the government cover to ban all public assemblies) and the introduction of the National Security Law (NSL) in July 2020, brought the protests to an abrupt end. Since then, the criminal prosecution of thousands of protesters and the imprisonment of nearly all leading democratic politicians under the NSL have thoroughly dismantled civil society: Critical newspapers have been forcibly closed; political groups and NGOs related to human rights have been dissolved, among them the important teachers' union and the *Hong Kong Alliance in Support of Patriotic Democratic Movements of China*, which for many years had organized the June 4 vigil in remembrance of the victims of Tiananmen; and all public expression of dissent has been silenced—even clothing with the phrase "Hong Kong add oil" was banned from the city's annual marathon. Hong Kong lies frozen in a state of shock: some suffer posttraumatic stress disorder and depression, many have migrated to Taiwan or to the West, including over 200 Protestant pastors, around 5 percent of the pastoral staff in Protestant churches;[26] and a few are relieved that the turmoil is finally over, and business can resume.

The protests' long-term impact on church–state relations in Hong Kong are still to be seen. During the hot summer and autumn of 2019, pro-Beijing newspapers, speaking as always for the central government, fiercely attacked Christians, calling some churches "warehouses for rioters" or "shields for thugs." They claimed that the churches were infiltrated and steered by CIA agents who wanted to trigger a "color revolution" to destabilize China, and that young people were being misled by clergy who used their positions in schools to foment turmoil and confrontation.[27] Such rhetoric heightened the pressure on the local government to move towards less church-friendly policies and to tighten the supervision of Christian schools and social-service organizations. Precisely because many churches of mainline denominations have been using schools and social service centers as places of worship, they did not purchase their own properties. This has hampered their bargaining power. Land-use and politics are thus intertwined. As Hong Kong is increasingly led by Beijing, it is likely that the mainland model for church–state relations will more and more become the norm for Hong Kong. Perceived as a "foreign religion" linked to a global church, Christianity is *a priori* under official suspicion,[28] yet, on this basis, the government will distinguish between cooperative groups that support the overall direction of the city, the state, and the party, and that will enjoy the benefits of this cooperation, and uncooperative ones, which will be marginalized. Churches feel an informal pressure to tone down their prophetic criticism and to adopt the policy of sinicization. Some church leaders worry that they will be required to sign statements in support of the government, include patriotic teachings in their sermons, and cast out anything not in conformity with socialist teaching.[29] A climate of fear fosters self-censorship. Churches have become cautious with their online recordings and public statements, careful not to cross the invisible red lines. The arrest of the nonagenarian Cardinal Zen in May 2022 over collusion with foreign forces makes the city's Catholics wonder whether they all are in danger of prosecution under the National Security Law, as the Vatican is not only a church but also a state.

Passion for Politics: A Question of Identity

The question is: Why did Christians join in such large numbers and with so much passion? To be clear, the protest movement was a broad-based social movement supported by a large segment of Hong Kong's population. It was not a Christian movement and Christian participants were a minority. Yet, Christians did actively participate, many in a prominent position. This was surprising to many who used to know them as rather inward-looking, morally conservative, and politically apathic. This section thus asks more narrowly: Why did Christians get involved in this movement? What were the driving motives and inner reasons specifically related to the Christian faith, beyond the previously mentioned economic and political factors that affected Christians and non-Christians equally?

A first factor, important not so much in itself but as one of several triggers, was that the extradition bill directly threatened Christians' mission in China and their fellowship with believers across the border. Even though not all Christians and churches are involved in mission in China, the proposal brought the mainland Chinese judiciary a step closer, which meant that *religious freedom*, already deteriorating for years in China, as easily seen from Hong Kong, could become more tenuous in Hong Kong as well. Facing the prospect of a deterioration in religious freedom, the interests of progressive ecumenical Christians, with their long tradition of advocacy in social campaigns, and conservative evangelical Christians, with their traditional distrust regarding a central government that fails to observe basic religious rights, converged.

Second, protesters, Christians and non-Christians alike, clearly expressed the conviction that they were driven by a quest for *justice*. The values of justice, fairness, care for the marginalized, and democracy had been an important element in the liberal education teaching of local schools. For Christians, these values converged with the churches' teaching of righteousness. They saw their participation as practicing their faith, as shown by a survey of the Fellowship of Evangelical Students.[30] For them, social inequality, a lack of public accountability, and the government's long-term neglect of people's livelihoods stood in radical contrast to basic Christian values.

Another factor was that in this moment of crisis, perhaps subconsciously, Christians received inspiration from an undercurrent of *dissent* that permeates the Bible and the Christian faith tradition, and that had come to Hong Kong not least through the pietist missionary tradition, which bequeathed to local Christianity an element of critical opposition to the socially dominant culture.[31] Although Christians have historically and globally adapted to all possible political systems, they have ultimately (and with the exception of a few traditions past and present—German Christians in the past, the Russian Orthodox Church today) always kept some critical distance from earthly authorities' claims over people's hearts and minds and maintained that they ultimately belong to another King. Faith always means that the will of God "supersedes that of any earthly ruler."[32] The foundational stories of the Christian faith community—the prophetic words addressed to the kings of Israel, Jesus' proclamation of God's Kingdom, his embodiment of an alternative Kingship, his bold standing before Pilate, his crucifixion, the early Christians' willingness to endure martyrdom—stand in radical tension to worldly governments and have the potential to destabilize any accommodation to the political system of the day. In spring 2019, this dissenting tradition broke out from its captivity in tame religious life centered on regular worship and Bible study.

Yet, this dissenting element, so much in contrast to traditional Chinese values of obedience, receives its strength not just from the biblical tradition, but also from biographic experiences of many Hong Kong Christians. In contrast to many other places around the globe, Christianity in Hong Kong has not simply merged with the dominant culture. The sociologist *Lida V. Nedilsky*, in her book *Converts to Civil Society*, looks at the relationship between the Christian faith and civil engagement in Hong Kong and describes conversion as "establish[ing] the individualism necessary for civil society," and as a "key to understanding how Hong Kong people committed to religion become committed to the public sphere."[33] She describes how the conversion to the Christian faith is for many an individual act that goes against the wishes of the family. While many local Christians question Nedilsky's view of conversion or regard it as describing the situation in the past when conversions had the potential of causing family conflicts, and while many rather observe a wish of parents for their children to become Christian, conversion to the Christian faith clearly is a break with one's clan, a renunciation of a family-based collectivism, and a step into an alternative, a voluntary and faith-based collectivism with a distinct lifestyle. The first step in a person's faith journey is thus a critical departure from an ultimate loyalty to family and culture, and a commitment to a higher form of obedience. This critical distance from the dominant culture and this higher form of obedience are the crucial contribution of Christian conversion to civil society and ultimately to Christians' bold participation in protests; they go together with a rejection of filial piety as the core virtue and ideological basis of Chinese society and of religious practices centered on ancestor worship, which was traditionally the spiritual basis of a nation based on obedience to family, clan, and emperor. To be clear, Hong Kong Christians are fully dedicated to their families, treasure familial relations, love their parents, and maintain a high level of obedience to them. However, familial relations do not assume quasi-religious status but are framed by a more fundamental "family," the faith-based community.

Christians will therefore remain critical of the family metaphor so commonly used in Chinese politics and social life and so inherently linked to the idea of a fatherly head (Grandpa Xi, or "Xi Ye Ye"). Vice versa, the family image is the key to understanding how Beijing sees its relationship with Hong Kong and why it interprets Hongkongers' political dissent in moral and psychological categories, and rejects its political character.[34] According to the official Chinese narrative, the Hong Kong protests happened (if not because of the infiltration of foreign agents) because Hongkongers were brought up by an alien mother and thus lack gratitude and proper moral education—their hearts have not yet fully returned to China. The family metaphor and the subsidiary parent–child metaphor (used to describe the China–Hong Kong relationship) imply an eternal subordination of the child under the parents, leaving the child with only a derived identity, one dependent on the parents.[35] For Christians in Hong Kong, this metaphor has lost credibility not just through the events on the ground but also spiritually, as their conversion has reframed the traditional understanding of family. Joining the Christian faith community establishes a new allegiance, one that transcends blood relationships to family and clan, incorporating Christians into a global community. This is a quality particularly manifest in the Catholic tradition, which has its head in Rome and where priests, due to their required celibacy, maintain a stronger personal independence from familial and national allegiances than do most Protestant clergy. But whether Catholic or Protestant, the Christian embeddedness in a transnational community contributes to an identity that transcends the local and the national,[36] and converges with Hongkongers' self-understanding as both indigenous and cosmopolitan. Being part of a global community strengthens Christians' potential for dissent, as they do not so much depend on a local or national government but on a value- and faith-based community.

An extreme form of dissent is the willingness to accept *martyrdom*. Many young protesters said they were prepared to sacrifice themselves for the future of Hong Kong.[37] A similar willingness to bear the radical consequences of dissent was already expressed at the end of Occupy Central, when the founding members, together with Cardinal Zen and thirty other protesters, turned themselves in, accepting the legal consequences of their occupation of the public space. The three founders Tai, Chu, and Chan explained their act of surrender:

> We three have abided by the law throughout our lives, but in order to challenge this unjust system, we are willing to face all consequences. To surrender and bear the legal consequences is to respect the rule of law. Surrendering is not an act of cowardice, but the courage to act on a promise. To surrender is not to fail, but a silent denunciation of a heartless government.[38]

The motif of martyrdom can be found among leading proponents of the protest movement: *Jimmy Lai*, owner of the *Apple Daily* newspaper and a devout Catholic, had sufficient chance to leave the territory, yet he decided to stay until he was arrested in 2020, fully aware of the possible consequences. Today, he is in prison and spends his time drawing devotional paintings and reading spiritual literature. *Lee Cheuk Yan*, who had worked with the CIC since 1980 and had moved on to become the leader of the *Hong Kong Confederation of Trade Unions* (CTU) and a leading politician, was convicted for organizing and taking part in an unauthorized assembly. Before his sentencing in April 2021, he wrote the following words in a letter of mitigation to the court:

> Your Honor, I plead guilty, but I've done no wrong in affirming the rights of people to peaceful procession [protest] and I believe history will absolve me. May I give you more on my background so as your Honor can understand why I decided to march with the people for the future of Hong Kong. As a Christian, during Easter when the scripture was read, I was reminded how Christ went to meet his fate on the cross, sacrificing for mankind to reconcile sinners with God. From his arrest to his prosecution to his death sentencing by Pilate, he was a political prisoner who had committed no crime apart from being seen to be a threat to the Jewish hierarchy by serving the poor and oppressed and preaching the good news. Throughout the history of mankind, the rights that humankind now enjoys were pioneered by political prisoners from Gandhi to Martin Luther King to Nelson Mandela. I was the chairman of Hong Kong's anti-apartheid movement back in the 80s and I always remember the determination of Nelson Mandela when he said during his trial back in 1963: "an ideal for which I am prepared to die." [. . .]
>   My lifetime ideal is the empowerment of the poor and oppressed to speak out, to rise up for their rights. [. . .]

I humbly submit myself to your sentencing and whatever your sentence, I have no regret for standing up for the rights of the people.[39]

Faith that goes against familial resistance becomes a strong faith. Conversion that happens against a family's expectations creates a strong identity. The strength of Christian participation in politics at a critical time in the city's history has to do with *identity*. The passion of Christians joining the protests was grounded in their awareness that at this moment, the core of their identity was at stake. For local Christians, faith is not just one among several equally important elements of a person's identity but the base that impacts and guides the whole person. This is different from places where the Christian faith is a kind of default choice or where Christianity is the majority faith. Several high government and civil service officials were aware how much their faith could lead them into tension with their government service. One senior official waited until his retirement to become president of a denomination because he recognized the potential conflict between his civil-service and church-leadership posts. Donald Tsang, the second Chief Executive, is a devout Catholic who frequently referred to his faith in public and who, even during his time in the city's highest office, started every day with a short visit to the Catholic church for prayer and reflection. When he was considered for appointment as Chief Executive in 2005, he reminded the national leaders in Beijing of his faith and of his regular church attendance. Tsang was immediately assured that this would not be a problem, because religious freedom prevailed in China. Indeed, since 1997 there had been no official objection to his continued daily church attendance when he was in mainland China on business or leisure trips. But this episode reveals a misunderstanding rooted in two completely different frameworks of understanding religious faith: Donald Tsang knew that his identity is linked to God and to the Catholic Church, and that his ultimate loyalty belongs not to any earthly ruler. He wanted to make this transparent to the Chinese leaders who, from their side, could not see any problem in Tsang's faith as, for them, a religious community is naturally subordinate to the political government—for them, political identity supersedes spiritual identity.[40]

A final reason to explain Christians' participation in the 2019 protests is that they were led and inspired by a unique *religious experience*. Several interviewed Christians explained that the experience of the 2014 movement—the peace, and the mutual respect shown during the seventy-nine days of occupation—was, for them, a reflection of God's Kingdom. It showed that an alternative life, one dominated by values of solidarity and trust, without leaders but based on mutual respect, was possible.[41] Even the government's eventual crackdown on the Occupy Movement in December 2014 and the police violence in 2019, although painful, did not come as a surprise. For these

Christians, it was always evident that the path to heaven goes through the cross. After years of congregational Bible study, they saw their life in the light of the experiences of Jesus and his followers; more than that, their own experiences *merged* with the biblical narratives.

At this point, the Bible becomes more than just a guide for Christian life. Instead, local Christians recognize a deep concordance between their experiences and those of Jesus and the early Christians. They understand that the "struggle is not against flesh and blood, but against the rulers, against the authorities, against the powers of this dark world" (Eph 6:12 NIV).[42] As Christians read about the Roman Army, about the Roman Governor Pilate, about the local King Herod, about the religious establishment in the temple, they recognize their own situation. Lessing's famous "ugly broad ditch" between then and now is bridged by an amazing congruence. This congruence came to me when talking to a Christian friend from the business world, as I was struggling with new security requirements in the prisons that I visited and was reminded: "Be nice to the Roman soldiers!" Although my friend's social status made her part of the establishment, as a Christian she instinctively understood what I, what all of Hong Kong, was facing. It is this congruence that helps protesters spiritually understand what is happening and gives resilience to imprisoned Christians. Vicarious suffering becomes their own experience, and, idling in prison, hope is indeed based on what is unseen. They feel connected to biblical prison experiences, as in the story of Acts where Paul and Silas are portrayed spending the night in the innermost part of the prison singing and worshipping until triggering an earthquake that opened the prison doors. One Christian political prisoner knows that the time in captivity is the time to learn forgiveness, not in weakness but in strength, in the same way that the crucified Jesus reached out in forgiveness. Another one, drawing from images in the Old and the New Testament, expressed it in the following way:

> It is like standing at the well, drawing from the living water; it is like a journey through the wilderness—I am here now, in the wilderness, in the prison, and I have nothing left except of God. The only thing that I am left with is depending on God. So I am really in the wilderness, but I do not need to be thirsty because I have the living water of Christ, I have a basis of faith that carries me through the time in the wilderness. I am living in the resurrection hope.[43]

A threat to religious freedom, a desire to practice Christian values, a dissenting biblical tradition that receives strength from biographic experiences of dissent, a concern about the core of believers' identity, and a recognition of an amazing congruence of experiences—these are some of the motives that caused Christians to leave the comfort zone of their pews and enter the messy protests in the streets. Today, after Covid and the National Security Law, the streets are empty—or back to being filled with consumers. Christians are back to their regular devotional life—at home, as a diaspora community abroad, and not a few in prison, where imprisoned pastors and lay leaders gather their fellow inmates for worship. The dark clouds are still hanging over the territory: the impacts of the NSL on Christian life are still to be seen; the emigration of many faithful believers and the long periods of Covid-related restrictions have severely impaired churches. Yet, there is a resiliency in local Christianity that comes from a solid faith, from a collective history of constant change, and from the annual experience of typhoons making landfall. Local churches will continue to be an important element in civil society in a context where public life is dominated by an economic elite and a disinterested government, both eager to please the higher authorities in Beijing. As Christians face a decline in the freedoms that they had enjoyed, they remember, in the words of a political prisoner, that they are with Israel on a journey through the desert. Had the Israelites known that their journey would take forty years, they would not have left the fleshpots of Egypt.

8

Towards a Local Theology

I came to Hong Kong in the late 1990s from Zurich, Switzerland, fresh from completing doctoral studies in systematic theology. The Swiss-based Basel Mission, engaged in Hong Kong since 1847, gave me only one initial task: to learn Cantonese—a difficult task that easily filled my first two years. The kindness of locals and—alas!—a captive audience in prison, where I served as chaplain, helped me pass the initial stages of linguistic brokenness and have kept me on a path of learning ever since. The experience of learning a radically new language from scratch coincided with the necessary process of unlearning of what I had taken—theologically, spiritually, and culturally—for granted. I learnt to bid farewell to the apparently universal character of the theology I had studied, and I discovered the value of testimonies and personal stories as expressions of local theologies. I recognized the autobiographical character of *all* theology (hence this introduction), where the individual and the community intertwine and develop theologies that reflect their stories.

This chapter thus asks: What are some of the local theologies in Hong Kong, what are their important elements, and how did they develop? The chapter identifies several features of locally lived theology, outlines how a more explicit local theology emerged, and discusses two strands of locally produced theology: postcolonial and Sino-Christian theology.

Lived Theology in Hong Kong

Lived theology understands that theology finds expression not just in theological treatises and explicit statements of faith but also in individual and communal religious practices and in the lived experience of individuals and groups within the Christian faith community. This perspective has emerged in recent decades, as theologians such as Jürgen Moltmann have turned to a more holistic understanding of the workings of the Holy Spirit and of human beings, including believers' experiences, and as scholars in religious studies have broadened their understanding of how individuals and communities communicate their faith. Known as "lived religion," this concept has been developed by scholars such as Nancy Ammerman, Meredith McGuire, Robert Orsi, and David Hall. Lived theology narrates experiences of lived lives and makes "space for life-narratives, testimonials, observed experience, and biography." It is based on the idea that faith-based practices and actions, as concrete expressions of God's presence, are the actual building blocks of theology.[1]

Lived theology in Hong Kong shares many general characteristics of broader Chinese Christianity: an overall conservative character; a deep love of the Bible; a primarily cognitive approach to faith that sees faith less as an experience than as a process of learning and understanding, expressed in lengthy sermons; and an emphasis on morals and rules that moves Christian faith towards a path of self-cultivation, but risks forfeiting the centrality of God's forgiving grace even while, rhetorically, upholding it. In short, it is not difficult to see the continuing Confucian influence in much of local church life.

Arguably the most prominent feature of lived theology in Hong Kong is, as highlighted repeatedly in this book, the *family as a focal point and as a metaphor describing the Christian community*.[2] Among the most popular songs of many congregations are "*In Jesus, We Are One Family*" and "*We Become One Family*."[3] Much of local churches' strength and cohesion comes from this sense of family. The self-understanding of Protestant Christians as embodying a unique family is expressed in the common phrase "brothers and sisters," adopted from the Pietist forefathers and perfectly fitting Hong Kong's family-centered culture. The understanding of the church as family is a main reason why many Christians show such enormous generosity with their money and their time. Local Protestant Christians are primarily members of a congregation rather than of the church as such. Once joining a congregation, they maintain a very high level of loyalty—in particular to the senior pastor, a relationship that can turn unhealthily dependent, where a member's break with a congregation is experienced as a painful separation. This Protestant view stands in sharp contrast to that of Catholic Christians, who see themselves as members not of one specific congregation but of the church overall. Other problems of the ecclesial image of the family are that leadership is still male-dominated; that many young Christians' voices are not heard; that leadership transitions, particularly in independent, non-denominational churches, are often difficult; and that tensions between senior pastors and church elders are not uncommon, as both claim paternal authority.

Another feature is a common belief that *bigger is better*, and that "bigger" is a true sign of God's blessing. In this city centered on trade and finance, where success is measured numerically, a can-do spirit and a positive attitude to wealth have shaped local Christians, who see God at work in expanding congregations, in increasing conversions, and in swelling donations. In short, the ABC of the local church is higher **A**ttendance, bigger **B**uildings, and more **C**ash. The public prestige of a pastor—commonly described as "face"—is a direct result of his or her success. To support the vision of "biggering," local churches have adopted various recipes for church growth. Children ministry and youth ministry are the keys—the former because it retains the whole family, the latter because the youth, it is hoped, will soon become the engine of the church, both financially and manpower-wise. This vision is goading Christians into serving more and working harder and has led many to feel burnt out, as shown in Snelgrove's interviews (Chapter 3). Christians' hope for growth is nurtured by an atmosphere of activism and an orientation towards results, and it is supported by popular beliefs expressed in ubiquitous symbols expressing hope for a prosperous life—the cat beckoning money, the goldfish, the carp.[4] Yet, on a deeper level, what galvanizes the notion of "bigger is better" is the vision of the whole family coming together in unity and jointly celebrating around a round banquet table. While this ideal has continuously mobilized Christians to evangelize their families, their neighborhoods, and their workplaces, it is ultimately an *anti*-missional attitude because the world becomes irrelevant other than as a reservoir for new recruits. It is an *introverted* theology that reduces contact with the world and keeps its eyes firmly on the church as an extended family, and it is a *patriarchal* theology that remains solidly focused on the senior pastor and/or the church elders.

A third feature of lived theology is a *separatism or at least distinctiveness from the world*, which finds expression in a *continuous and visible demarcation between those inside and those outside the Christian community*. Practices such as saying grace before eating—whether in a McDonald's, a sushi bar, an upmarket Chinese restaurant, or a *cha chaan teng*, a typical local neighborhood restaurant that offers fast service, low prices, and a unique East-West cuisine—are emblematic for local Christians to emphasize their difference from the world. The same applies to abstaining from smoking, gambling, and playing the lottery (except for the stock market), as well as to keeping a distance from places "contaminated" by popular religion or by triads. Indeed, the most important demarcation is from Chinese religious practices such as kowtowing and incense burning at the graves of relatives. Only Catholics and a small minority of Protestant churches and individual Christians show tolerance regarding the integration of Chinese features into Christian practices.[5] Many local Protestants also distance themselves from Catholics and regard them as not much better than those venerating ancestors and worshipping idols. Other demarcating practices are refusing to bless weddings between believers and non-believers, rejecting divorce, repudiating equal rights for sexual minorities, and abstaining from pre-marital sex. Whether the latter is rhetoric or reality is hard to say—at least rhetorically, the rule is widely insisted upon and a couple failing to observe it may receive public criticism from others in the church. This clear demarcation from the world is one reason why Christians place such high value on baptism: it a decision that is taken for life, disrupts the traditional family allegiance, and brings believers into a new family. For most Chinese people who have decided to receive baptism, their deepest hope is that their remaining family members will follow suit.

Christian separatism is closely linked to a *negative view of the world and a pessimistic view of history*. At this point, the influence of various religious traditions, social contexts, and historical experiences converge and mutually reinforce each other: the separatism and otherworldliness of fundamentalist Christian missionaries; the historical experience of a diasporic community that was not allowed to participate in society, and, in fact, had little interest in doing so; the broad-based pessimism of dissenting religious traditions and millenarian groups in the history of China, from historical Daoist sects such as the Yellow Turban to the Buddhist White Lotus and the Christian-inspired Taiping in the nineteenth century;[6] and the uncertainty and turmoil experienced in twentieth-century China. All these have nurtured a negative view of the world that has cemented the cohesion of the Christian family as a beleaguered community surrounded by darkness. The sense that Hong Kong is "a borrowed place on borrowed time" (a common saying in colonial Hong Kong, a sense that everything is fluid and can vanish in the blink of an eye, or under a tidal wave) is reinforced by events since 2019, seen by many as a sudden disappearance of the values that made Hong Kong such a special place.

However, there is an obvious tension between this pessimistic stand and local Christians' active engagement in the community reflecting Hongkongers' hard-working, life-affirming, and pragmatic attitude, and the joviality and extroversion of southern Chinese. This hands-on, outgoing faith grows out of a specific context: the typical coastal community's openness towards the world, the experience of a refugee community that worked hard to raise itself from abject poverty to wealth in only a few decades, and a can-do spirit fostered by a period of tremendous growth in which the city became a shining financial center. The tension between engagement with and separation from the world is basic to Christianity, and the church in Hong Kong offers a near-perfect combination of these two contrasting—but perhaps complementary—faith practices.

The importance of *matters relating to death and of the related question of salvation* is another feature of locally lived theology. The urgency to convert parents on their deathbeds and the efforts made to conduct funerals properly are fueled by a deep concern for the well-being of the deceased and a strong bond reaching beyond death, both fundamental to the surrounding religious culture.[7] Against the clear relational, spatial, and temporal separation between the living and the dead that is commonly taught in Western Protestant theology (and in Western psychology!), local Christians, steeped in Daoism, maintain more elements of a continuous bond and interaction with the deceased. An important motive in the passion with which many local Christians evangelize their parents is the hope for the eschatological family reunion in heaven, finally restoring the disruption caused by the conversion of only parts of the family. Filial piety lives on in the hope for a heavenly extension of the parent–child relationship.

Local Christianity is young. Its youthfulness offers spiritual space for theological creativity, playful experimentation, freedom from old and foreign traditions, and a focus on what works. Comparing local Christianity with the situation in Europe, where worship often takes place in centuries-old church buildings, the functionality and newness of local worship venues is striking— and liberating. As a result, local Christians, much like local people overall, are *practical and pragmatic, actively engaged in the world, uninterested in theological subtleties, and focused on tangible results.* Faith is more than just a spiritual attitude but should, in local Christians' minds, be visible and find expression in transformed lives. Morality matters not just as a mark of distinction from the world but also as a mark of a transformed life. In contrast, theological debates, unless they relate to the practical aspects of Christian life (e.g., sexuality or politics), are mostly pursued with little passion and with pragmatic tolerance. Charismatic practices such as blessing ceremonies in a new house, cleansing rituals after spiritual contamination, spiritual-warfare prayers and exorcisms are popular among local Christians exactly because they claim to have a tangible impact on life. These practices allow interaction between the spiritual and material worlds that stands in contrast to the strict separation taught by most Western missionaries.

In sum, locally lived theology integrates elements from global evangelicalism, the global Pentecostal-charismatic movement, and the worldwide ecumenical movement; transforms them by absorbing elements of Confucian teaching and Daoist religious practices and amalgamates them with the needs of a global city and financial center. Global evangelicalism's influence is noticeable in the churches' teaching and in church-growth models; the Pentecostal-charismatic influence is perceptible in worship practices and church organization, and the ecumenical influence is manifest in Christian engagement in society. Similar to the situation in South Korea, where evangelical (Presbyterian) Christianity has been described as ethically confucianized and Pentecostal Christianity as spiritually shamanized,[8] Christianity in Hong Kong shows an elective affinity between evangelical Christianity and Confucianism on one hand and between Pentecostal-charismatic Christianity and popular-religious Daoism on the other hand. Local Christians reflect Confucian teachings ethically and Daoist practices spiritually. To be clear, a strict demarcation between Christianity and popular religious practices is a fundamental feature of local Christians. However, the popular-Daoist underground enters Christian spirituality and religious practice in other forms, as described above. Hong Kong Christians have built a distinct community that treasures its difference from the world while passionately engaging with the world. They successfully balance loyalty to popular practices and traditional teachings with a curiosity and open-minded receptiveness towards the teachings and practices of global Christianity, and they create a space to find release from some constraints of local life and from repressive elements of their own culture—even while adhering to the stricter rules of their faith community.

The Emergence of a Local Theology

While considering Christian engagement in local society and culture (Chapters 4 and 5), we saw the 1970s as a time when Hong Kong developed a unique identity. It was a time when the economy boomed, when Hong Kong became an important center of cultural production, and when social movements advocated for industrial workers and the urban poor. Thus, it does not come as a surprise that the 1970s was also a decade of important developments in local theological production. However, both local identity-building and local theologizing have deeper roots. The former can be traced back to the early years of Hong Kong, when locals acted as traders and intermediaries between China and the West.[9] The latter began in the first decades of the twentieth century: on the ecumenical side, with the ideas of veteran Chinese theologians such as Liu Tingfang and Zhao Zichen, calling for churches and theology to engage in the world and become independent of missionaries; on the conservative-evangelical side, with those like Wang Mingdao or Nee Tuosheng who passionately resisted missionary-led Christianity. In the middle of the twentieth century, the two dominant themes in local theology were the dialogue between Christianity and Chinese culture and philosophy, and the study of Christian developments in a China that was largely closed to the outside world.[10] Several mainland scholars escaped the turmoil in China and found refuge in Hong Kong, among them Xie Fuya and Xu Dishan. Together with Western missionaries and church leaders such as K.L. Reichelt and Bishop Hall, and local theologians such as Ho Sai-Ming, Lee Shiu Keung, and Peter Lee King-Hung, they sought to root the Christian faith in Chinese soil and to help Christianity contribute to the revitalization and modernization of China.

nstitutionally, the *Christian Study Centre on Chinese Religion and Culture (CSCCRC)* and the *Tao Fong Shan Christian Institute*, which in 1979 merged as the *Tao Fong Shan Ecumenical Centre (TFSEC)*, and their respective publications *Ching Feng* and *Bridge* have played a key role in the study of Christianity in China and in the development of a local theology. In the 1980s, they were joined by other publications such as *Theology and Life* and the *China Studies Series*, published by the Lutheran Theological Seminary, and, on the Catholic side, by the *Holy Spirit Study Centre* and by several journals reflecting on contextual theology (*Tripod, Theology Annual,* and *Spirit*).[11]

These theologians prepared the ground for the emergence of local theological schools such as the ecumenical one within Chung Chi College (1963), part of the Chinese University of Hong Kong,[12] and the evangelical China Graduate School of Theology (1975). When Western missions, after the Communist victory, withdrew their personnel from China, Hong Kong became an important base for theological studies, with several denominational and missionary-led schools relocating to the city from the mainland. Gradually, these schools have become localized, contributing to theological proliferation in Hong Kong. Today, there are over forty seminaries and Bible schools in the city, most of which are quite small. Some are still linked to a specific denominational tradition or even to only one large congregation; some serve a particular focus group such as charismatic churches, grassroots ministries, or students who already have an academic degree and seek higher academic training. As elsewhere, theology in Hong Kong has been shaped by an ecumenical/evangelical divide, stemming from an earlier divide between fundamentalists and modernists in theological education in China.[13] This divide lives on and was only temporarily dissolved in the cooperation during the 2019 social movement.

One local theologian who left a unique mark was Raymond Fung, who led the Christian Industrial Committee from 1969 to 79. He pioneered theological engagement within the specific context of Hong Kong, by focusing on reading the Bible from the perspective of industrial workers and developing social action on that basis, instead of dealing more generally with Chinese Christianity and culture. The CIC's 1970 workers' declaration (see Chapter 5) expresses the core ideas of *local* liberation theology, such as a conscious position at the side of the underprivileged industrial workers, independently from the more famous Latin American forms, with the timing of the Hong Kong declaration excluding any direct influence. In a city based on free trade and populated with refugees from the excesses of Chinese socialism, most theologians were (and still are) suspicious of Marxist categories. Although liberation theology did inspire some local theologians in subsequent decades, its traditional Marxist criticism of capitalist economy never received much sympathy. The theology and practice of the CIC was modeled instead after Korean *minjung* theology. Responding to criticism from liberation theologians during his time working in Geneva, Fung referred to a theological distinction that he had already introduced in the 1970s—a person is always a *sinner and sinned-against*, a perpetrator of sin *and* its victim[14]—and insisted that such an understanding is theologically both more profound and more accurate, i.e., expressing the ambiguity to which the poor are subject. Remaining passionately dedicated to justice for industrial workers, Fung paved the way for theologizing beyond the common binary opposition of oppressor and oppressed, a path that subsequent theologians would resume. His theological reflection influenced the understanding of the social and structural dimensions of sin—in Hong Kong and beyond.

The 1980s saw the beginning of the Sino-British negotiations about the future of the city and the Joint Declaration in 1984, which affirmed that Hong Kong was inseparable from China and made a future under Chinese sovereignty an unalterable fact. The political negotiations had largely happened without the involvement of local people, causing Lo Lung-Kwong to call for Hongkongers to regain their status as subjects of history rather than objects of other powers' political considerations.[15] In this period, the question of Hongkongers' identity carried an unprecedented urgency, not only in theology but also in society overall, with a significant number of Hongkongers, among them many church leaders, choosing to emigrate. A pressing question for Christians staying behind was regarding their role in society. Against people's fears about the future loss of religious freedom and other civil rights, evangelical Christian leaders, prominent among them Carver Yu Tat Sum, reaffirmed that:

> God, the Lord of creation, redemption and judgment, is the master of history, therefore any future change in Hong Kong shall take place under His countenance . . . [O]ur historic identity is inextricably related to that of the Chinese people as a whole. Therefore, we should not be concerned only with the interests of Hong Kong but should also care for and participate in the development of mainland China.[16]

Local Christians faced a difficult balancing act between expressing belonging to and solidarity with the people in China and preserving precious civil rights. Two positions faced each other.[17] On one side stood those who called for churches to play a *prophetic role* in seeking justice. A prominent voice among them was *Kwok Nai Wang*, who, in 1988, frustrated about the increasing dominance of conservative church leaders and their silence regarding democracy and human rights, resigned as general secretary of the HKCC. Standing on the other side of the theological divide was *Arnold Yeung Muk Kuk* (1945–2002). His book *Theology of Reconciliation and Church*

Renewal (1987, in Chinese)[18] suggested that both local Hongkongers and mainland Chinese needed healing because both had been wounded, by the tragedies of China's recent history—the Great Famine and the Cultural Revolution—or by some Hongkongers' animosity towards the government and the Three-Self church and an occasionally xenophobic and condescending attitude towards mainland Chinese. Christians should thus play a reconciliatory, priestly role, Yeung said, a position attractive to politically conservative evangelicals. Yet, this call for reconciliation sounded quite different only two years later, when the student demonstrations in Tiananmen Square ended tragically. Reconciliation, so it appeared to locals, was not on the agenda of mainland authorities.

The 1990s thus began with a sense of great uncertainty and with renewed fear that the city's economic prosperity and political stability might end. The cause of the demonstrating students in Beijing had brought conservative and progressive Christians in Hong Kong closer together. Many evangelical Christians had stood side by side with fellow ecumenical Christians in a broad movement of solidarity with the students in Beijing, many for the first time joining a protest. On the other side, approaching the 1997 handover, many ecumenical theologians understood that the inevitable fact of Chinese control over Hong Kong made healthy relations and pragmatic cooperation with Chinese authorities necessary for the sake of local people. In subsequent decades, the divide between prophetic and priestly voices, between progressive ecumenical and conservative evangelical voices continued to fluctuate, always shaped by social and political events on the ground. Yet, parallel to this tension, a new movement, critical of dualistic theological positions and concerned about the unique identity of Hong Kong at the end of British colonial times, emerged. This movement—postcolonial theology— emphasized *the multiple ambiguities* in any given context.

Postcolonial Theology in Hong Kong

No other global theological movement has received as significant a contribution from Hong Kong theologians as postcolonial theology. The city's colonial experience was unique: a place shaped by Western intellectual, social, cultural, and legal traditions; a refuge for those seeking stability; a home to people who treasure and maintain their Chinese cultural heritage; a city at the heart of Asia yet somehow distant from common images of poor, suffering Asians.[19] Living at the intersection of power networks and colonial relationships, theologians in Hong Kong are ideally placed to reflect on the ambiguities and hybrid identities inherent in colonialism. Yes, Christianity entered Hong Kong and other places in the Global South in conjunction with colonial powers, but, ask local theologians, does this mean that Christianity is nothing more than a colonial religion? Does Christianity in post-colonial times need to shed all its colonial elements to become fully indigenous, or, in official parlance, fully sinicized? What would such an indigenized faith look like? Is not its "standing-in-between" what best describes the local context and what is thus the most appropriate contextualization of Christianity in Hong Kong? Responding to such questions, local theologians have taken inspiration from postcolonial studies to develop a theology that challenges the traditional binary constructions of colonial and anti-colonial, East and West, missionary and indigenous.

Postcolonial theologies emerged locally in the 1990s, the fruit of critical discussions that begun in the 1970s about the need for a decolonization of the mind and the liberation of theology from its colonial shackles. The conversation was led by theologians of the Global South such as the Sri Lankan R.S. Sugirtarajah, the Botswanan Musa Dube, the Cuban-American Fernando Segovia, the Hong Kong-born Kwok Pui-Lan and Benny Liew, and the Argentinian Marcella Althaus-Reid. The movement was deeply influenced by cultural critic Edward Said, whose ground-breaking book *Orientalism* (1978) is commonly regarded as the beginning of postcolonial studies. Postcolonial critics question "the hegemonic systems of thought, textual codes, and symbolic practices, which the West constructed in its domination of colonial subjects."[20] They challenge the eurocentrism of Western scholars who, in their intellectual practice, construct images of the oriental and colonially subject other in a binary order of "us and them"; in addition, they show the long history of such binary constructions, which persist in people's minds and in cultural and scholarly production even after the political processes of decolonization and independence. Postcolonial studies in Hong Kong were advanced by biblical scholars such as Archie Lee Chi-Chung, Philip Chia and, more recently, Sonia Wong Kwok, and theologians such as the already mentioned Kwok Pui-Lan, Angela Wong Wai-Ching, and Simon Kwan Shui-Man.

Since the early 1990s, Archie Lee has pursued a *cross-textual reading* of the Bible.[21] According to him, an approach based only on the text of the Bible fails to give meaning to the reality of people's lives in Asia. Even a "text-context hermeneutics," which consciously relates the text to the context, fails to do justice to the traditions and sacred texts of Asia, Lee says, because it tends to be a one-way relation (the Bible speaking to the context) that prevents the context speaking to the text. Cross-textual hermeneutics, in contrast, allows the biblical text and the religious texts of Asian cultures, or the "text" of present-day Hong Kong, to stand next to each other, to dialogue on an equal footing and thus to enrich each other, one forming "the contour against which the other text is perceived with some new spectra of colors unrecognized before."[22] A "text" can be a literary or a non-literary work, including cultural heritage, historical traditions, religious beliefs and folk tales reflecting the collective wisdom from all ages. As much as the Greek and the Latin traditions were fundamentally woven into the writings and early translations of the Bible, cross-textual practices affirm Asian traditions, religiosities, and social realities. As a result, Asian cultures and languages will not be just *bearers* of biblical revelation. They will be *contributors* to the revelatory truth.[23] In this way, Lee reads the texts of the Confucian or Daoist traditions, the *Analects* or the *Dao De Jing*, or the text of the social and political reality of Hong Kong alongside biblical texts and thus "destabilizes any claims to primacy of the biblical text."[24]

Likewise, Kwok Pui-Lan places the Bible within the multi-faith context of Asia, taking a similar cross-textual approach to feminist postcolonial theology, as in this quote from her Korean colleague Chung Hyun-Kyung: "Asian women theologians should realize that we are the text, and the Bible and tradition of the Christian church are the context of our theology." She points out that Asian women face double colonization by both foreign powers and by men who essentialize women as "servile, weak, and docile," and that they experience multiple forms of oppression because of "race, class, militarism, and colonialism." Kwok challenges the stereotypical images established by Western *and* Asian male elites to discover an in-between space that offers new possibilities for negotiating identity and exploring cultural hybridity. On this basis, aware of the need to avoid an essentialized view of women, and bringing together feminist theological discourses from various contexts, she reclaims the authority for women to be theological subjects, emphasizes women's experiences as a foundation for theology, and endeavors to reconstruct the image of God within the pluralistic context of Asia.[25]

In a landmark essay two years after the handover, Archie Lee addressed the burning issue of local identity by comparing the situation in Hong Kong with that of Israel returning from exile (Is 56–66). After 150 years of British colonial rule, Lee wrote, locals' identity "is highly hybridized . . . culturally Chinese and yet pragmatically British," displaying at the same time "a strong sense of identification with China and an unexplainable fear of being national Chinese."[26] He diagnosed a fundamental dilemma: Hong Kong had gone through its handover to China, which has always regarded the city as too westernized and not sufficiently authentic Chinese, and which has now subjected it to a "hegemonic state power which upholds a totalizing nationalistic vision of a homogenous Chinese people."[27] Yet, local people have never developed a hostile, anti-colonial attitude and wished in no way to distance themselves from the legacy of the colonizer. They were and are caught in a double impossibility—for them, it is both impossible to submit to Chinese nationalist and nativist repossession, and impossible to submit to British colonialism.[28] More simply, Hongkongers enjoy being both fully Chinese and Western, but refuse to enjoy being one by excluding the other. Discussing this unique identity of Hongkongers, Lee uses the term "hybridity," as introduced by Homi K. Bhabha, another leading postcolonial thinker, in his book *The Location of Culture* (1994). Hybridity is more than a value-free description of a mixed entity, for being neither one nor the other challenges any reductionist construction of a "culture" such as "Asian" or "Western" or "Chinese"—and is a deliberate resistance to any hegemonial claim of cultural homogeneity.

The importance of Bhabha's thought is also seen in the work of other local postcolonial theologians. In a context where the indigenization discourse, once used as a tool of decolonization, has been redeployed as a tool of recolonization, and where indigenization has become instrumentalized as "sinicization," which propagates nationalism, recolonizes Christianity, and integrates it into the overriding rationale of the Party and the state, Simon Kwan discovers in Bhabha's notions of ambivalence, mimicry, and hybridity, effective resistance strategies that subvert colonial or recolonizing relationships.[29] He insists on incomplete and non-binary indigenization that resists the claim of *complete* indigenization, which would eradicate traces of the missionary past and would remain stuck in a binary logic between "us" and "the foreigners." Drawing on Bhabha, Michel Foucault, and James Scott, Kwan contends that the relationships between the colonizer and the colonized are always more than the neat dichotomy of powerful-colonizer versus powerless-colonized. Religious practice can be part of a hidden form of resistance.

For Angela Wong, a leading Asian feminist and postcolonial theologian, the hybridity of dual identities and traditions, British and Chinese, is a mixed blessing for Chinese Christian women. They can hardly feel at home with either identity, as patriarchal domination was at work as much in traditional/local religion as in the religion of the colonizers. Furthermore, the Christian faith as it developed in Hong Kong estranged local Chinese from their own cultural heritage, which is inextricably linked to religious acts such as the veneration of ancestors, burials, marriage, and communal festivals. However, Christianity offered women a creative space for negotiating, on behalf of the cause of women, an extra-territory and training ground for independence, and a bridge to the world.[30] As Wong shows, throughout the city's history Christian women have played an active role in social change, from their work as female missionary teachers to the movement against the *mui tsai* system (cf. Chapter 5), as well as the 1990s campaign against discriminatory inheritance rights in rural Hong Kong.[31]

In the views of both Kwan and Wong, the location of Hong Kong at the margins of the British Empire, which, for a long time, regarded the local population with disdain, and at the margins of China, which regarded the city as not properly Chinese, resulted in Hongkongers standing in-between. In the case of local Christians, their being different was further exacerbated by their appearing unfaithful to their own traditions while still not becoming fully

British. This is what Kwan, with reference to Bhabha, calls "colonial mimicry"—almost the same but not quite.[32]

In sum, postcolonial theology, with its emphasis on hybridity, ambiguity, and resistance, is significant in both method and content: it is theological thinking in the local context, *and* a contextually relevant theology. The proper place for doing theology is at the margins and in the spaces in between the empires. It is from the periphery—from Taipei, Hong Kong, or from overseas' Chinese communities—that the renewal of Chinese society emerges.[33] Accordingly, more recent postcolonial scholars such as Sonia Wong have pointed out the analogy with the location of the ancient Israelites, who found themselves between Babylon and Egypt. These theologians stress the anti-hegemonial character of the biblical texts, and they recognize the same deep congruence of present and past that we discovered at the end of the last chapter, as Hongkongers' own experiences and those of biblical times converge.

Sino-Christian Theology

Not far from the Chinese University of Hong Kong, the institutional base for much of Hong Kong's postcolonial theological reflection, stands another hill, the Tao Fong Shan, which is the place for a very different, yet somehow similar kind of theological work. At the site of Reichelt's Christian mission to Buddhists, the *Institute for Sino-Christian Studies (ISCS)*, established in 1995, undertakes a Christian mission to Chinese intellectuals. Yet, this mission is not to be mistaken as evangelization, but should be seen as a joint pursuit and discovery of truth.[34] On this beautiful site among the hills of the New Territories, where monkeys and boars roam, scholars from China and the West come together to share in a vision similar to the one that Archie Lee suggested in his cross-textual reading, namely, that the Eastern and Western learning mutually enrich each other and that their joint reading deepens the human understanding of revelatory truth.[35]

From its beginning, the ISCS worked with Chinese scholars interested in Christianity outside of the churches, thus affirming the wider dimension of Christianity. These mainland scholars refrain from joining a church, partly due to institutional and political restrictions (Party members are not allowed to be church members), and partly because they are on an intellectual quest and do not see a need for baptism. They include senior scholars from departments of philosophy or religious studies at major mainland Chinese and Taiwanese universities, among them Liu Xiaofeng and He Guanghu (both regarded as prime proponents of the movement), Gao Shining, Yang Huilin, Tao Feiya, Zhuo Xinping, Zhang Qingxiong, and Thomas Qu Xutong. At the same time, the ISCS invites Western scholars interested in Chinese studies and connects them with universities in China; this group has included prominent theologians such as Hans Küng, Jürgen Moltmann, Michael Welker, Chloe Starr, David Jasper, and Markus Bockmuehl.

Sino-Christian theology emerged in the late 1980s as an intellectual movement within Chinese academia. The description points to a core tension within the movement—is it a movement of Christians thinking about Christianity from within, or a movement of people simply interested in Christianity and thinking about Christianity from without? Lai Pan-Chiu, a Hong Kong theologian, has introduced a widely accepted distinction between *a broader* use of the term, referring to any theology written in the Chinese language, to which the Chinese term for Sino-Christian theology, "theology in Chinese language" alludes, and a *narrow* use, designating the theological thinking of some cultural Christians. Jason Lam Tsz-Shun, another local theologian connected to Tao Fong Shan, describes three groups within Sino-Christian theology: those who have no religious commitment and simply study Christianity as a major foreign religion but in comparison to Chinese culture; those who, still without a faith commitment, study Christianity through an even more value-neutral lens, from within the framework of social and human sciences; and those who have a personal commitment to the Christian faith. It is this third group that is sometimes called "cultural Christians."

Sino-Christian theology, by its use of the Chinese language, is a Chinese contextual theology shaped by Chinese cultural, religious, political, and social contexts. Yet, it is not commonly regarded as a Hong Kong theology, except in the sense that Hong Kong is part of China and much of its theological production is in the Chinese language. But the city contributes with its strengths, theologizing in the in-between space of East and West, brokering the encounter of the two and serving as their meeting place. Local theologians playing key roles in Sino-Christian theological circles are Lai Pan-Chiu, Milton Wan Wai-Yiu, Jason Lam Tsz Shun, Daniel Yeung, director of the ISCS, and Kwok Wai-Luen from the Baptist University's *Center for Sino-Christian Studies*. Alongside others such as Kwok Hung-Biu, Tang Siu-Kwong, or Lo Wing-Kong, who have been trained in the West and are familiar with the Chinese cultural traditions, these scholars facilitate Sino-Christian theological debates and transmit Chinese theology to the West.

Perhaps the most significant local contribution has come from Lai Pan-Chiu, who draws from both Western doctrinal tradition and Chinese philosophy to offer new perspectives on long-lasting theological problems. His work includes a broad range of thoughts and studies: he proposes, similar to Archie Lee, the joint reading of texts from the Christian tradition and from Chinese religions and philosophies to demonstrate how they mutually enrich each other; he reviews the tradition of the Church of the East, *Jingjiao*, which built the first encounter of Christianity with China, to critically point out how this tradition developed independent of Nestorius, who was condemned by the Western Church as a heretic; he retrieves early forms of contextualization in China, as for example the concept of God as "Great-Father-Mother," found in the texts of Chinese Catholics during the Ming dynasty (1368), to show how they integrate traditional Chinese concepts with Christian theology; he experiments in comparative theology, as when he interprets Christology within the framework of Mahayana Buddhism, to establish this as a method through which Chinese Christian theology can make a global contribution; and he revisits traditional doctrinal sticking points, such as the two natures of Christ, to demonstrate how some of the classical problems of Christianity arose in the context of an Aristotelian logic, where humanity and divinity are mutually exclusive, but look different if seen from a Chinese perspective. Lai's intentional blending of Chinese and Western traditions provides Chinese material for the articulation of a Christian theology that is relevant for theologians also in non-Chinese contexts. In other words, Lai advances the development of a Chinese theology to contribute to a decentered understanding of Christianity.

To conclude, the two movements, postcolonial and Sino-Christian theology, are important local contributions to the theologies of global Christianity. While they take place in an academic environment, in some distance from congregational life, and hardly known to the majority of Christians, they express in theologically reflected form a basic sentiment of many local Christians by connecting Chinese and Western traditions. One does so with a stronger emphasis on the particularity of the city and the other with a stronger emphasis on the city's belonging to China, yet both are united in a passion to link Chinese and Western learning. The differences between the two theological movements reflect the ongoing tension within the concept of "one country, two systems," the basis of the city's post-1997 political status: different attitudes regarding Hong Kong and China that ultimately derive from different identities. Many of Hong Kong's older generation are mainland-born refugees to the city. Among them, some regard the city as a place of transition from which to move on to better shores. Others are looking to return to China, which they still regard as their true "home." Still others are happy to have left the mainland behind; they regard Hong Kong as their new home. And a growing group of locally born Hongkongers knows the mainland only from occasional family visits. They have no deeper attachment to China, other than as a place to engage for the sake of the gospel, yet they see in the recent developments on the mainland an empire that increasingly threatens local existence. The two theological strands are faith-based expressions created by the collective biography of the city and by the local identities it engenders. While important developments in local identity-building happened in the 1970s and 80s, fear about the future soon gained the upper hand.[36] Hongkongers sensed that the wealth accumulated during those years might be gone anytime. Recent events have reinforced the city's status as a place of transition from which local people are scattered around the globe. Yet, local Christians' faith moves beyond fear and connects them to the story of the peregrinating people of God, who are never sovereigns but always sojourners.

Epilogue

The first ideas for this book came to me in January 2021, during a three-week quarantine, when, due to the city authorities' paramount fear of the spread of the Covid-19 virus, I was locked up in a hotel room in Hong Kong. It was one and a half years after the hot summer of 2019, when political demonstrations had rocked the city, and half a year after the introduction of the National Security Law. Hong Kong was still in a state of shock and in a collective depression. Many well-educated people, young families, and those engaged in social movements were preparing to leave or had already done so. The writing of this book took place against the background of widespread fear that the freedoms that the city had enjoyed would be gone for a long time.

What the coming years may bear is impossible to predict. Many residents worry about a deterioration of civil liberties and about Hong Kong becoming just like any city on the mainland. In response to this, more than a hundred thousand Hongkongers have resettled around the globe. The absence of so many friends, colleagues, and young families is painfully felt. Yet, Hong Kong has an amazing ability to bounce back, to mobilize extra strengths, and to find creative ways to foster an unbroken spirit. Whether the recent developments are just a bump in the history of this amazing city or indeed the beginnings of Hong Kong losing its unique character, only history will tell.

Two quotes shall conclude this book's thoughts—one from China, the other from Germany, both places close to my heart, yet not quite my home. Ren Bumei, a theologian from Northeastern China who meanwhile lives in Canada, diagnosed China as caught in a tragic history of catastrophes that turned Chinese people into refugees. All of Chinese life is affected by a refugee mentality. Redemption to those scattered, most recently the Hongkongers who now live in exile, means to be found, to be integrated in the community of the chosen people, and to be brought back. Ren Bumei writes: "It is by the predestined grace of God throughout history that victims of catastrophes shall be found and become the elected people of God. [災民被尋回成為選民，同樣是神在歷史中預定恩典]" (Ren Bumei, Catastrophism, Hong Kong 2010,

386). As much as Christian faith has been a pillar of strength for the refugees flocking to Hong Kong over the past century, today's Hongkongers who live in exile abroad find strength in it and hear God's promise of a new community.

For those staying in the city, and for myself, the changes of the past two years have been a spiritual learning process and have deepened the understanding of the role and experience of Christians in the local community. I was reminded of the words of a German theologian and modern-day martyr, who, while in prison and waiting for his execution, profoundly reflected on the presence and the hiddenness of God in the world. With him, I experienced how Christians share in the inner-worldly pain, vulnerability and powerlessness of God, which has so paradoxically been exhibited in the cross. To him shall be the last word:

> The God who is with us is the God who forsakes us (Mark 15:34). The God who lets us live in the world without the working hypothesis of God is the God before whom we stand continually. Before God and with God we live without God. God lets himself be pushed out of the world on to the cross. He is weak and powerless in the world, and that is precisely the way, the only way, in which he is with us and helps us. Mt 8.17 makes it quite clear that Christ helps us, not by virtue of his omnipotence, but by virtue of his weakness and suffering.
>
> DIETRICH BONHOEFFER, *Letters and Papers from Prison*,
> Letter from July 16, 1944

Tobias Brandner
HongKong, December 30, 2022

Notes

Introduction

1 United Nations Development Programme (UNDP)'s Human Development Report Office 2020.

2 Numbers from a 2019 publication of the Society for Community Organization, *Life stories of the homeless* and from https://soco.org.hk/en/projecthome/cage-homes/ (accessed February 15, 2021). The calculation of the Gini coefficient varies, depending on whether taxes and social transfers are included.

3 Surprisingly, there is no comprehensive study in English of the history of Christianity in Hong Kong. Short information is available in encyclopedia articles or book chapters such as in Ying, "Hong Kong" (2020), Kwan, "Hong Kong" (2020), or Lo, "Taiwan, Hong Kong, Macau" (2011). A book-length historical study by Ying, *Introduction* [Chin.] (2004), is available only in Chinese. A good summary with a review of the study of the field until the late 1990s is M.K. Wong, "Survey" (1998), 1–40.

4 Ying "Hong Kong" (2020), 76.

5 T.F. Liu, "Conversion of the Urban Poor" (1996).

Chapter 1

1 Research Group, *2019 HK Church Survey [Chin.]*, 20. The census is based only on Protestant churches using one of the Chinese languages and covers neither Roman-Catholic nor international churches. If Catholic churches had been included, the numbers would look slightly different, with more free-standing and fewer upper-floor churches. The subsequent numbers and percentages in this chapter likewise include only Protestant churches; the 1,312 Chinese congregations are based on an updated report that integrates some recent developments, Research Group, *2021 Research [Chin.]*, 9. Most of the numbers in this chapter are based on the 2019 report and the lower number of 1305 (Chinese-speaking) congregations.

2 Statistics of the Diocese of Hong Kong (August 31, 2021). https://catholic.org.hk/en/statistics-of-the-diocese-of-hong-kong/.

3 Research Group, *2019 HK Church Survey [Chin.]*, 20: 301 of 1305 churches are located in commercial buildings, and 377 in residential buildings (including residential buildings where parts of the building are used commercially).

4 A case study of such an upper-floor church can be found in Yeung, "Constructing sacred space" (2011), 401–418.

5 Constable, *Christian Souls and Chinese Spirits* (1994).

6 Ap Chau Story Room, Sister Wai Yan Chan (Tai Po Church), www.tjchkga.com/eng/Testimony_ApChauStoryRoom.asp.

7 Heaver, "The abandoned churches of Sai Kung," SCMP Magazine, February 27 2016, www.scmp.com/magazines/post-magazine/article/1916619/abandoned-churches-sai-kung-how-italian-missionaries.

8 Sharpe, *Karl Ludwig Reichelt* (1984), 117.

9 Tong, *Tao Fong: Walk and Pray [Chin.]*, (2019).

10 See a summary of the history and some memories in a recent research project, Lee, *Cultural and Historical Studies* (2021).

11 See the memories of Bray, "Growing up in China" (1992), 199–213.

12 Carroll, *A Concise History of Hong Kong* (2007), 74–75.

13 For a history of the Christian cemeteries in Hong Kong, see Ying, *Between This and the Other Worlds [Chin.]* (2012).

14 Mayfield, *Pentecostal Hong Kong* (2021), 303.

15 Y.W. Chan, "Where to Die?" (2016), 312 and 339.

16 Ko, "Development of Cemeteries" (2001), 248.

17 Y.W. Chan, Where to Die?" (2016), 339.

18 Teather, "High-rise homes for the ancestors" (1999), 415.

19 Y.W. Chan, ibid., 323.

20 Keegan, "Real estate now more expensive for the dead" (2019). www.theguardian.com/cities/2019/apr/23/dead-pricey-hong-kong-burial-plots-now-more-expensive-than-living-space. Other sources quote lower prices, see Kao, "Private columbarium operators face stricter financial regulations," www.scmp.com/news/hong-kong/health-environment/article/2173476/private-columbarium-operators-face-stricter.

21 Quoted from Y.W. Chan, Where to Die?" (2016), 332.

22 Yang, *Religion in Chinese Society* (1961), 30.

23 Ibid., 31–43.

24 Ko, "Development of Cemeteries" (2001), 256–257.

25 Poon, *Hong Kong's Land Policy* (2011), 1. https://carnegieendowment.org/hkjournal/archive/2011_spring/3.htm.

26 Nissim, *Land Administration and Practice* (2012), 14.

27 Nissim, ibid., 13.

28 Fukushima and Doi, "Building process" (2013), 1431–1440.

29 Lai, "God or Mammon?" (2017), https://hongkongfp.com/2017/11/19/god-mammon-gains-hong-kongs-historic-churches-turned-blocks-flats/.

30 Fukushima and Doi, "Building process" (2013), 1431.

31 Based on calculations of World Bank national accounts data, and OECD National Accounts data files. https://data.worldbank.org/indicator/NY.GDP.MKTP.KD.ZG?end=2000&locations=HK&start=1970&view=chart.

32 K.K. Yeung, "Constructing sacred space," 405.

33 Research Group, *2021 Research*, 11.

34 Ellis, "Anglican Indigenization and Contextualization" (2019), 219–246, here 225.

35 Wickeri and Chen, "Contextualization and the Chinese Anglican Parish" (2015), 147.

36 Ellis, ibid. 237 and 240.

37 Coomans, "Sinicising Christian Architecture" (2016), 133–160; Coomans and Ho, "Architectural Styles and Identities" (2018), 81–109.

38 K.K. Yeung, ibid. 407.

39 Ibid., 415.

40 Smith, *Chinese Christians*, 129–131. Critical of the assumption that Ho was deliberately disguising his wealth Choa, *Life and Times of Sir Kai Ho Kai* (2000), 15.

Chapter 2

1 Hong Kong Yearbook 2019, Chapter 21, 329–330 (www.yearbook.gov. hk/2019/en/).

2 Research Group, *2019 HK Church Survey [Chin.]*, 25.

3 Study commissioned by the Centre for Christian Studies (DSCCC, CUHK) and conducted by (i) the Institute of Asia-Pacific Studies, CUHK (2009) and (ii) the Centre for Communication and Public Opinion Survey, School of Journalism and Communication, CUHK (2012). Chu, "Quantitative Analysis [Chin.]" (2009), 129.

4 Ray Bakke Centre, "How many Christians are there in Hong Kong?" (2018).

5 HKCC and DSCCC, Survey Report 2021 [Chin.].

6 Ray Bakke Centre, ibid.; Yip, "Know Yourself and Know Your Enemy [Chin.]" (2009), 109.

7 HKCC and DSCCC, Survey Report 2021 [Chin.], 12–15.

8 Chu, "Quantitative Analysis [Chin.]" (2009), 133.

9 2016 Population By-Census, www.bycensus2016.gov.hk/en/Snapshot-02.html

10 Census and Statistics Department, www.censtatd.gov.hk/en/press_release_ detail.html?id=4979

11 Ibid., www.censtatd.gov.hk/en/EIndexbySubject.html?scode=500&pcode =D5250038

12 Research Group, *2019 HK Church Survey [Chin.]*, 6 and 18; Research Group, *2021 Research [Chin.]*, 9.

13 Raiser (1991), *Ecumenism in Transition*, 3.

14 Bebbington, *Evangelicalism* (2005), 16.

15 Marsden, Fundamentalism and American Culture (2006), 235.

16 Anderson, *An Introduction to Pentecostalism*, 14. For a discussion of the problems of definition, see ibid., 9–15.

17 All numerical information from the diocesan website (as on August 31, 2021) https://catholic.org.hk/en/%E9%A6%99%E6%B8%AF%E6%95%99%E5% 8D%80%E6%95%99%E5%8B%99%E7%B5%B1%E8%A8%88-2/. The website offers a contradictory number of worship sites. The total number of Filipinos in the territory is 217,000, see Hong Kong Yearbook 2021, https:// www.yearbook.gov.hk/2021/en/

18 For the history of the first years, see Ha, *Foundation of Catholic Mission* (1998), 64–80.

19 Ha, *History of Evangelization in Hong Kong* (2006).

20 Malek, "Historiography and Spirituality of Religious Orders and Congregations" (2009), 2. The year numbers relating to their arrival are found in the articles related to the various orders in one of the volumes.

21 Westendorp, "Belonging to a global family of God" (2017), 117.

22 Beatrice Leung, "The Hong Kong Catholic Church: A Framing Role in Social Movement" (2009), 251.

23 Kwong and Wickeri, "Sheng Kung Hui" (2016), 259.

24 Ying, "R.O. Hall and the Christian Study Centre on Chinese Religion" (2015), 65–78.

25 Quoted from ibid., 76.

26 For a historical reconstruction of the ordination and related events, see Wickeri, "Ordination and Ministry of Li Tim Oi" (2018), 107–127.

27 A. Wong, "A Distinctive Chinese Contribution" (2018), 137.

28 For a detailed study of this whole process, see C.H. Chan, *Unity without uniformity [Chin.]*, (2013), particularly 86–103; and So, *Quest for Visible Unity*, 26–61.

29 Bays, *A New History of Christianity in China*, 109–111. C.H. Chan, ibid. 98; So, 31–34.

30 Following historical information is from the church's website www.methodist. org.hk/about/[Chin.].

31 Salvation Army Annual Report 2019-20. https://salvationarmy.org.hk/wp-content/uploads/2021/01/CCD-Annual-report-2019-2020.pdf

32 For the early history of the Basel Mission in China, see Schlatter, *Geschichte der Basler Mission* (1916). For the whole history of the TTM see Tong, *From the Basel Mission to the Tsung Tsin Mission* [Chin.] (2012).

33 For the early history of the Rhenish Church, see Law, *Missionary History of the Rhenish Church [Chin.]* (1968).

34 Smith, *Chinese Christians* (2005), 2–3; Lowe, "The Beliefs, Aspirations and Methods" (2000), 53.

35 These and other numbers of worship attendants and members in this section refer to the time pre-2019, that is, before the social movement of 2019, which led to many young people particularly from large churches, leaving their church. The changes through the Covid pandemic and the wave of migration since 2020 are also not reflected in these numbers. One of the references, although meanwhile outdated is K.K. Ng, *Ten Large Hong Kong Denominations* (2008).

36 C.H. Chan, "The contribution of Philip Teng [Chin.]" (2016). See also the portrait by K.L. Leung, "Portrait of a Chinese Evangelical of the 20th Century" (2016).

37 Ying, *Introduction* (2004), 117–118; see also the website of CNEC Lau Wing Sang Secondary School with a history of the denomination.

38 K.K. Chan, "Indigenous Mission Movement from China" (2013).

39 See the summary of its spiritual path, www.hkpec.org/pec_spir.php, 6.4 [Chin.].

40 „A Preliminary Study of 'The Church of God in Hong Kong,'" *Christian Times* No. 301 [Chin.], June 6, 1993.

41 Au, "From Collaborations to Independence" (2019), 85.

42 Au, "Hong Kong," (2021); on Mok Lai Chi, see Au, "Mok, Lai Chi" (2021).

43 Mayfield, *Pentecostal Hong Kong* (2021), 266.

44 Au, "From Collaborations to Independence" (2019), 87.

45 Au, "The Pentecostal Holiness Church's Mission" (2011), 28.

46 Mayfield, ibid., 347.

47 S. Chan, *Pentecostal Ecclesiology* (2011), 94.

48 https://foursquare.org.hk/%e9%97%9c%e6%96%bc%e6%88%91%e5%80%91/%e6%ad%b7%e5%8f%b2/ [Chin.]

49 Mayfield, ibid., 292.

50 Critical of such categorization Iap, "A Pioneer and Paradigm of Chinese Independent Pentecostal Churches" [Chin.], 86–90.

51 See overall Lian, *Redeemed by Fire*, 42–63, here 47.

52 Zheng, Notes on the History of the True Jesus Church [Chin.] (2015), 90. The earliest local missionaries' Chinese names are 邱馬利亞 and 尤玉英.

53 Lian, ibid., 155–178; Anderson, *Introduction*,135-6.

54 Lian, ibid. 194.

55 Tiedemann, *Reference guide* (2009), 245; Ying, *Introduction* (2004), 115–117.

56 A. Yeung, *Charisma and Diakonia [Chin.]* (2003), 45.

57 Olsen, *History of the Seventh-Day Adventists* (1926), 192, 652–653.

58 Research Group, *2019 HK Church Survey [Chin.]*, 18–19.

59 The story of Sam Lai is recounted in Cham Sha (Sea Sand), *Dawn Finally Comes* (2003); see also Pavey, *Theologies of Power and Crisis* (2011), 84–86.

60 See the doctoral dissertation by S.H. Chan, *The Making of Religious Universe* (1995).

61 For a more historical list until 1950, see Ying, *Introduction* (2004), 77–80.

62 Information from the Wikipedia entry, which seems to reflect editing by people close to the church.

63 Ying, *Introduction* (2004), 99. The church's own information gives 1976 as the year when the first church was established.

64 Ibid., 173–183.

65 Research Group, *2019 HK Church Survey [Chin.]*, 27.

66 Quoted from Brandner, "The Church as Family" (2019), 218. The following section summarizes the thoughts presented in this article; see also Chapter 8.

67 See among many, Cox, *Fire from Heaven*, 221–228.

68 See the discussion of growth factors in Singapore's Pentecostalism in Goh, "State and Social Christianity" (2010), 54–89.

69 Ned, "Rather Spirit-filled than Learned!" (2016).

70 Ray Bakke Center, *Preliminary Report on 'Churched & Dechurched' Survey* (2018).

71 Ray Bakke Center, *New Expressions of Churches Research* (2021).

72 Christian Times, September 30, 2020 https://christiantimes.org.hk/Common/ Reader/News/ShowNews.jsp?Nid=163488&Pid=2&Version=1727&Cid=589& Charset=big5_hkscs [Chin.].

Chapter 3

1 Based on the Research Group on 2019 Hong Kong Church Survey, *Report of 2019 HK International Church Survey* and the Research Group on 2014 Hong Kong Church Survey, *Report of 2014 HK English-speaking Church Survey (International Churches)* and further research; see more on this calculation below.

2 Information from the 2016 by-census, A105 "Population by Nationality and Year," www.bycensus2016.gov.hk/en/bc-mt.html.

3 See Chapter 2, footnote 17; Hong Kong Yearbook 2021, https://www. yearbook.gov.hk/2021/en/

4 Cheung a.o. "Abuse and depression among Filipino foreign domestic helpers" (2019), 121–127.

5 See also similar descriptions by the noted Filipino sociologist Randy David in Cruz (2010), "It Cuts Both Ways" (2010), 26–28.

6 Constable, "Telling Tales of Migrant Workers in Hong Kong" (2019), 312; Cruz, "Em-body-ing Theology," 67–68.

7 Ma, "Influence of Pentecostal Spirituality" (2020), 115–116. For a more thorough analysis see Cornelio, "Jesus is Lord" (2018), 127–155.

8 Cruz, "It Cuts Both Ways" (2010), 22–26.

9 Cornelio, ibid., 132–135.

10 Cheng, "Rick Warren's Saddleback Church Pushes Beyond U.S. Borders," *Gospel Herald*, October 5, 2013.

11 Interview with Senior Pastor of Yoido Full Gospel Church Hong Kong and calculated based on statistics from Moon, *The Korean Missionary Movement* (2016).

12 Klaver, *Hillsong Church* (2021), 22.

13 Based on an overall population of 6,309 Koreans in the city (2016 Population By-census. Thematic Report: Ethnic Minorities, www.statistics.gov.hk/pub/B11201002016XXXXB0100.pdf, 21) and assuming around 20 percent of them being Protestants. Around 20 percent is the estimated number of Protestant Christians in South Korea (the World Christian Database estimating 33 percent overall Christians, 11 percent of them Roman Catholic).

14 Kingdom Revival Times (HK), July 21, 2011, [Chin.] https://web.archive.org/web/20110721085404/http://www.krt.com.hk/modules/news/article.php?storyid=5755.

15 Gordon-Conwell Theological Seminary, *Christianity in its Global Context, 1970–2020: Society, Religion and Mission*, 2013, 38.

16 Research Group, *Report of 2019 HK International Church Survey*, 3.

17 www.thevine.org.hk/what-we-believe.

18 Chan, *No Strangers Here*, 151.

19 Quoted from ibid., 189.

20 Ibid., 187.

21 Fuentes, *Lived Experiences and Christian Faith of Catholic OFW Mothers in Hong Kong* (2021), 155–158.

22 Währisch-Oblau, *Missionary Self-Perception*, 2009.

23 E-mail from Judy Chan, formerly a staff member at the Hong Kong Christian Council (March 22, 2021).

24 68.7%. See Research Group, *Report of 2019 HK International Church Survey*, 12.

25 Ibid., 7.

26 Ibid., 11.

27 Steve Gaultney, quoted from Snelgrove, *Key Factors behind Hong Kong's Millennials Moving to International Churches* (2018), 105.

28 Ibid. 67–109. A summary of the study is published as Snelgrove, a.o. "Hong Kong millennial Christians" (2021), 1–16.

29 See the examples in Snelgrove, ibid., 90–91.

Chapter 4

1 Hong Kong Movie DataBase, https://hkmdb.com/db/people/view.mhtml?id=572&display_set=eng; see also Art. "Mui, Yee (Mei Qi) (1923-66)," in Stokes and Braaten, *Historical Dictionary of Hong Kong Cinema*, 348–9.

2 Tan, "Pentecostal and Charismatic Origins in Malaysia and Singapore" (2005), 288.

3 Testimony of Sammi Cheng on www.youtube.com/watch?v–hR6UiyOiE8&t=239s.

4 L. Yeung, "Fellowship of the Stars," *SCMP* September 5, 1994.

5 Yam, "Engagement in Television" (2005), 94–95.

6 See the critical discussion in Yam, "Interplay between Media and Religion" (2017), 42–44.

7 Important ideas for this paragraph come from two (unpublished) student papers written by Chloe Luo Ning, "Thirty-five Years of Hong Kong Artistes Christian Fellowship" and Wins Law, "Christianity and Entertainment in Hong Kong."

8 Christian Times September 12, 1999 [Chin.], https://christiantimes.org.hk/Common/Reader/News/ShowNews.jsp?Nid=6041&Pid=2&Version=628&Cid=7&Charset=big5_hkscs

9 Yam, "Engagement in Television" (2005), 95–96.

10 Ibid.

11 Yam, *A Study of Popular Hong Kong Cinema* (2008), 54.

12 Ibid., 70.

13 Shui Xiang San Mu (水巷三木), quoted in Yam (2008), 58.

14 Yam, "Engagement in Television" (2005), 97–98.

15 Ibid., 98.

16 Ibid., 101–102; further Yam, "Interplay between Media and Religion" (2017), 41.

17 For a critical discussion of the film's political message see J.T.H. Lee, "Despair and Hope" (2016), 76–81.

18 L.K. Lo, "Taiwan, Hong Kong, Macau" (2011), 186.

19 The following description of historical developments is largely based on an unpublished paper by Hung, "From Singing 'Out-of-tone' to Producing Contextualized Cantonese Hymns" (2021); additional information from O.Y. Wong, *Singing the Gospel Chinese Style* (2005), 68–77, W.K. Ho, *Contemporary Christian Music in Hong Kong* (2011), and from an interview with Roger Chung, a local Christian music producer and singer (November 22, 2021).

20 Lim, "Nashville and Sidney Are Not the World" (2020), 149.

21 Wong, ibid., 122–167.

22 Ibid., 183.

23 Hung, ibid. 15–16.

24 Tam, Wai Kwok testimony [Chin.], June 16, 2004, www.smchk.org/testimony2.php; Lee, Wai-sze testimony, March 11, 2008 [Chin.], www.smchk.org/testimony8.php.

25 Information in this section is based on an interview with Johnny Yiu Yuk Hing. Some of the information on the SIC is based on a course paper submitted by Ho Wai Hong, a local student who has been involved in SIC's ministry.

26 He, *Sports and life* [Chin.] (2011), 10–12.

27 Y.C. Lee, "Preface" (2011), vi.

28 Coakley, *Sports in Society*, 2015, 497.v

29 See the sociological observations of Overman, *The Protestant Work Ethic and the Spirit of Sport* (2011).

30 Ong, *Flexible Citizenship* (1999).

31 Kwok Wai Luen, quoted from Yam, "Engagement in Television" (2005), 94.

Chapter 5

1 The overall number of schools is from the education bureau's website (www.edb.gov.hk/en/edu-system/primary-secondary/primary/index.html). The number of Christian schools is from a website on the Hong Kong school system, www.schooland.hk/ss/; www.schooland.hk/ps/, which reports the overall number of schools as around 10 percent lower than the official number given by the government.

2 http://www.hkskh.org/content.aspx?id=42&lang=1; https://www.hkcccc.org/en/?page_id=114; https://www.hkcccc.org/en/?page_id=117.

3 Following numbers from the HKSAR 2020, Hong Kong Yearbook, 329–330, www.yearbook.gov.hk/2019/en/pdf/E21.pdf and other government numbers.

4 Kwan "Hong Kong" (2020), 374; S.H. Chan, "Development of Christian Social Services" (1998), 66 (with numbers referring to 1995). According to the member list of The Hong Kong Council of Social Service (July 2018), about 127 out of 465 members are Christian NGOs (about 27.3 percent).

5 Eitel, *Europe in China* (1895), 291.

6 Carroll, *Concise History* (2007), 39.

7 Ibid., 47–53.

8 Sinn, *Power and Charity* (2003), 4.

9 Mason, "Wilhelm Lobscheid" Biographical Dictionary of Chinese Christianity. http://bdcconline.net/en/stories/lobscheid-wilhelm

10 See overall Bosch, *Transforming Mission* (1991), 284ff.; Etherington, "Schools and Education in the Missionary Enterprise" (2016), 166–175.

11 Endacott and She (The Diocese of Victoria, Hong Kong), quoted from K.H. Leung, *The Impact of Mission Schools* (1987), 91.

12 Smith, *Chinese Christians* (2005), 9; see for further examples ibid., Chapter 8.

13 Gimelli, "'Borne upon the Wings of Faith'" (1994), 239–240.

14 Here, and for the following, K.H. Leung, *The Impact of Mission Schools* (1987), 78–82.

15 J.H. Kang, "Trained to Care" (2018), 169–171; see further Carroll, *Concise History* (2007), 63–66.

16 Yung, "Visions and Realities in Hong Kong Anglican Mission Schools, 1849–1941" (2021), 259. See also Rawski, "Elementary Education in the Mission Enterprise," (1985), 140–142.

17 Endacott and Hinton, Fragrant Harbour, 68, quoted from K.H. Leung, *The Impact of Mission Schools* (1987), 85.

18 Yung, "Visions and Realities" (2021), 262.

19 K.H. Leung, ibid., 130.

20 S.L. Lau, *Interaction of Church and Society* (2018), 163.

21 W.C. Wong, "Negotiating Gender Identity" (2003), 155–156.

22 W.C. Wong, ibid., 157; see overall Lutz, "Women's Education and Social Mobility" (2010), 393–420, especially 397–399.

23 See overall Lutz, "Chinese Emigrants" (2009). For a discussion of the indenture system, see Allen, "Asian Indentured Labor" (2017).

24 Lutz, "Chinese Emigrants" (2009), 141.

25 T.K. Wong, "Chinese Migration to Sabah" (1999), 138–141.

26 Choa, *The Life and Times of Sir Kai Ho Kai* (2000).

27 Carroll, *Concise History*, 80–81.

28 On the following, see Smith, "The Chinese Church, Labour and Elites and the Mui Tsai Question" (1981); here 91.

29 W.C. Wong, "Negotiating Gender Identity" (2003), 160–161.

30 Carroll, *Concise History*, 112; Pedersen, "The Maternalist Moment in British Colonial Policy" (2001).

31 Numbers from Hong Kong Statistics 1947-1967, Census and Statistics Department Hong Kong (1969) https://www.censtatd.gov.hk/en/data/stat_report/product/B1010003/att/B10100031967AN67E0100.pdf and Saw and Chiu. "Population Growth" (1975), 126–127.

32 For a more extended description of the following, see Ying, *Wandering in Hong Kong [Chin.]* (2018), 30-35; S.H. Chan, „Development of Christian Social Services [Chin.]" (1998), 67–74; S.L. Lau, *Interaction of Church and Society [Chin.]* (2018), 173–194.

33 Elliot, *Autobiography* (1988) and *Colonial Hong Kong in the eyes of Elsie Tu* (2003).

34 Mok, "Challenges of Catholic Schooling" (2007), 757.

35 S.H. Chan, "Development of Christian Social Services [Chin.]" (1998), 73–74.

36 K.W. Tsang, *Study of Bishop Ronald Hall* (1983), 49–51. For the following, see ibid., 11–32; Paton, *Life and Times* (1985), 91–95 and 115–127; Chan-Yeung, *The Practical Prophet*, 85–184.

37 K.W. Tsang, 29; Chan-Yeung, 91ff.

38 Paton, 172.

39 See the biography by Morrissey, *Thomas F. Ryan SJ* (2010).

40 Ying, *Wandering in Hong Kong [Chin.]* (2018), 32.

41 Ibid., 33.

42 Ying, *Your Kingdom Come [Chin.]* (2002), 103-24. The former three were built with funds from the Methodist Committee for overseas Relief (MCOR), the latter by funds from the Plummer Relief Fund.

43 The following is based on Fung, *The Gospel is not for Sale* (2005), 17–40. For a description of the historical contexts of the riots, see Carroll, *Concise History*, 150–159; Tsang, *Modern History* (2004), 183–190.

44 Bianchi, "Secular Ecumenism" (1969).

45 Fung, *The Gospel is not for Sale* (2005), 31.

46 See W.Y. Wong, *An Ecumenical Experiment in Colonial Hong Kong* (2019).

47 Ying, *Wandering in Hong Kong [Chin.]* (2018), 37.

48 Ying and Lai, "Diasporic Chinese Communities" (2004), 149; B. Leung and Chan, *Changing Church and State Relations* (2003), 26ff.

49 Kwong and Wickeri, "Sheng Kung Hui" (2016), 263. The study counts 98 service centers if including those in Macau that are also part of the HKSKH province.

50 S.L. Lau, *Interaction of Church and Society [Chin.]* (2018), 197; B. Leung and Chan, *Changing Church and State Relations* (2003), 44.

51 Fung, *The Gospel is not for Sale* (2005), 35.

52 Yuen, "The Catholic Church and Civil Society in Hong Kong" (2021), 186–188.

53 Ibid.

54 Carroll, *Concise History* (2007), 170.

55 S.H. Chan, "Development of Christian Social Services [Chin.]" (1998), 80; Ying, *Wandering in Hong Kong [Chin.]* (2018), 46–47.

56 Here and in the following see W.C. Wong, "A Distinctive Chinese Contribution," 136–138.

57 See overall N. Kang, "Reclaiming Theological Significance" (2010).

58 See her book: Wu, *Liberating the Church from Fear* (2000).

59 "Objectives." Annual Report 2004–2005, quoted from S.H. Chan, "Governance crisis" (2008), 76; see further N.W. Kwok, *Hong Kong 1997* (1991), 54–55.

60 For a longer version of this famous saying, see the Confucian book *The Great Learning*, http://classics.mit.edu/Confucius/learning.html.

61 For a detailed analysis, see W.C. Wong, "Politics of Sexual Morality" (2013).

62 Douglas (ed.), *Let the Earth* (1975), 3–9 (Paragraph 6).

63 Ying, *Wandering in Hong Kong [Chin.]* (2018), 141–142.

64 See for instance McGavran, *Understanding Church Growth* (1990), 23.

65 See Cape Town Commitment. Part I. Section 10 B.

66 Ying and Lai, "Diasporic Chinese Communities" (2004), 149–150.

67 Mok Chan, "Christian Drug Rehabilitation" (2004), 94. See also a related government website, www.nd.gov.hk/en/list_of_major_organisations_providing_drug_treatment_and_rehabilitation_services.html.

68 W.L. Kwok, "Social Participation of Hong Kong Young Evangelicals [Chin.]" (2002), 148.

69 Fung, *The Gospel is not for Sale* (2005), 59.

70 W.L. Kwok, ibid., 159; see overall ibid., 159–171.

71 Fung *The Gospel is not for Sale* (2005), *58.*

72 Ibid., 55.

73 Miller and Yamamori, *Global Pentecostalism: The New Face of Christian Social Engagement* (2007).

74 See Oxfam inequality report 2018 (numbers refer to the 2016–17 tax period), 12. www.oxfam.org.hk/f/news_and_publication/16372/Oxfam_inequality%20 report_Eng_FINAL.pdf.

75 Ibid., 11.

Chapter 6

1 See the portraits of local missionaries working with Western missionaries in the earliest time in Lutz and Lutz, *Hakka Chinese* (1998). See also ibid., "Karl Gützlaff's Approach to Indigenization" (1996), 269–291.

2 Department of Intercultural Studies, ABS, Chinese missionaries on the move (2017); Fan "Seize the Opportunity of this Era [Chin.]" (2020), 1; https:// cmacuhk.org.hk/%E8%AA%8D%E8%AD%98%E5%AE%A3%E9%81%93 %E6%9C%83/.

3 The following numbers are based on the *HKACM 2020 Annual Report [Chin.]* (https://hkacm.net/), 28–31; see further HKACM, "Briefing on Missionaries sent by the Hong Kong Church [Chin.]" (https://hkacm.net/infowall/). Important contribution comes from Elim Mok who analyzed the data of HKACM for a student paper.

4 Based on an estimated 20,000 missionaries from South Korea, see Moon, *The Korean Missionary Movement* (2016).

5 Fan, "Seize the Opportunity" (2020), 1.

6 Here and in the following Research Group, *HK Church Census 2019* [Chin.], 55–57.

7 See on the cooperation of locals with visiting mission teams from the perspective of the recipients, Brandner, "Emerging Christianity in Cambodia" (2020).

8 For a summary of estimations about the growth of Christianity in China and general information, see Brandner, "A Besieged Boom: Christianity in China" (2019).

9 Leung, "China's Religious Freedom Policy" (2005), 902.

10 Liu, "Pentecostal-Style Christians in the 'Galilee of China'" (2014), 161.

11 Hirono, *Civilizing Missions* (2008), 101–129.

12 Wordie, "Hong Kong priest," SCMP, June 6, 2015.

13 Leung, "Church—State Relations in Hong Kong and Macau" (2001).

14 Leung, "The Hong Kong Catholic Church: A Framing Role in Social Movement" (2009), 253.

15 Madsen, "Religious policy in China" (2020), 26. For a summary of religious policy under Xi see ibid., 26–32; further Ying, "The politics of cross demolition" (2018).

16 Chan, *Christian Times*, April 26, 2019, https://christiantimes.org.hk/Common/Reader/News/ShowNews.jsp?Nid=157789&Pid=102&Version=0&Cid=2141&Charset=big5_hkscs.

17 Tam, "Renegotiating religious transnationalism" (2019), 67.

18 Yang, "Chinese Christian Transnationalism" (2002), 130.

19 Ibid.

20 Huang and Hsiao, "Chinese evangelists on the move" (2015), 381–382; similar, with reference to CCCOWE, Nagata, "Christianity among Transnational Chinese," 122.

21 www.cccowe.org/index.php#aboutus (translation by TB); for a critical discussion of CCCOWE, see Nagata, ibid., 122–124; further examples of CCCOWE's construction of a pan-Chinese identity in Tam, "Renegotiating religious transnationalism" (2019).

22 Tam, ibid., 67–68.

23 Ibid., 73; Huang and Hsiao (2015), 385.

24 Similar Huang and Hsiao, 390.

25 https://lausanne.org/news-releases/inaugural-mission-china-2030-conference.

26 For a detailed analysis of the movement, see Brandner, "Mission, Millennium, and Politics" (2009).

Chapter 7

1 B. Leung and Chan, *Changing Church and State Relations in Hong Kong* (2003), 18ff.

2 Ibid., 27.

3 S.H. Chan, "Christian social discourse" (2007), 461.

4 Yuen, "The Catholic Church and Civil Society in Hong Kong" (2021), 186.

5 See the detailed description in Brown, "Hong Kong's Catholic Church and the Challenge of Democratization" (2006), 187–193.

6 S.H. Chan "Christian social discourse" (2007), 463.

7 Lau, "'An Unholy Alliance': Protestant Liberals accuse Leaders of Bowing to Peking." *Far Eastern Economic Review.* December 24, 1987, 23; similarly, N.W. Kwok, *Hong Kong Braves 1997.* Hong Kong: Hong Kong Christian Institute. 1994; both quoted from Pavey, *Theologies of Power and Crisis* (2011), 62.

8 Regarding the latter, see B. Leung and Chan (2003), 37–38.

9 Ibid., 33.

10 See the analysis of S.H. Chan, "Governance and Public Policy" (2013), 171–197. For a discussion of the role of the Catholic Church, see Yuen, (2021), 184ff.

11 S.H. Chan, "Governance crisis" (2008), 78.

12 S.H. Chan, "Christian social discourse" (2007), 455–456.

13 See more on these United Front activities Ying, "Hong Kong Religious Sectors" (2018), 83.

14 A concept summarized in the Chinese expression "zheng zhu jiao cong" 政主教從, see Ying (2018), 85–86.

15 S.H. Chan, "Christians and Building Civil Society" (2021a), 201.

16 Ibid., 209.

17 Quoted from S.H. Chan, "Political Influence of Mainline Protestant Churches" (2021b), 226.

18 Chow and Lee, "Almost Democratic" (2016), 262.

19 For a summary of the events, see Ho, "A Critical Review" (2021), 15–37.

20 See more on the cultural and strategic elements of the movement in Hung, "If Not Us, Who?" (2021), 55–74.

21 Quoted from Ying, "Entanglement between Religion and Politics" (2021), 131.

22 See for this and the following Ying, ibid.

23 Ibid., 120.

24 Research Group, Report on 2021 Research on Hong Kong Church in the Midst of Crisis, 27–28 (Table 23).

25 Ying, ibid. 127.

26 Based on research by the Hong Kong Church Renewal Movement, which bases its information on questionnaires sent to Protestant churches. It is assumed that the migration movement among Catholic clergy is far less an issue, as many of those leaving are young families.

27 Ta Kung Pao, June 14; Wen Wei Po, Sept, 19 and 20; Ta Kung Pao, August 12; quoted from Ying, ibid. (2021), 125, 129, and 119.

28 Madsen, "Civil Societies and Christianities" (2021), 28.

29 McKeown, "Hong Kong priest: China trying to control religion in Hong Kong." *Catholic News Agency.* April 26, 2022.

30 Ying, "Entanglement between Religion and Politics" (2021), 127.

31 Chow and Tse, "Almost democratic" (2016), 265.

32 Madsen, "Civil Societies and Christianities" (2021), 29–30.

33 Nedilsky, *Converts to Civil Society*, 26. For the following, see particularly 32–63.

34 See for this Kung, "Parent–Child and Center-Edge Metaphors" (2019) and Guo, "So Many Mothers, So Little Love" (2022).

35 Kung, ibid., 394.

36 Westendorp, "Belonging to a global family of God" (2017), 117.

37 Kung, "Crucified People, Messianic Time" (2021), 142.

38 "Occupy Central Trio's Letter to the Hong Kong People," December 2, 2014, quoted from S.H. Chan, "Christians and Building Civil Society" (2021a), 223–224.

39 Slightly edited excerpt from mitigation speech, CitizenNews 7. April 2021 www.hkcnews.com/article/40085/831-%E6%9C%AA%E7%B6%93%E6%8 9%B9%E5%87%86%E9%9B%86%E7%B5%90-40085/lee-cheuk-yan-i-plead-guilty-but-i%E2%80%99ve-done-no-wrong.

40 Personal conversation, recounted with permission.

41 See also the story recounted by Bruce Lui, a veteran journalist, quoted in S.H. Chan, "Christians and Building Civil Society" (2021a), 200.

42 See also the thoughtful reflection on the "demonic" in Yip, "For Our Struggle Is Not Against Flesh and Blood" (2021), 109–116.

43 Conversation with a prisoner, March 2021.

Chapter 8

1 See overall Marsh a.o. (eds.), *Lived Theology* (2016), 8.

2 For an extended discussion see Brandner, "The Church as Family" (2019), 217–223 and above, Chapter 2.

3 "Zai Yesu li, women shi yi jia ren" (在耶穌裡我們是一家人) and "women chengwei yi jia ren" (我們成為一家).

4 Yang, *Religion in Chinese Society*, 76-80; Brandner, "Pentecostals in the Public Sphere" (2017), 132. See also Chapter 5.

5 See also Constable, *Christian Souls and Chinese Spirits* (1994), 99.

6 See overall Brandner, "Premillennial and Countercultural Faith" (2011), 14–21.

7 For the following, and offering plenty of examples from local bereavement practice, see Kwan, "Decolonizing 'Protestant' Death Rituals" (2021) and Kwan, "Hope for the Dead" (2010).

8 Yim Sung-bihn and Kang Namsoon, keynote presentations at the Global Ecumenical Theological Institute, Seoul and Busan, October 25 to November 9, 2013.

9 Kwan, "I leave peace to you [Chin.]" (2022), 3.

10 For this early period, see Kwan and England, "Contextual Theology in Hong Kong" (2004), 230–243; Yu, "Theological Development [Chin.]" (1998), 104–117.

11 Kwan and England, ibid., 239.

12 See Ying, "Chung Chi in the Development of Chinese Theological Education" (2014) and https://youtu.be/s7ahiVpU0K8.

13 See Yao, *Fundamentalist Movement among Protestant Missionaries* (2003), 101–182.

14 See for instance Fung, *Evangelistically Yours* (1992), 1–2 (1982).

15 Yu, "Theological Development [Chin.]" (1998), 123.

16 "Proposed Statements of Faith for Hong Kong Christians in the Face of Social and Political Change." Quoted from Leung and Chan, *Changing Church and State Relations* (2003), 162 and 164.

17 See on the following H.L. Wong, "Hong Kong Protestant Theologies" (2022), 7–11.

18 For a critical discussion of Yeung's position, see Kung, "Parent–Child and Center-Edge Metaphors" (2019), 400–401.

19 W.C. Wong, *The Poor Woman (1997)*, 274–281, 289.

20 Sugirtarajah, *Asian Biblical Hermeneutics and Postcolonialism* (1998), 17.

21 C.C. Lee, "Biblical Interpretation in Asian Perspectives" (1993).

22 C.C. Lee, "The Divine–Human Encounter" (2018), 370.

23 C.C. Lee, "Cross-Textual Interpretation" (2019).

24 P.L. Kwok, "Response to Archie Lee's Paper on 'Biblical Interpretation in Postcolonial Hong Kong'" (1999), 183.

25 Quotes from P.L. Kwok, *Introducing Asian Feminist Theology* (2000), 38, 17, and 46; see overall 65ff.

26 C.C. Lee, "Returning to China" (1999), 157.

27 Ibid.

28 Rey Chow, quoted in Lee, ibid., 157–158.

29 Kwan, "Decolonizing 'Protestant' Death Rituals" (2021), 248–249; Kwan, "Theological Indigenisation" (2009).

30 W.C. Wong, "Negotiating between Two Patriarchies" (2014), 159 and 162; W.C. Wong, "Negotiating Gender Identity" (2003), 171.

31 W.C. Wong, ibid., (2003), 155–169.

32 Kwan, "Theological Indigenisation" (2009), 25; Bhabha, *The Location of Culture* (1994), 122–123.

33 Richard Madsen (1993), quoted in Nedilsky, "The Liberalizing Role of Startups" (2021), 173.

34 H.N. Yeung, "On the idea of mission" (2022), 20.

35 For an overview, see the introductory chapter of Lai and Lam in their edited volume *Sino-Christian Theology* (2010), 1–17, and the chapters of Lai, "Theological Translation" 83–99, and Lam, "Emergence of Scholars" 21–33 in the same volume; further, Lam, "Is Sino-Christian Theology Truly "Theology"?" (2020), 97–119.

36 Kwan, "I leave peace to you [Chin.]" (2022), 4.

Bibliography

Allen, Richard B. "Asian Indentured Labor in the 19th and Early 20th Century Colonial Plantation World." *Oxford Research Encyclopedia of Asian History*. March 29, 2017. https://oxfordre.com/asianhistory/view/10.1093/acrefore/9780190277727.001.0001/acrefore-9780190277727-e-33.

Anderson, Allan Heaton. *An Introduction to Pentecostalism: Global Charismatic Christianity*. 2nd ed. Cambridge: Cambridge University Press, 2013.

Au, Connie Ho Yan. "The Pentecostal Holiness Church's Mission in the Anti-Christian Movement in China (1920–30)." *Asian Journal of Pentecostal Studies* 14:1 (2011), 27–55.

Au, Connie Ho Yan. "From Collaborations with Missionaries to Independence: An Early History of the Hong Kong Pentecostal Mission (1907–1930)." In *Asia Pacific Pentecostalism*, edited by Denise A. Austin, Jacqueline Grey, and Paul W. Lewis. Leiden: Brill, 2019. https://doi.org/10.1163/9789004396708_006

Au, Connie Ho Yan. "Hong Kong." In *Brill's Encyclopedia of Global Pentecostalism Online*, edited by Michael Wilkinson, Connie Au, Jörg Haustein, and Todd M. Johnson. Leiden: Brill, 2021a. doi:http://dx.doi.org/10.1163/2589-3807_EGPO_COM_033768.

Au, Connie Ho Yan. "Mok, Lai Chi." In *Brill's Encyclopedia of Global Pentecostalism Online*, edited by Michael Wilkinson, Connie Au, Jörg Haustein, and Todd M. Johnson. Leiden: Brill, 2021b. doi:http://dx.doi.org/10.1163/2589-3807_EGPO_COM_038294.

Bays, Daniel H. *A New History of Christianity in China*. Chichester, West Sussex; Malden, MA: Wiley-Blackwell, 2012.

Bebbington, David W. *Evangelicalism in Modern Britain: A History from the 1730s to the 1980s*. London and New York: Routledge, 2005 [1989].

Bhabha Homi K. *The Location of Culture*. London: Routledge, 1994.

Bianchi, Eugene C. "Secular Ecumenism." *Thought: Fordham University Quarterly* 44, no.1 (1969): 83–99.

Bosch, David J. *Transforming Mission: Paradigm Shifts in Theology of Mission*. New York: Orbis, 1991.

Brandner, Tobias. "Mission, Millennium, and Politics: A Continuation of the History of Salvation—from the East." *Missiology: An International Review* 37, no. 3 (2009): 317–332.

Brandner, Tobias. "Premillennial and Countercultural Faith and its Production and Reception in the Chinese Context." *Asian Journal of Pentecostal Studies* 14, no. 1 (2011): 3–26.

Brandner, Tobias. "Pentecostals in the Public Sphere: Between Counterculturalism and Adaptation (Observations from the Chinese Context in Hong Kong)." *PentecoStudies* 16, no. 1 (2017): 117–137.

Brandner, Tobias. "A Besieged Boom: Christianity in China." *Theology Today* 76, no. 3 (2019): 194–199.

Brandner, Tobias. "The Church as Family: Strengths and Dangers of the Family Paradigm of Christianity in Chinese Contexts." *Theology Today* 76, no. 3 (2019): 217–223.

Brandner, Tobias. "Emerging Christianity in Cambodia: People Movement to Christ or Playground for Global Christianity?" *International Bulletin of Mission Research* 44, no. 3 (2020): 279–289.

Bray, Denis. "Growing up in China: Lecture to the Royal Asiatic Society Hong Kong Branch, 14 May 1993." *Journal of the Royal Asiatic Society Hong Kong Branch* 32 (1992): 199–213.

Brown, Deborah A. "Hong Kong's Catholic Church and the Challenge of Democratization in the Special Administrative Region." In *Religious Organizations and Democratization. Case Studies from Contemporary Asia*, edited by Tun-Jen Cheng and Deborah A. Brown, 180–220. Armonk, NY: M.E. Sharpe, 2006.

Carroll, John M. *A Concise History of Hong Kong*. Lanham, MD: Rowman & Littlefield, 2007.

Census and Statistics Department Hong Kong. "Hong Kong Statistics 1947–1967," www.censtatd.gov.hk/en/data/stat_report/product/B1010003/att/B10100031967AN67E0100.pdf

Cham, Sha 沙沙. *"Heiye jin chu shi liming: Miao jie mushi Li Zhen Man he yixie miao jie ren de gushi"* 黑夜盡處是黎明：「廟街牧師」黎振滿和一些廟街人的故事 [*Dawn Finally Comes After the Long Dark Night. The Stories of Temple Street Pastor Sam Lai and Some People in Temple Street*]. Hong Kong: Yue Niao Wen Hua 越鳥文化, 2003.

Chan, Chi-Hang Louis 陳智衡. *"Heyi fei yilü: Zhonghua Jidujiaohui lishi"* 合一非一律：中華基督教會歷史 [*Unity without uniformity. History of the Church of Christ in China*]. Hong Kong: Alliance Bible Seminary 建道神學院, 2013.

Chan, Chi-Hang Louis 陳智衡. "Teng Jin Hui Mushi dui jiaohui heyi de gongxian." 滕近輝牧師對教會合一的貢獻 [The contribution of Philip Teng to an alternative ecumenism among Chinese churches]. *Jiandao xuekan* 建道學刊 45 (2016): 93–104.

Chan, Judy. *No Strangers Here. Christian Hospitality and Refugee Ministry in Twenty-First-Century Hong Kong*. Eugene, OR: Pickwick Publications, 2017.

Chan, Kim-kwong. "The Indigenous Mission Movement from China." *ChinaSource*, April 13, 2013. www.chinasource.org/resource-library/articles/the-indigenous-mission-movement-from-china-a-historical-review/.

Chan, Shun Hing. "The Making of Religious Universe: A Study of a Charismatic Church in Hong Kong." PhD diss., The Chinese University of Hong Kong, 1995.

Chan, Shun Hing. "Xianggang Jidujiao shehui fuli shiye de fazhan 香港基督教社會福利事業的發展 [The Development of Christian Social Services in Hong Kong]." *CGST Journal* 中國神學研究院期刊 25, no. 7 (1998): 65–85.

Chan, Shun Hing. "Christian Social Discourse in Postcolonial Hong Kong." *Postcolonial Studies* 10, no. 4 (2007): 447–466.

Chan, Shun Hing. "Governance Crisis and Social Mobilization of the Christian Churches in Hong Kong." In *Politics and Government in Hong Kong*, edited by Ming Sing, 72–98. London: Routledge, 2008.

Chan, Shun Hing. "Governance and Public Policy under the Donald Tsang Administration — Critical Voices from the Christian Community in Hong Kong." In *The Second Chief Executive of Hong Kong SAR: Evaluating the Tsang Years 2005-2012*, edited by Joseph Y.S. Cheng, 171–197. Hong Kong: City University of Hong Kong Press, 2013.

Chan, Shun Hing. "Christians and Building Civil Society in Hong Kong. The Case of the Occupy Movement." In *Citizens of Two Kingdoms: Civil Society and Christian Religion in Greater China*, edited by Shun-hing Chan and Jonathan W. Johnson, 201–229. Leiden: Brill, 2021.

Chan, Shun Hing. "The Political Influence of Mainline Protestant Churches in Hong Kong." *China Review* 21, no. 4 (2021): 225–258.

Chan, Simon K.H. *Pentecostal Ecclesiology. An Essay on the Development of Doctrine*. Blandford Forum, Dorset, England: Deo Publishing, 2011.

Chan, Yuk Wah. "Where to Die? Death Management and the Politics of Death Space in Hong Kong." In *Religion, Place and Modernity: Spatial Articulations in Southeast Asia and East Asia*, edited by Michael Dickhardt and Andrea Lauser, 312–342. Leiden: Brill, 2016.

Chan-Yeung, Moira M.W. *The Practical Prophet: Bishop Ronald O. Hall of Hong Kong and His Legacies*. Hong Kong: Hong Kong University Press, 2015.

Cheng, Claudia. "Rick Warren's Saddleback Church Pushes Beyond U.S. Borders." *Gospel Herald*, 5 Oct 2013.

Cheung, J. T. K., V. W. Y. Tsoi, K. H. K. Wong, and R. Y. Chung. "Abuse and Depression among Filipino Foreign Domestic Helpers. A Cross-sectional Survey in Hong Kong." *Public Health* 166 (2019): 121–27.

Choa, Gerald Hugh. *The Life and Times of Sir Kai Ho Kai: A Prominent Figure in Nineteenth-century Hong Kong*. Hong Kong: Chinese University Press, 2000.

Chow, Christie Chui-Shan, and Joseph Tse-Hei Lee. "Almost Democratic: Christian Activism and the Umbrella Movement in Hong Kong." *Exchange* 45, no. 3 (2016): 252–268.

Chu, Lui Julia 朱蕾. "'Xianggang Jidu Xinjiao de jichu shehuixue yanjiu' dingliang fenxi baogao. 「香港基督新教的基礎社會學研究」定量分析報告 [Quantitative Analysis Report on 'Basic Sociological Research on Protestantism in Hong Kong']" In *Pastoral Conference Series II: The Vocation of Pastoral Ministry: Theology, Spirituality, and Practices*, edited by Simon Siu Chuen Lee, 126–147. Hong Kong: The Divinity School of Chung Chi College, 2009.

Coakley, Jay J. *Sports in Society: Issues and Controversies*. Eleventh edition. New York, NY: McGraw-Hill Education, 2015.

Constable, Nicole. *Christian Souls and Chinese Spirits. A Hakka Community in Hong Kong*. Berkeley, Los Angeles, London: University of California Press, 1994.

Constable, Nicole. "Telling Tales of Migrant Workers in Hong Kong: Transformations of Faith, Life Scripts, and Activism." *The Asia Pacific Journal of Anthropology* 11, no. 3–4 (2010): 311–329.

Coomans, Thomas. "Sinicising Christian Architecture in Hong Kong: Father Gresnigt, Catholic Indigenisation, and the South China Regional Seminary, 1927–31." *Journal of the Royal Asiatic Society Hong Kong Branch* 56 (2016): 133–160.

Coomans, Thomas, and Puay-peng Ho. "Architectural Styles and Identities in Hong Kong: The Chinese and Western Designs for St Teresa's Church in

Kowloon Tong, 1928–32." *Journal of the Royal Asiatic Society Hong Kong Branch* 58 (2018): 81–109.

Cornelio, Jayeel Serrano. "Jesus is Lord. The Indigenization of Megachurch Christianity in the Philippines." In *Pentecostal Megachurches in Southeast Asia. Negotiating Class, Consumption and the Nation*, edited by Terence Chong, 127–155. Singapore: ISEAS–Yusof Ishak Institute, 2018.

Cox, Harvey. *Fire from Heaven. The Rise of Pentecostal Spirituality and the Reshaping of Religion in the Twenty-first Century*. Reading, Massachusetts: Addison-Wesley, 1995.

Cruz, Gemma Tulud. "Em-body-ing Theology. Theological Reflections on the Experiences of Filipina Domestic Workers in Hong Kong." In *Body and Sexuality: Theological-Pastoral Perspectives of Women in Asia*, edited by Agnes M. Brazal and Andrea Lizares Si, 60–74. Manila: Ateneo de Manila University Press, 2007.

Cruz, Gemma Tulud. "It Cuts Both Ways: Religion and Filipina Domestic Workers in Hong Kong." In *Gender, Religion, and Migration: Pathways of Integration*, edited by Glenda Tibe Bonifacio and Vivienne S.M. Angeles, 17–36. Lanham, MD: Lexington Books, 2010.

Department of Intercultural Studies, Alliance Bible Seminary. Eds. 建道神學院跨越文化研究系主編. "*Zhouliu sifang: Wushi zhi liushi niandai Jiandao xiaoyou de xuanjiao*" 周流四方：五十至六十年代建道校友的宣教 *[Chinese missionaries on the move: ABS graduates in world mission, 1950s-1960s]*. Hong Kong: Alliance Bible Seminary 建道神學院, 2017.

Douglas, James Dixon (ed.). *Let the Earth Hear His Voice. Official Reference Volume. International Congress on World Evangelism, Lausanne*. Minneapolis: World Wide Publications, 1975.

Eitel, Ernest J. *Europe in China. The History of Hong Kong from the Beginning to the Year 1882*. London and Hong Kong: Luzac & Company and Kelly & Walsh, 1895.

Elliot, Elsie. *An Autobiography. Rev. Edition*. Hong Kong: Longman, 1988.

Elliot, Elsie. *Colonial Hong Kong in the Eyes of Elsie Tu*. Hong Kong: Hong Kong University Press, 2003.

Ellis, James. "Anglican Indigenization and Contextualization in Colonial Hong Kong: Comparative Case Studies of St. John's Cathedral and St. Mary's Church." *Mission Studies* 36, no. 2 (2019): 219–246.

Etherington, Norman. "Schools and Education in the Missionary Enterprise." In *The Wiley Blackwell Companion to World Christianity*, edited by Lamin Sanneh and Michael J. McClymond Malden, 166–175. Oxford, UK: Wiley, 2016.

Fan, Guo Guang 范國光. "Bawo shidai jiyu. Rang Xianggang Xuandaohui zhou gengyuan de lu" 把握時代機遇—— 讓香港宣道會走更遠的路 [Seize the Opportunity of this Era, Set the Longer Path for Hong Kong C&MA]. *XuanXun* 宣訊 1 (2020): 1.

Fuentes, Philip Lajo. "A Phenomenological Understanding of the Interplay between the Lived Experiences and the Christian Faith of the Catholic OFW Mothers in Hong Kong in the Light of the Catholic Church's Pastoral Theology of Migration." PhD diss., The Chinese University of Hong Kong, 2021.

Fukushima, Ayako, and Yoshitake Doi. "The Building Process and the Laity Involvement of Our Lady of Mount Carmel Church in Wanchai." *Journal of*

Architecture and Building Science. Architectural Institute of Japan 78, no. 688 (2013): 1431–1440.

Fung, Raymond. *Evangelistically Yours. Ecumenical Letters on Contemporary Evangelism*. Geneva: WCC Publications, 1992.

Fung, Raymond. *The Gospel is not for Sale. The Story of the Hong Kong Christian Industrial Committee*. Hong Kong: Hong Kong Christian Industrial Committee, 2005.

Gimelli, Louis B. "Borne upon the Wings of Faith": The Chinese Odyssey of Henrietta Hall Shuck, 1835–1844." *Journal of the Early Republic* 14, no. 2 (1994): 221–245.

Goh, Daniel P.S. "State and Social Christianity in Post-Colonial Singapore." *Sojourn: Journal of Social Issues in Southeast Asia* 25, no. 1 (2010): 54–89.

Gordon-Conwell Theological Seminary. *Christianity in its Global Context, 1970–2020: Society, Religion and Mission*. South Hamilton, MA: Center for the Study of Global Christianity, 2013.

Guo, Ting. "So Many Mothers, So Little Love": Discourse of Motherly Love and Parental Governance in 2019 Hong Kong Protests." *Method & Theory in the Study of Religion* 34, no. 1–2 (2021): 3–24.

Ha, Keloon Louis. *The Foundation of the Catholic Mission in Hong Kong, 1841–1894*. Hong Kong: University of Hong Kong, 1998.

Ha, Keloon Louis. *The History of Evangelization in Hong Kong. Wun Yiu, Ting Kok, Yim Tin Tsai*. Hong Kong: The Diocesan Ad Hoc Committee for the Year of Evangelization, 2006.

He, Zhibin 何志彬. "*Yundong yu rensheng: Yesu jiao wo da paiqiu (Daoshi ben)*" 運動與人生：耶穌教我打排球 (導師本) [Sports and life: Jesus taught me volleyball (teacher edition)]. Hong Kong: Hancheng wenhua youxian gongsi 漢域文化有限公司, 2011.

Heaver, Stuart. "The Abandoned Churches of Sai Kung: How Italian Missionaries Established Hakka Congregations in Hong Kong." *SCMP Magazine*, 27 Feb 2016.

Hirono, Miwa. *Civilizing Missions. International Religious Agencies in China*. New York: Palgrave Macmillan, 2008.

Ho, Ben Siu-pun. "A Critical Review of Events during the Hong Kong Protests of 2019." In *The Hong Kong Protests and Political Theology*, edited by Pui-Lan Kwok and Francis Ching-Wah Yip, 15–37. London: Rowman and Littlefield, 2021.

Ho, Wing-Ki. "Contemporary Christian Music in Hong Kong: Mediating Religion through Song, Performance and Stardom." PhD diss., The Chinese University of Hong Kong, 2011.

Hong Kong Association of Christian Missions. *"Polang qianxing:2020 Nianbao"* 破浪前行: 2020 年報 [Breaking the Waves: 2020 Annual Report]. Hong Kong: Hong Kong Association of Christian Missions, 2021.

Hong Kong Christian Council and Divinity School of Chung Chi College, The Chinese University of Hong Kong. *Xianggang Shimin Dui Jidujiao de Guangan Diaocha baogao 2021* 香港市民對基督教的觀感調查報告 2021 [Survey Report on Public Perception of Protestantism in Hong Kong 2021]. Hong Kong: Hong Kong Christian Council, 2022.

Huang, Yuqin, and I-hsin Hsiao. "Chinese Evangelists on the Move: Space, Authority, and Ethnicisation among Overseas Chinese Protestant Christians." *Social Compass* 62, no. 3 (2015): 379–395.

Hung, Shin Fung. "From Singing 'Out-of-tone' to Producing Contextualized Cantonese Hymns: Hong Kong in the Decentralization of Chinese Christianity." Paper presented at AAR Annual Meetings, Denver, CO, November 22, 2021a.

Hung, Shin Fung. "'If Not Us, Who?' Youth Participation and Salient Aspects of the Protests." In *The Hong Kong Protests and Political Theology*, edited by Pui-Lan Kwok and Francis Ching-Wah Yip, 55–74. London: Rowman and Littlefield, 2021b.

Iap, Sian-chin 葉先秦. "Huaren Wuxunjiepai zili jiaohui de xiansheng he fanxing——Gangjiu Wuxunjie hui yu Jiulong Wuxunjie hui" 華人五旬節派自立教會的先聲和範型——港九五旬節會與九龍五旬節會 [A Pioneer and Paradigm of Chinese Independent Pentecostal Churches: The Pentecostal Mission, Hong Kong and Kowloon]. *Logos & Pneuma: Chinese Journal of Theology* 基督教文化評論 54 (2021): 62–100.

Kang, Jong Hyuk David. "Trained to Care: The Institutionalization of Nursing in Hong Kong (1887–1900)." In *The Church as Safe Haven: Christian Governance in China*, edited by Lars Peter Laamann and Joseph Tse-Hei Lee, 152–175. Leiden: Brill, 2018.

Kang, Namsoon. "Reclaiming Theological Significance of Women's Religious Choice-in-Differential: Korean Women's Choice of Christianity Revisited." *Journal of World Christianity* 3, no. 1 (2010): 18–46.

Kao, Ernest. "Private Columbarium Operators face Stricter Financial Regulations as Government tries to address Hong Kong's shortage of urn spaces." *South China Morning Post*, November 16, 2018.

Keegan, Matthew. "Hong Kong Real Estate now More Expensive for the Dead than the Living." *The Guardian*. April 23, 2019.

Klaver, Miranda. *Hillsong Church: Expansive Pentecostalism, Media, and the Global City* (Palgrave Studies in Lived Religion and Societal Challenges). Cham, Switzerland: Palgrave Macmillan, 2021.

Ko, Tim-keung. "A Review of Development of Cemeteries in Hong Kong: 1841–1950." *Journal of the Hong Kong Branch of the Royal Asiatic Society* 41 (2001): 241–280.

Kung, Lap Yan. "Parent–Child and Center-Edge Metaphors: A Theological Engagement with the Social Imaginary of 'One Country, Two Systems'." *Political Theology* 20, no. 5 (2019): 392–410.

Kung, Lap Yan. "Crucified People, Messianic Time, and Youth in Protest." In *The Hong Kong Protests and Political Theology*, edited by Pui-Lan Kwok and Francis Ching-Wah Yip, 133–147. London: Rowman and Littlefield, 2021.

Kwan, Shui-Man Simon. "Theological Indigenisation as Anti-Colonialist Resistance: A Chinese Conception of the Christian God as a Case Study." *Studies in World Christianity* 15, no. 1 (2009): 22–50.

Kwan, Shui-Man Simon. "Hope for the Dead: Protestant Death Rituals and the Psychology of the Continuing Bond." *International Journal of the Humanities* 8, no. 9 (2010): 1–14.

Kwan, Shui-Man Simon. "Hong Kong." In *World Christian Encyclopedia. Third edition*, edited by Todd M. Johnson and Gina A. Zurlo, 372–375. Edinburgh: Edinburgh University Press, 2020.

Kwan, Shui-Man Simon. "Decolonizing 'Protestant' Death Rituals for the Chinese Bereaved: Negotiating a Resistance that is Contextually Relevant." *International Journal of Practical Theology* 25, no. 2 (2021): 243–262.

Kwan, Shui-Man Simon. "Wo liuxia ping an gei nimen 我留下平安給你們" [I leave peace to you]. *Divinity School of Chung Chi College Newsletter* 73 (2022): 1–5.

Kwan, Shui-Man Simon and John C. England "Contextual Theology in Hong Kong." In *Asian Christian Theologies. Research Guide to Authors, Movements, Sources. Volume 3*, edited by John C. England et al., 216–292. Delhi: ISPCK; Quezon City: Claretian Publishers; Maryknoll, NY: Orbis Books, 2004.

Kwok, Nai-Wang. *Hong Kong 1997: A Christian Perspective*. Hong Kong: Christian Conference of Asia, Urban Rural Mission, 1991.

Kwok, Nai-Wang. *Hong Kong Braves 1997*. Hong Kong: Hong Kong Christian Institute, 1994.

Kwok, Pui-Lan. "Response to Archie Lee's Paper On 'Biblical Interpretation in Postcolonial Hong Kong'." *Biblical Interpretation* 7, no. 2 (1999): 182–186.

Kwok, Pui-Lan. *Introducing Asian Feminist Theology (Introductions in Feminist Theology, 4)*. Sheffield: Sheffield Academic Press, 2000.

Kwok, Pui-Lan, and Francis Ching-Wah Yip (eds.). *The Hong Kong Protests and Political Theology*. London, UK: Rowman & Littlefield, 2021.

Kwok, Wai Luen 郭偉聯. "Qishi niandai Xianggang fuyin pai qingnian jidutu zhi shehui canyu." 七十年代香港福音派青年基督徒之社會參與 [The Social Participation of Hong Kong Young Evangelicals in the Seventies.] *CGST Journal* no. 32 (2002): 145–190.

Kwong, Paul, and Philip Wickeri. "Sheng Kung Hui: The Contextualization of Anglicanism in Hong Kong." In *The Oxford Handbook of Anglican Studies*, edited by Mark Chapman, Sathianathan Clarke, and Martyn Percy, 256–270. Oxford, UK: Oxford University Press, 2016.

Lai, Catherine. "God or Mammon? Who Gains When Hong Kong's Historic Churches Are Turned into Blocks of Flats." *Hong Kong Free Press*, November 19, 2017.

Lai, Pan-Chiu. "Theological Translation and Transmission between China and the West." In *Sino-Christian Theology. A Theological Qua Cultural Movement in Contemporary China*, edited by Lai Pan-Chiu and Jason Lam, 83–99. Frankfurt am Main: Peter Lang, 2010.

Lai, Pan-Chiu and Jason Lam. "Retrospect and Prospect of Sino-Christian Theology: An Introduction." In *Sino-Christian Theology. A Theological Qua Cultural Movement in Contemporary China*, edited by Lai Pan-Chiu and Jason Lam, 1–17. Frankfurt am Main: Peter Lang, 2010.

Lam, Jason Tsz Shun. "The Emergence of Scholars Studying Christianity in Mainland China. In *Sino-Christian Theology. A Theological Qua Cultural Movement in Contemporary China*, edited by Lai Pan-Chiu and Jason Lam, 21–33 Frankfurt am Main: Peter Lang, 2010.

Lam, Jason Tsz Shun. "Is Sino-Christian Theology Truly 'Theology'? Problematizing Sino-Christian Theology as a Public Theology." *International Journal of Public Theology* 14, no. 1 (2020): 97–119.

Lau, Siu Lun 劉紹麟. "*Jiema Xianggang Jidujiao yu shehui mailuo: Xianggang jiaohui yu shehui de hongguan hudong*" 解碼香港基督教與社會脈絡：香港教會與社會的宏觀互動 [The interaction of the church and society in Hong Kong]. Hong Kong: Chinese Christian Literature Council 基督教文藝出版社, 2008.

Law Yin-Bun 羅彥彬. "*Lixianhui zai huachuan jiaoshi (1847–1947)*" 禮賢會在華傳教史 (1847–1947) [The Missionary History of the Rhenish Church in China

(1847–1947)]. Hong Kong: The Chinese Rhenish Church Hong Kong Synod 中華基督教禮賢會香港區會, 1968.

Lee, Archie Chi-Chung. "Biblical Interpretation in Asian Perspective." *Asia Journal of Theology* 7, no. 1 (1993): 35–39.

Lee, Archie Chi-Chung. "Returning to China: Biblical Interpretation in Postcolonial Hong Kong." *Biblical interpretation* 7, no. 2 (1999): 156–173.

Lee, Archie Chi-Chung. "Cross-Textual Interpretation as Postcolonial Strategy in Bible Translation in Asia." In *The Oxford Handbook of Postcolonial Biblical Criticism*, edited by R.S. Sugirtharajah (online edn, Oxford Academic, November 7, 2018). https://doi.org/10.1093/oxfordhb/9780190888459.013.16

Lee, Archie Chi-Chung. "The Divine–Human Encounter in the Hebrew Wisdom of the Writings and the Confucian Analects." In *The Oxford Handbook of the Writings of the Hebrew Bible*, edited by Donn F. Morgan, 369–383. London and Oxford: Oxford University Press, 2018.

Lee, Miriam. "Cultural and Historical Studies for Pui O, Shui Hau and Neighbouring Areas at Lantau. Additional Scope on Yi Tung Shan." Draft Report v1 (unpublished). Chinese University of Hong Kong, 2021.

Lee, Tse-Hei Joseph. "Despair and Hope: Political Cinema in Hong Kong." In *Hong Kong and Bollywood: Globalization of Asian Cinemas,* edited by Joseph Tse-Hei Lee and Satish Kolluri, 69–84. New York, NY: Palgrave Macmillan, 2016.

Lee, Tse-Hei Joseph. "Christian Witness and Resistance in Hong Kong: Faith-based Activism from the Umbrella Movement to the Anti-Extradition Struggle." *Tamkang Journal of International Affairs* 24, no. 3 (2021): 95–140.

Lee, Yiu-Chuen. "Li xu 李序 [Preface]." In He, Zhibin. *Yundong yu rensheng: Yesu jiao wo da paiqiu (Daoshi ben)* 運動與人生：耶穌教我打排球（導師本） *[Sports and life: Jesus taught me volleyball (teacher edition)]*. Hong Kong: Hancheng wenhua youxian gongsi 漢域文化有限公司, 2011.

Leung, Beatrice. "Church—State Relations in Hong Kong and Macau: From Colonial Rule to Chinese Rule." *Citizenship Studies* 5, no. 2 (2001): 203–219.

Leung, Beatrice. "China's Religious Freedom Policy: The Art of Managing Religious Activity." *The China Quarterly* 184 (2005): 894–913.

Leung, Beatrice. "The Hong Kong Catholic Church: A Framing Role in Social Movement." In *Social Movements in China and Hong Kong: The Expansion of Protest Space*, edited by Khun Eng Kuah-Pearce and Gilles Guiheux, 245–258. Amsterdam University Press, 2009. www.jstor.org/stable/j.ctt46mxv6.16.

Leung, Beatrice and Shun-hing Chan. *Changing Church and State Relations in Hong Kong, 1950–2000*. Hong Kong: Hong Kong University Press 2003.

Leung, Ka-Lun 梁家麟. "Ershi shiji huaren fuyin xinyang zhe de mianpu——Teng Jin Hui Mushi de sixiang he shigong" 二十世紀華人福音信仰者的面譜——滕近輝牧師的思想和事工 [The Portrait of a Chinese Evangelical of the 20th Century—Pastor Philip Teng's Thought and Ministry]. *Jiandao xuekan* 建道學刊 45 (2016): 1–52.

Leung, Kwong-hon. "The Impact of Mission Schools in Hong Kong (1842–1905) on Traditional Chinese Education. A Comparative Study." PhD diss., Institute of Education, University of London, 1987.

Lian, Xi. *Redeemed by Fire: The Rise of Popular Christianity in Modern China*. New Haven, CT: Yale University Press, 2010.

Lim, Swee Hong. "Nashville and Sidney Are Not the World: The Transnational Migration of Sources for Contemporary Chinese Praise & Worship Songs." In

Essays on the History of Contemporary Praise and Worship. edited by Lester Ruth, 146–159. Eugene, OR: Wipf and Stock, 2020.

Liu, Tat Fong Agnes. "Conversion of the Urban Poor." In *Sharing the Good News with the Poor. A Reader for Concerned Christians*, edited by B.J. Nicholls and B.R. Wood, 230–240. Grand Rapids, MI: Baker Book House, 1996.

Liu, Yi. "Pentecostal-Style Christians in the "Galilee of China." *Review of Religion and Chinese Society* 1, no. 2 (2014): 156–172.

Lo, Lung-Kwong. "Taiwan, Hong Kong, Macau." In *Christianities in Asia*, edited by Peter C. Phan, 173–195. Malden, MA: Wiley-Blackwell, 2011.

Lowe, Kate. "The Beliefs, Aspirations and Methods of the First Missionaries in British Hong Kong, 1841-5." *Studies in Church History Subsidia* 13 (2000): 50–64.

Lutz, Jessie G. "Chinese Emigrants, Indentured Workers, and Christianity in the West Indies, British Guiana and Hawaii." *Caribbean Studies* 37, no. 2 (2009): 133–154.

Lutz, Jessie G. "Women's Education and Social Mobility." In *Pioneer Chinese Christian Women. Gender, Christianity, and Social Mobility*, edited by Jessie G. Lutz, 393–420. Bethlehem: Lehigh University Press, 2010.

Lutz, Jessie G., and Roland R. Lutz. "Karl Gützlaff's Approach to Indigenization: The Chinese Union." In *Christianity in China: From the Eighteenth Century to the Present*, edited by D.H. Bays, 269–291. Stanford: Stanford University Press, 1996.

Lutz, Jessie G., and Roland R. Lutz. *Hakka Chinese Confront Protestant Christianity, 1850–1900: with the Autobiographies of Eight Hakka Christians, and Commentary.* Armonk, NY: M.E. Sharpe, 1998.

Ma, Julie. "Influence of Pentecostal Spirituality to Asian Christianity." *Asian Journal of Pentecostal Studies* 23 (2020): 107–122.

Madsen, Richard. "Religious policy in China." In *Handbook on Religion in China*, edited by Stephan Feuchtwang, 17–33. Cheltenham: Edward Elgar Publishing, 2020.

Madsen, Richard. "Civil Societies and Christianities in a Diverse and Changing China." In *Citizens of Two Kingdoms: Civil Society and Christian Religion in Greater China*, edited by Shun-hing Chan and Jonathan W. Johnson, 17–31. Leiden: Brill, 2021.

Malek, Roman. "Historiography and Spirituality of Religious Orders and Congregations in the Chinese Context." In *History of Catholic Religious Orders and Missionary Congregations in Hong Kong. Volume Two: Research Papers*, edited by Louis Ha and Patrick Taveirne, 1–26. Hong Kong: Centre for Catholic Studies, The Chinese University of Hong Kong, 2009.

Marsden, George. *Fundamentalism and American Culture.* 2nd Edition. New York: Oxford University Press, 2006.

Marsh, Charles, Peter Slade, and Sarah Azaransky (eds.). *Lived Theology: New Perspectives on Method, Style, and Pedagogy.* New York, NY: Oxford University Press, 2016.

Mason, Laura. "Wilhelm Lobscheid." *Biographical Dictionary of Chinese Christianity.* http://bdcconline.net/en/stories/lobscheid-wilhelm.

Mayfield, Alex R. "Pentecostal Hong Kong: Mapping Mission in Global Pentecostal Discourse, 1907–1942." PhD diss., Boston University, 2021.

McGavran, Donald. *Understanding Church Growth. Third Edition*. Revised and edited by C. Peter Wagner. Grand Rapids, MI: William B. Eerdmans, 1990.

McKeown, Jonah. "Hong Kong Priest: China Trying to Control Religion in Hong Kong." *Catholic News Agency*. April 26, 2022.

Miller, Donald E., and Tetsunao Yamamori. *Global Pentecostalism: The New Face of Christian Social Engagement*. Berkeley: University of California Press, 2007.

Mok, Mo-ching Magdalena. "Challenges of Catholic Schooling in Hong Kong." In *International Handbook of Catholic Education. Challenges for School Systems in the 21st Century*, edited by Gerald R. Grace and Joseph O'Keefe, SJ, 751–769. The Netherlands: Springer, 2007.

Mok, Chan Wing Yan. "Christian Drug Rehabilitation in Hong Kong: Issues in Wholistic Urban Mission." *Transformation* 21, no. 2 (2004): 92–100.

Moon, Sang-Cheol Steve. *The Korean Missionary Movement: Dynamics and Trends, 1988–2013*. Pasadena, CA: William Carey Library, 2016.

Morrissey, Thomas J. *Thomas F. and Ryan SJ: From Cork to China and Windsor Castle, 1889–1971*. Dublin: Columba Press, 2010.

Nagata, Judith. "Christianity among Transnational Chinese: Religious versus (sub) Ethnic Affiliation." *International Migration* 43, no. 3 (2005): 99–130.

Nedilsky, Lida V. *Converts to Civil Society. Christianity and Political Culture in Contemporary Hong Kong*. Waco, TX: Baylor University Press, 2014.

Nedilsky, Lida V. "The Liberalizing Role of Startups in Hong Kong Religion and Politics." In *Citizens of Two Kingdoms: Civil Society and Christian Religion in Greater China*, edited by Shun-hing Chan and Jonathan W. Johnson. Leiden: Brill, 2021. doi: https://doi.org/10.1163/9789004459373_008

Nel, Marius. "Rather Spirit-filled than learned! Pentecostalism's Tradition of Anti-Intellectualism and Pentecostal Theological Scholarship." *Verbum et Ecclesia* 37, no. 1 (2016): 1–9.

Ng, Kwok Kit 吳國傑. "*10 Da Xianggang zongpai xunli: Toushi zhuyao Jidujiao zongpai*" 10 大香港宗派巡禮：透視主要基督教宗派 *[A Tour of Top 10 Hong Kong Denominations: Insights into Major Christian Denominations]*. Hong Kong: Shatin Baptist Church, 2008.

Nissim, Roger. *Land Administration and Practice in Hong Kong*. 3rd Edition. Hong Kong: Hong Kong University Press; London: Eurospan Distributor, 2012.

Olsen, Mahlon Ellsworth. *History of the Origin and Progress of the Seventh-Day Adventists*. Maryland: Review and Herald Publishing Association, 1926.

Ong, Aihwa. *Flexible Citizenship: The Cultural Logics of Transnationality*. Durham, NC: Duke University Press, 1999.

Overman, Steven J. *The Protestant Work Ethic and the Spirit of Sport*. Macon, GA: Mercer University Press, 2011.

Paton, David M. *The Life and Times of Bishop Ronald Hall of Hong Kong*. Hong Kong: Diocesan Association, 1985.

Pavey, Stephen Carl. *Theologies of Power and Crisis: Envisioning / Embodying Christianity in Hong Kong*. American Society of Missiology Monograph Series 10. Eugene, OR: Pickwick Publication, 2011.

Pedersen, Susan. "The Maternalist Moment in British Colonial Policy: The Controversy over 'Child Slavery' in Hong Kong 1917–1941." *Past & Present* 171 (2001): 161–202.

Poon, Alice. "Hong Kong's Land Policy: A Recipe for Social Trouble." *Hong Kong Journal Archive* October 2006, Issue 4, 2011.

Raiser, Konrad. *Ecumenism in Transition: A Paradigm Shift in the Ecumenical Movement?* Geneva: WCC Publications, 1991.

Rawski, Evelyn. "Elementary Education in the Mission Enterprise." *In Christianity in China: Early Protestant Missionary Writings,* edited by Suzanne Wilson Barnett and John King Fairbank, 135–151. Cambridge, MA: Harvard University Press, 1985.

Ray Bakke Centre for Urban Transformation. "How Many Christians Are There in Hong Kong?" September 3, 2018. https://en.bethelhk-rbc.org/researcheng/how-many-christians-are-there-in-hong-kong%3F.

Ray Bakke Centre for Urban Transformation. "Preliminary Report on "Church & Dechurched" Survey." Oct 10, 2018. https://en.bethelhk-rbc.org/researcheng/preliminary-report-on-%E2%80%9Cchurched-%26-dechurched%E2%80%9D-survey.

Ray Bakke Centre for Urban Transformation. "New Expressions of Churches in Hong Kong\\ – Qualitative Research." June 7, 2021. https://en.bethelhk-rbc.org/researcheng/%22new-expressions-of-churches-in-hong-kong%22---qualitative-research.

Ren Bumei 任不寐. „*Zai bian lun. Zhong guo ren liu qin piao dang ji qi jiu shu*" 災變論. 中國人流禽飄蕩及其救贖 [*Catastrophism. Chinese people's restless wandering and redemption*]. Xiang Gang: Guo ji zheng zhu xie hui 国际证主协会 (香港), 2010.

Research Group on 2014 Hong Kong Church Survey. *Report of 2014 Hong Kong English-speaking Church Survey (International Churches)*. Hong Kong: Hong Kong Church Renewal Movement Ltd. 2015.

Research Group on 2019 Hong Kong Church Survey. "2019 *Xianggang jiaohui pucha jianbao*" 2019 香港教會普查簡報 [*Report on 2019 Hong Kong Church Survey*]. Hong Kong: Hong Kong Church Renewal Movement Ltd., 2020.

Research Group on 2019 Hong Kong Church Survey. *Report of 2019 Hong Kong English-speaking Church Survey (International Churches)*. Hong Kong: Hong Kong Church Renewal Movement Ltd., 2021.

Research Group on 2021 Research on Hong Kong Church in the Midst of Crisis. "2021 *Nijing zhong Xianggang jiaohui genjin yanjiu jianbao.*" 2021逆境中香港教會跟進研究簡報. [*Report on 2021 Research on Hong Kong Church in the Midst of Crisis*]. Hong Kong: Hong Kong Church Renewal Movement Ltd., 2021.

Saw, Swee-Hock, and Chiu Wing-Kin. "Population Growth and Redistribution in Hong Kong, 1844–1975." *Southeast Asian Journal of Social Science* 4, no. 1 (1976): 123–131.

Schlatter, Wilhelm. *Geschichte der Basler Mission, 1815–1915: Mit Besonderer Berucksichtigung der ungedruckten Quellen*. Basel: Basler Missionsbuchhandlung, 1916. (Chinese edition: Zhen guang zhao Kejia. Base Chaihui zaoqi lai hua xuanjiao jianshi. 1839–1915. Hong Kong: Tsung Tsin Mission Church, 2008.)

Sharpe, Eric J. *Karl Ludvig Reichelt: Missionary, Scholar and Pilgrim*. Hong Kong: Tao Fong Shan Ecumenical Center, 1984.

Sinn, Elizabeth. *Power and Charity: A Chinese Merchant Elite in Colonial Hong Kong*. Hong Kong: Hong Kong University Press, 2003.

Smith, Carl T. "The Chinese Church, Labour and Elites and the Mui Tsai Question in the 1920's." *Journal of the Hong Kong Branch of the Royal Asiatic Society* (1981): 91–113.

Smith, Carl T. *Chinese Christians: Elites, Middlemen, and the Church in Hong Kong*. Hong Kong: Hong Kong University Press, 2005.

Snelgrove, John H. "Key Factors behind Hong Kong's Millennials Moving to International Churches." DMin diss., Bethel Bible Seminary, 2018.

Snelgrove, John, Natalie Chan, and Kar Yan Alison Hui. "Why Hong Kong Millennial Christians Switch from Chinese Local Churches to International Churches: A Qualitative Study." *Missiology: An International Review* 49, no. 4 (2021): 332–347.

So, Shing Yit Eric. *The Quest for Visible Unity. A Study of the Theological Understandings of Church Unity, from Organic Union to Conciliar Fellowship to Koinonia*. Hong Kong: Divinity School of Chung Chi College, 2021.

Stokes, Lisa Odham and Rachel Braaten. *Historical Dictionary of Hong Kong Cinema*. Second Edition. London: Rowman and Littlefield, 2020.

Sugirtarajah, R.S. *Asian Biblical Hermeneutics and Postcolonialism: Contesting the Interpretations*. Maryknoll, NY: Orbis Books, 1998.

Tam, Jonathan. "Renegotiating Religious Transnationalism: Fractures in Transnational Chinese Evangelicalism." *Global Networks* 19, no. 1 (2019): 66–85.

Tan Jin Huat. "Pentecostal and Charismatic Origins in Malaysia and Singapore." In *Asian and Pentecostal. The Charismatic Face of Christianity in Asia*, edited by Allan Anderson and Edmond Tang, 281–306. Baguio, Philippines: Regnum, 2005.

Teather, Elizabeth K. "High-Rise Homes for the Ancestors: Cremation in Hong Kong." *Geographical Review* 89, no. 3 (1999): 409–430.

Tekenaka, Masao. *The Place Where God Dwells: An Introduction to Church Architecture in Asia*. Hong Kong and Geneva: World Council of Churches, 1995.

Tiedemann, Rolf G. *Reference Guide to Christian Missionary Societies in China: From the 16th to the 20th Centuries*. Armonk, NY: M.E. Sharpe, 2009.

Tong, Wing Sze 湯泳詩. "*Yige huanan Kejia jiaohui de yanjiu: Cong Basehui dao Xianggang Chongzhenhui*" 一個華南客家教會的研究：從巴色會到香港崇眞會 [A Study of the Hakka Church in South China. From the Basel Mission to the Tsung Tsin Mission of Hong Kong]. Hong Kong: Christian Study Centre on Chinese Religion and Culture 基督教中國宗教文化研究社, 2012.

Tong, Wing Sze 湯泳詩. "*Daofeng xing tao: Daofengshan feng wu chi*" 道風行禱：道風山風物志 [Walk and Pray in Tao Fong: A Record of Tao Fong Shan Landscape]. Hong Kong: Tao Fong Shan Christian Center 道風山基督教叢林, 2019.

Tsang, Kwok-wah. "A Study of Bishop Ronald Halls' Contribution (1895–1975) to Hong Kong Education and Social Welfare." Master's diss., The University of Hong Kong, 1993.

Tsang, Steve. *A Modern History of Hong Kong*. Hong Kong: Hong Kong University Press, 2004.

Tse, Justin K.H. and Jonathan Y. Tan (eds.). *Theological Reflections on the Hong Kong Umbrella Movement*. New York, NY: Palgrave Macmillan, 2016.

Währisch-Oblau, Claudia. *The Missionary Self-Perception of Pentecostal/Charismatic Church Leaders from the Global South in Europe: Bringing Back the Gospel*. Leiden: Brill, 2009.

Westendorp, Mariske. "Belonging to a Global Family of God in Hong Kong: the Relevance of Religion in Facing an Uncertain Future." *Asian Anthropology* 16, no. 2 (2017): 116–132.

Wickeri, Philip L. "The Ordination and Ministry of Li Tim Oi. A Historical
   Perspective on a Singular Event." In *Christian Women in Chinese Society. The
   Anglican Story*, edited by Angela Wai Ching Wong and Patricia P.K. Chiu,
   107–127. Hong Kong: Hong Kong University Press, 2018.
Wickeri, Philip L. and Ruiwen Chen. "Contextualization and the Chinese Anglican
   Parish: A Case Study of St. Mary's Church, Hong Kong (1912–41)." In *Christian
   Encounters with Chinese Culture: Essays on Anglican and Episcopal History in
   China*, edited by Philip L. Wickeri, 135–153. Hong Kong: Hong Kong University
   Press, 2015.
Wolfendale, Stuart. *Imperial to International: A History of St. John's Cathedral,
   Hong Kong*. Hong Kong: Hong Kong University Press, 2013.
Wong, Ho Lun Donald. "Hong Kong Protestant Theologies in the 1980s and
   1990s Responding to the Handover of Hong Kong to China." *Asia Journal
   Theology* 36, no. 1 (2022): 1–19.
Wong, M. K. Timothy "A Survey of English and Chinese Sources Materials
   Related to the History of Christianity in Hong Kong," *Ching Feng* 41 no.1
   (1998): 1–40.
Wong, Connie Oi-Yan. "Singing the gospel Chinese style:" Praise and worship"
   music in the Asian Pacific." PhD diss., University of California, Los Angeles,
   2006.
Wong Tze-Ken, Danny. "Chinese Migration to Sabah before the Second World
   War." *Archipel* 58, no. 3 (1999): 131–158.
Wong, Wai Ching Angela. "The Poor Woman: A Critical Analysis of Asian Theology
   and Contemporary Chinese Fiction by Women." PhD diss., University of
   Chicago, 1997.
Wong, Wai Ching Angela. "Negotiating Gender Identity: Postcolonialism and
   Hong Kong Christian Women." In *Gender and Change in Hong Kong:
   Globalization, Postcolonialism, and Chinese Patriarchy*, edited by Eliza Wing-
   Yee Lee, 151–176. Vancouver and Toronto: University of British Colombia
   Press. 2003.
Wong, Wai Ching Angela. "The politics of sexual morality and evangelical
   activism in Hong Kong." *Inter-Asia Cultural Studies* 14, no. 3 (2013):
   340–360.
Wong, Wai Ching Angela. "Negotiating between Two Patriarchies: Chinese
   Christian Women in Postcolonial Hong Kong." In *Gendering Chinese Religion:
   Subject, Identity, and Body*, edited by Jinhua Jia, Xiaofei Kang, and Ping Yao,
   157–179. Albany, NY: State University of New York Press, 2014.
Wong, Wai Ching Angela. "A Distinctive Chinese Contribution. The Ordination of
   the First Five Women Priests in Chung Hua Sheng Kung Hui." In *Christian
   Women in Chinese Society: The Anglican Story*, edited by Angela Wai Ching
   Wong and Patricia P. K. Chiu, 129–153. Hong Kong: Hong Kong University
   Press, 2018.
Wong, Wai-Yin Christina. "An Ecumenical Experiment in Colonial Hong Kong: The
   Start of the Tsuen Wan Ecumenical Social Service Centre (1973 to 1997) and
   Its Local Praxis." *Religions* 10, 294, no. 5 (2019): 1–15.
Wordie, Jason. "The Hong Kong Priest who was the Ultimate China Watcher."
   South China Morning Post, June 6, 2015.
Wu, Rose. *Liberating the Church from Fear: The Story of Hong Kong's Sexual
   Minorities*. Hong Kong: Hong Kong Women Christian Council, 2000.

Yam, Chi-Keung. "Engagement in Television by Protestant Christians in Hong Kong." *Studies in World Christianity* 11, no. 1 (2005): 87–105.

Yam, Chi-Keung. "A Study of Popular Hong Kong Cinema from 2001 to 2004 as Resource for a Contextual Approach to Expressions of Christian Faith in the Public Realm after the Reversion to Chinese Sovereignty in 1997." PhD diss., University of Edinburgh, 2008.

Yam, Chi-Keung. "Regarding the Interplay between Media and Religion in Hong Kong," in *Religion and Media in China: Insights and Case Studies from the Mainland, Taiwan and Hong Kong*, edited by Stefania Travagnin, 35–52. New York: Routledge, 2017.

Yang Ching-Kun. *Religion in Chinese Society: A Study of Contemporary Social Functions of Religion and Some of Their Historical Factors*. Berkeley, CA: University of California Press, 1961.

Yang, Fenggang. "Chinese Christian Transnationalism: Diverse Networks of a Houston Church." In *Religion Across Borders: Transnational Immigrant Networks*, edited by Helen Rose Ebaugh and Janet Saltzman Chafetz, 129–148. New York, Oxford: Altamira Press, 2002.

Yao, Kevin Xiyi. *The Fundamentalist Movement among Protestant Missionaries in China, 1920–1937.* New York: University Press of America, 2003.

Yeung, Arnold 楊牧谷. "*Kuang biao hou de wei sheng: Lingen yu shifeng*" 狂飆後的微聲：靈恩與事奉 [*The Whisper After Cyclonus: Charisma and Diakonia*]. Hong Kong: Ming Feng Press 明風出版, 2003.

Yeung, Hei Nam Daniel. "On the Idea of Mission: Discovering Truth Together with All Truth-Seekers." *Institute of Sino-Christian Studies Newsletter* 20 (2022).

Yeung, Gustav Kwok-Keung. "Constructing Sacred Space under the Forces of the Market: A study of an 'Upper-Floor' Protestant Church in Hong Kong." *Culture and Religion* 12, no. 4 (2011): 401–418.

Yeung, Linda. "Fellowship of the Stars." *South China Morning Post*, September 5, 1994.

Ying Fuk-tsang. 邢福增 "*Yuan ni de guo jianglin—Zhan hou Xianggang 'Jidujiao xin cun' de gean yanjiu*" 願祢的國降臨：戰後香港「基督教新村」的個案研究 [*Your Kingdom Come: A Case Study of the 'Christian Cottage Villages' in Postwar Hong Kong*]. Hong Kong: Alliance Bible Seminary 建道神學院, 2002.

Ying Fuk-tsang. "*Xianggang Jidujiao shi yanjiu daolun*" 香港基督教史研究導論 [*Introduction to Christian Church History of Hong Kong*]. Hong Kong: Alliance Bible Seminary 建道神學院, 2004.

Ying Fuk-tsang. "*Cishi yu tashi zhi jian: Xianggang Jidujiao muchang de lishi yu wenhua*" 此世與他世之間：香港基督教墳場的歷史與文化 [*Between This and the Other Worlds: History and Culture of Hong Kong Christian Cemeteries*]. Hong Kong: Chinese Christian Literature Council 基督教文藝出版社, 2012.

Ying Fuk-tsang. "Chung Chi in the Development of Chinese Theological Education." *Divinity School of Chung Chi College Newsletter* 15 (2014): 1–5.

Ying Fuk-tsang. "R.O. Hall and the Christian Study Centre on Chinese Religion." In *Christian Encounters with Chinese Culture. Essays on Anglican and Episcopal History in China*, edited by Philip Wickeri, 65–78. Hong Kong: Hong Kong University Press, 2015.

Ying Fuk-tsang. "*Bianju xia de paihuai. Cong zhanhou dao hou jiuqi Xianggang jiaohui sheguan shilun*" 變局下的徘徊：從戰後到後九七香港教會社關史論

[Wandering in Hong Kong: Church and Society from Post-War to Post-97].
Hong Kong: In Press 印象文字, 2018.

Ying Fuk-tsang. "The Politics of Cross Demolition: A Religio-Political Analysis of the 'Three Rectifications and One Demolition' Campaign in Zhejiang Province." *Review of Religion and Chinese Society* 5, no. 1 (2018): 43–75.

Ying Fuk-tsang. "Hong Kong Religious Sectors under the Shadow of China's Sharp Power." In *China's Sharp Power in Hong Kong*, edited by Benny Yiu-ting Tai, 80–89. Hong Kong: Hong Kong Civil Hub, 2018.

Ying Fuk-tsang. "Hong Kong." In *Christianity in East and Southeast Asia*, edited by Kenneth R. Ross, Francis D. Alvarez, and Todd M. Johnson, 74–86. Edinburgh: Edinburgh University Press, 2020.

Ying Fuk-tsang. "The Entanglement between Religion and Politics: Hong Kong Christianity in the Anti-Extradition Bill Movement." *Review of Religion and Chinese Society* 8, no. 1 (2020): 111–142.

Ying, Fuk-tsang, and Pan-chiu Lai. "Diasporic Chinese Communities and Protestantism in Hong Kong during the 1950s." *Studies in World Christianity* 10, no. 1 (2004): 136–153.

Yip, Francis Ching Wah 葉青華. "'Zhiji zhibi' yanjiu jihua: Shehuixue yanjiu dui Xianggang 'jiaohui xiankuangxue' de gongxian." 「知己知彼」研究計劃：社會學研究對香港「教會現況學」的貢獻. ["Know Yourself and Know Your Enemy" Research Project. The Contribution of Sociological Research to the "Church Situation Study" in Hong Kong]. In *Pastoral Conference Series II: The Vocation of Pastoral Ministry: Theology, Spirituality, and Practices*, edited by Simon Yiu-Chuen Lee, 104–110. Hong Kong: The Divinity School of Chung Chi College, 2009.

Yip, Francis Ching Wah. "For Our Struggle Is Not Against Flesh and Blood:" The Demonic in Hong Kong. In *The Hong Kong Protests and Political Theology*, edited by Pui-Lan Kwok and Francis Ching-Wah Yip, 109–116. London: Rowman and Littlefield, 2021.

Yu, Tat-Sum Carver 余達心. . "Xianggang shenxue fazhan sishi nian" 香港神學發展四十年 [Theological Developments of the Hong Kong Christian Community in the Last Forty Years.] *China Graduate School of Theology Newsletter* 25 (1998): 103–132.

Yuen, Mary Mee-Yin. "The Catholic Church and Civil Society in Hong Kong: Contributions of the Hong Kong Catholic Commission for Labor Affairs." In *Citizens of Two Kingdoms: Civil Society and Christian Religion in Greater China*, edited by Shun-hing Chan and Jonathan W. Johnson, 177–199. Leiden: Brill, 2021.

Yung, Tim. "Visions and Realities in Hong Kong Anglican Mission Schools, 1849–1941." *Studies in Church History* 57 (2021): 254–276.

Zheng, Jia-zheng 鄭家政. "*Zhen Yesu jiaohui lishi jiangyi*" 真耶穌教會歷史講義 [*Notes on the History of the True Jesus Church*]. Taichung City: Philemon 腓利門書房, 2015.

Index